CAREER EXPLORATION AND PREPARATION FOR THE SPECIAL NEEDS LEARNER

CAREER EXPLORATION AND PREPARATION FOR THE SPECIAL NEEDS LEARNER

Allyn and Bacon, Inc.

L. ALLEN PHELPS ~ RONALD J. LUTZ

The Pennsylvania State University

Central Michigan University

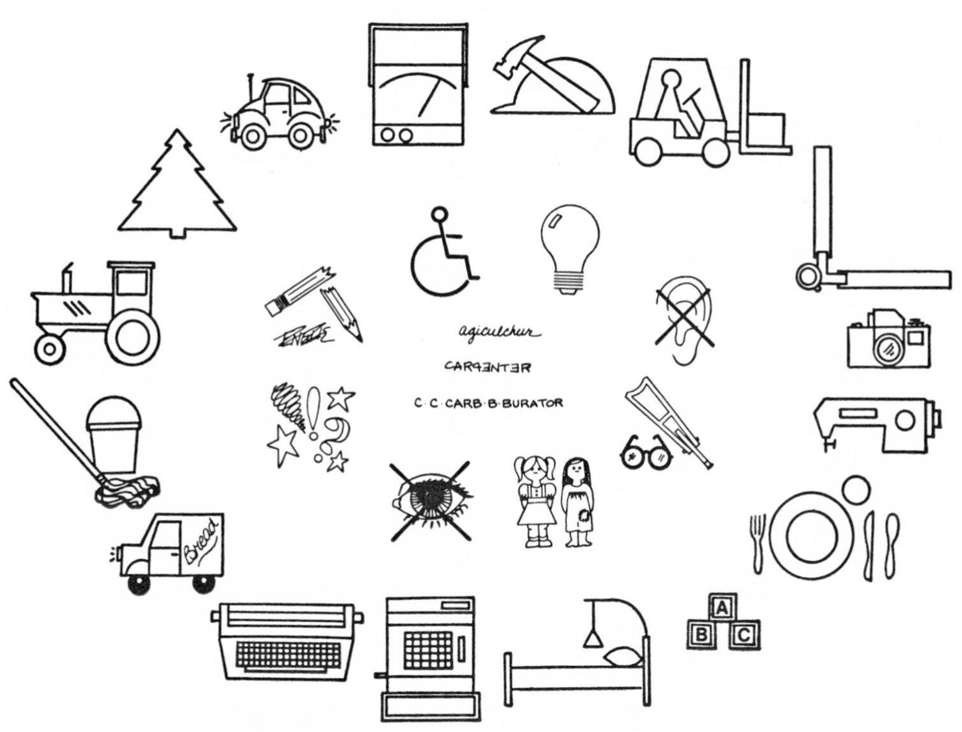

Boston, London, Sydney

LIBRARY OF CONGRESS CATALOGING IN PUBLICATION DATA

Phelps, L Allen, 1948-
Career exploration and preparation for the special needs learner.

Includes bibliographies and index.
1. Handicapped children—Education. 2. Teachers of handicapped children. 3. Vocational education.
I. Lutz, Ronald J., 1939- joint author. II. Title.
LC4019.P48 371.9 77-21999

Illustrations on the title page produced by Instructional Materials Production Department, Central Michigan University. Adapted from *Cluster Guide* (Series), Central Michigan University, 1973.

CONTENTS

FOREWORDS

THE VOCATIONAL EDUCATION PERSPECTIVE

For many years a large proportion of vocational educators have taken pride in the diversity of students they can serve simultaneously. Other vocational educators have sought or have been forced by circumstances to restrict enrollments to the "best" who apply. It is clear, however, that almost all vocational educators are now seeing and will continue to see a greater diversity of students enrolled in their programs at every educational level. Not only are enrollments of special needs students certain to increase with the new federal and state legislation for special education, but large numbers of students are also entering vocational education programs as a result of the gradual phasing out of the general education curriculum at the secondary school level. Vocational education has never been asked to serve this diverse an audience. The challenge of providing a quality, comprehensive vocational education to *all* who can benefit is both significant and immediate.

This book is an attempt to assist vocational educators in meeting that challenge. However, its most crucial and penetrating message is that vocational educators cannot—and must not—address the task alone. Part One tells why by describing special needs students and by indicating ways in which cooperative efforts can work to serve them better than can the efforts of any single group of specialists. Functional strategies for communicating and working closely with special educators, parents, counselors, and other important service providers can be found in nearly each chapter.

A very broad view of vocational education is maintained throughout. This should make the book useful to junior high school, high school, and postsecondary practical arts, career education, and vocational teachers. The occupational cluster analysis approach suggested in Chapter 8 emphasizes the need to develop a curriculum that provides students with career exploration, job seeking, and personal adjustment skills as well as appropriate and marketable occupational skills. Numerous local, state, and national studies have noted that the employment opportunities of special needs individuals have been severely restricted because they were not provided these critical skills in school.

With the expanded diversity of students participating in vocational education comes the imperative to individualize the instruction being provided. Teaching and planning techniques developed by the field of special education must be acquired and used by vocational teachers, just as special educators must learn of the techniques developed by vocational educators. Practical guidelines for developing modules of instruction for individual students, assessing the learner's needs, and other useful procedures are described by the use of case studies. These chapters in Part Two are particularly helpful because vocational educators will be involved in developing the Individual Educational Plans (IEP's) for handicapped students required by Public Law 94-142.

To a major extent, the effectiveness of vocational education will be judged on the successful placement of handicapped and disadvantaged learners in the full range of occupations or educational programs entered by nonspecial needs students. This is a monumental challenge confronting all vocational educators, as well as other regular class teachers, counselors, and specialists. This book is directed toward addressing this challenge effectively.

Rupert N. Evans
Professor of Vocational and Technical Education
University of Illinois at Urbana-Champaign

THE SPECIAL EDUCATION PERSPECTIVE

It is with great pleasure that I provide a foreword for this book that so directly meets one of the major unmet responsibilities of education. For many years individuals and organizations such as the National Advisory

Committee on the Handicapped and special study groups in organizations like the American Association on Mental Deficiency have decried the lack of secondary education programming for children with special needs. Some typical recommendations are noted below.

> Promote and conduct workshops in career and vocational education in conjunction with state and national convention of the AAMD.
>
> Develop career and vocational education materials and guides for professionals engaged in preservice and inservice training.
>
> Identify programs that successfully integrate the mentally retarded into career and vocational education.
>
> Charles Kokaska, Chairperson — AAMD Committee on Secondary Education

The history of special education has clearly indicated a much stronger emphasis on the primary and elementary areas, with special programs for these exceptional youngsters often stopping, or being drastically reduced, at the secondary level. It is precisely at this age level, where the transition between school and work becomes most significant to the student, that we have been least able to provide an individualized and special orientation to the student with special needs. We seem poorly prepared to train either special educators interested in the topic or regular educators who sought special knowledges that would enable them to work more effectively with these youngsters.

During the time that I worked with the Bureau of Education for the Handicapped in the U.S. Office of Education (1967–1969), we discussed those priority areas that needed attention. In the total developmental scheme of finding handicapped children and providing a continuous training for them and help for their families, two major areas stood out as needing special attention. One special emphasis was early childhood, and major programs have been developed to take care of that deficit. The second area of deficit was secondary education and career education, and that has developed more slowly. It is for this reason that the U.S. Congress provided in 1969 that 10 percent of federal vocational education funds were mandated to be spent on program needs for children with special needs.

This book by Phelps and Lutz provides one of the first documents I have seen that effectively addresses in very concrete fashion what the nature of the educational experience should be with secondary-aged children with special needs. I resonate particularly to the case study approach that allows for detailed individual descriptions and specific educational planning and also allows for the portrayal of the great diversity of problems and program alternatives that can be provided to this set of students. There is a wealth of practical data in the text, not the least of which are examples of forms and procedures that define the program dimensions to be attacked and outline a practical guide for assessment of the results of the program.

I hope that this book will be attractive to two major audiences. The first would be those in special education whose knowledge encompasses the needs of the child but who are limited in specialized program dimensions such as drafting, printing, agriculture, and so on, since such content areas are the focus of concern for the career-interested youngster. Second would be those people whose work lies in the area of career and vocational education but who have personal experience and interest and wish to provide effective training for exceptional youngsters despite their special needs. The book provides a wealth of practical detail that should be widely and gratefully received by educators in both of these major groups.

One of the major sections of the book deals with cooperative planning and cooperative teaching. The authors state that it is not often that one finds genuine cooperation within school systems, and that statement is undoubtedly true. It is also true that very few individuals carry all of the knowledges and skills necessary to provide an effective vocational education experience for a multiply handicapped child, a deaf adolescent girl, or a mentally retarded young man. It is the kind of situation that cries out for a multidisciplinary team approach. It is to the authors' credit that they spend a good section of the text discussing the nature of that cooperation and how it can be enhanced.

This is a topic that needs careful consideration by educators, particularly at a time when the concepts of *mainstreaming* and *normalization* have become such an important part of the educational scene. With strong pressures on the schools to bring children with special needs into the mainstream, there will be pressure to incorporate children with special needs more into the general program of career education and vocational education. What needs to be grasped most firmly is that handicapped individuals do make fine workers if they are provided with the appropriate training and opportunities. It is not only the employers who need to understand that concept but educators as well.

I hope that this book will signal the beginning of additional major attempts to provide practical models and training materials to meet the needs stated here. This book is a fine start in that direction and should be of enormous value to many different educators.

James J. Gallagher, Director
Frank Porter Graham Child Development Center
Kenan Professor of Education
University of North Carolina at Chapel Hill

PREFACE

In recent years educational programs for individuals with special educational needs have received increasing attention. This has resulted, in large part, from the growing societal concern for the protection of individual human rights. In education this movement has been reflected in the passage of federal and state legislation that assures that all handicapped learners will receive a free and appropriate education. Almost simultaneously, there has been an increasing concern for the ability of the educational system to prepare individuals for meaningful, productive, and satisfying occupational roles in society. Career education has gained recognition as a reform movement in American education. Most observers agree that the movement is basically calling for increased emphasis on the career awareness, exploration, and preparation objectives of the educational system. This book focuses upon the commonality of these concerns: career exploration and preparation programming for special needs learners.

The text is intended to facilitate the expansion and improvement of occupational programs serving handicapped and disadvantaged learners at the secondary level. The intended audience includes teachers, work experience coordinators, counselors, consultants, supervisors, and program administrators who are involved in any capacity with handicapped or disadvantaged learners enrolled in some form of occupational programming. The strategies, concepts, and examples presented in the book are appropriate for both junior high level exploratory programs and senior high level job preparation programs. A close examination of the table of contents reveals that this is primarily a curriculum or instructional development book, designed for practicing educators, graduate students, and advanced undergraduates. An effort has been made to provide examples and illustrations for all areas and levels of occupational education.

Two basic principles are critical to the successful utilization of the curriculum construction strategies presented in this book. First, in order for instructional efforts to be fully effective for special needs learners, the expertise of occupational and special needs educators (special education personnel, teachers of the disadvantaged, remedial staff, and so on), parents, employers, and supportive agency personnel (such as rehabilitation counselors) must be coordinated in a team effort. Second, the team effort must be focused on the *individual and unique* needs of each learner. When operationalized, these basic principles foster the commitment needed to provide the special needs learner with the competencies to function in an independent occupational life role in society.

Part One clarifies several basic concepts and perspectives that are critical to effective interdisciplinary instructional planning for special needs learners. The nature of special needs learners, career exploration and preparation programming, and cooperative teaching are discussed, illustrated, and exemplified. Part Two presents a series of specific processes designed to aid in developing and managing individualized instructional programs. A systematic approach to planning, implementing, and evaluating instruction is utilized in providing functional "how-to-do-it" information and planning forms. Learner identification and assessment, resource and job analysis, cooperating strategies, instructional module planning, instructional implementation, and evaluation of learner progress are among the processes described.

Two authors have carefully blended their mutually complementary experiences, interests, and philosophies in the preparation of this book. As a result of this joint endeavor, the quality of the work is beyond that which would have resulted from individual efforts. It may be helpful to the reader, however, to know that Ronald J. Lutz was responsible for the preparation of Part One and L. Allen Phelps was responsible for Part Two.

Many individuals have participated in different ways in the preparation of this book. The majority of the concepts and ideas presented here have come from the authors' teaching experiences as well as their involvement with teachers, counselors, administrators, graduate students, and others through workshops and graduate courses over the past fifteen years. It would be impossible to begin to recognize the several hundred individuals who have warmly and willingly shared their effective techniques, materials, and attitudes. Each of these inputs was and is much appreciated. A special note of appreciation is extended to Tim L. Wentling, University of Minnesota; Rupert Evans, Jacob Stern, and Elizabeth Abbas, University of Illinois at Urbana; Gary M. Clark, University of Kansas; and Leslie H. Cochran, Central Michigan University, all of whom have reviewed portions of the manuscript and offered suggestions for its improvement. Appreciation is also extended to a number of teachers and colleagues who have, in other ways, shaped the philosophy and concepts reflected in this text: Marc W. Gold, Merle B. Karnes, Norman Gronlund, and M. Stephen Lilly of the University of Illinois; Thomas S. Baldwin of the North Carolina Division of Services for the Blind; Larry K. Brentro of the Star Commonwealth for Boys; and James J. Gallagher of the University of North Carolina.

This book is dedicated to all those who have, who are, and who will be working with learners with special needs, as well as to our families, who have provided patience, encouragement, and support during the preparation stages. To mention a few we include Susan, Lisa, and Stacey Phelps and Carolyn, Becky, Jon, Rhonda, Lori, Joe, Delbert, and Ida Lutz.

L. Allen Phelps

Ronald J. Lutz

CAREER EXPLORATION AND PREPARATION FOR THE SPECIAL NEEDS LEARNER

TEACHING COOPERATIVELY TO PREPARE SPECIAL NEEDS LEARNERS FOR CAREERS

PART ONE

In some schools various faculty members are cooperatively planning and implementing effective career education programs with special needs students. Much of the success of these cooperative arrangements is predicated upon teachers' sharing a common understanding of teaching philosophy and basic concepts. If barriers exist, either for the vocational education-practical arts teacher due to misunderstood special education philosophy or for the special education teacher because of unclear vocational technical concepts, the cooperative relationship suffers. Another factor that deserves careful attention is the individualization of instruction and evaluation. Teaching individuals—as opposed to teaching classes—can mean the difference between success and failure for the learner with special needs. ∾ The first chapter provides a simplified overview of "learners with special needs" and is written primarily as an introduction for the vocational and practical arts teacher who may have questions concerning terminology and philosophy which are common knowledge to the special needs teacher. The discussion, however, is intended to stimulate thinking for special education teachers as well, but more as a review of the very broad interpretations of special education. Each learner described represents a real person whose name has been changed so that the sound of the name and that of the particular learning difficulty are similar, for example, Mark and Ed are examples of mentally retarded and emotionally disturbed learners respectively. ∾ The second chapter provides a workable definition and brief explanation of a few concepts related to vocational-practical arts in career exploration and preparation programs. Although numerous definitions and interpretations are available, those selected seem to be the most simple and straightforward and are included primarily as an introduction for the special education and regular classroom teachers who may have questions, because of the many different viewpoints, concerning the career education movement. The discussion is intended to provide a review for the vocational-practical arts teachers.

Both of the first two chapters are intended to whet the reader's appetite for additional information from professional journals, hundreds of excellent textbooks and, most important, from other professionals in the same school system.

Chapter 3 summarizes some of the educational work experience backgrounds of a variety of vocational-practical arts and special education teachers for the purpose of enlightening potential cooperating teachers and expanding their understanding. Each teacher represents a real person in a classroom or laboratory who works effectively with (1) learners with special needs and (2) learners who do not suffer significantly from learning difficulties. The examples of curriculum materials and techniques have been reviewed, developed, and/or utilized by them in the classroom.

The fourth chapter enhances the philosophy that "two heads are better than one" and encourages teachers from two different disciplines to merge their efforts to accomplish the most important goal in education—providing meaningful and relevant experiences for the special needs learner. In most cases at least two teachers are working with a special needs learner, such as the vocational-practical arts teachers and the special education teacher plus special therapists or consultants.

LEARNERS WITH SPECIAL NEEDS

Frequently, teachers have differing opinions about general terms such as special needs, the handicapped, and the disadvantaged. These differing opinions and the lack of a mutual understanding of varied educational terminology relating to mental, physical, and emotional impairments hamper productive planning, cooperative teaching, and effective learner evaluation.

This chapter is intended to provide a common knowledge of many terms used by teachers who work with special needs learners and to enhance communication between occupational and special education teachers. The examples of special needs learners in various occupational areas represent actual individuals who are struggling to overcome their learning difficulties and are becoming successful in a chosen occupation. Much of their success is based upon the continued cooperative instructional planning and communi-

1

cation between the occupational and special needs personnel. This cooperative involvement requires a mutual understanding of the terminology expressed in these illustrative examples. The reader is encouraged to develop a greater depth of understanding by studying from the references at the end of the chapter.

Many words are used to describe the person being taught such as a pupil, student, and learner. *Learner* is preferred for a variety of reasons. First, a learner acquires a broad background of all kinds of knowledge, skills, and attitudes based upon his or her interests and aptitudes. Learning both in school and out of school is expected and recognized. In contrast, the phrase "good student" is often synonymous with an academically successful person but may be less appropriate for one who demonstrates a high mechanical aptitude but low academic abilities. Secondly, the term learner implies a "teacher helping" role as each person searches and prepares for a place in society. It subtly implies varied individual learning styles, teaching styles, and a meshing of the two.

WHO ARE LEARNERS WITH SPECIAL NEEDS?

Special suggests something that is different, unique, exceptional, or highly individualized. As human beings, each of us has characteristics that are special, including personality traits, physical characteristics, occupational choices, and preferred learning styles.

The word *needs* relates to a want or demand that must be satisfied if success is to be attained. Each term independently implies an unsolved mystery and, when combined, the phrase *learner with special needs* implies the necessity for arriving at a personal solution to each individual's "learning mystery." Very simply, a person who has not been making normal progress through school and who appears to be headed for failure in school may be identified as a learner with special needs. Even though learning difficulties are specific to each person, a variety of common terms are used to describe them.

Special needs is an umbrella term that includes both the populations of the handicapped and the disadvantaged. The learner with special needs and the school personnel may become involved in adjustments to one or a

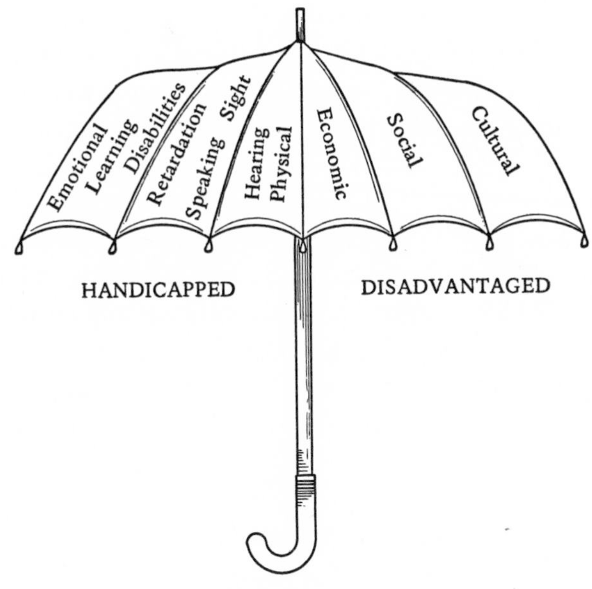

FIGURE 1-1. SPECIAL NEEDS

combination of handicaps—related emotional instability, learning disabilities, retardation, speaking difficulties, sight and hearing impairments, or physical handicaps. Other special needs might be a lack of opportunity for learning because of social, cultural, or economic disadvantages. Basically we all have or have had special needs, but the key factor is whether or not we have been able to adjust to or overcome the handicaps or learning disadvantages that we once experienced.

WHAT ARE LEARNING DIFFICULTIES?

Most students in school do not evidence serious learning difficulties. Some have had serious learning difficulties and have made an adequate adjustment, but a few have serious learning difficulties and have not been successful in adjusting to their special needs. If a unique or obvious type of help is deemed necessary to reverse a negative trend for a student, special services may be appropriate and should be explored. Using their professional judgment, teachers and other school personnel 1) determine whether or not a specific student needs supplementary assistance to avoid educational disaster, 2) make responsible decisions as to the specific nature of the student's learning difficulty, and 3) prescribe specific assistance through cooperative planning.

The purpose of devising categories to describe learning difficulties is to develop ways of diagnosing and, more important, to create ways of prescribing help. A title such as "National Honor Society student" is interpreted as being scholarly, whereas "special needs student" energizes one's curiosity about why the distinction and what to do about it. The why question will be discussed only in an attempt to clarify labels so teachers may share a common terminology. The greater emphasis will be placed on what we can do about the learning difficulties.

Often a referral from teachers about a certain student's difficulties draws needed attention to the student's difficulties, which may not have been previously observed, or tends to substantiate prior diagnoses. Teacher referrals commonly add justification for additional help in terms of support staff, equipment modification, unique learning media, or any of a number of other instructional program modifications or special services.

The inexperienced teacher may simply refer to "one of those kids," whereas the more experienced teacher may recognize and describe definite relationships between a special needs student and terms such as special education students, the exceptional, the handicapped, or the disadvantaged. Both experienced and inexperienced teachers may find that for the special needs student additional sophistication is needed when assessing student potential, planning curriculum, managing classroom activities, and evaluating student progress.

WHO IS RESPONSIBLE FOR LEARNERS WITH SPECIAL NEEDS?

At one time parents were made to feel totally responsible for the personal, social, and educational development of their handicapped child. Today the responsibility is shared—in some states by law—by groups of people. In the schools the initial determination of who will be eligible for special needs services is made by a carefully organized team of people with personal and professional commitments to help those experiencing unusual learning difficulties. This team is sometimes called an educational planning and placement committee (EPPC) and may be composed of one or more of the following: special education teacher, parent, occupational instructor, administrator, one of several therapists or specialists, and in most instances the learner who is having difficulty. Based on federal, state, and local guidelines and comprehensive data on an individual learner, the team will help make a series of independent professional decisions about the learner's future educational needs. These decisions may include:

1. What career opportunities are most consistent with the learner's interests and abilities?
2. What career exploration and preparation programs are available?
3. Does the learner qualify for special needs services?
4. What services can the learner be provided to increase his or her chances of becoming successful?

Additionally the committee may monitor the learner's progress, modify the occupational program if necessary, and provide follow-up for school to work experiences.

A later chapter, "Identifying School and Community Resources," describes the organization and function of various other organizations and committees that are helpful in providing supportive services.

WHO HAVE SPECIAL NEEDS?

Practically speaking, all learners with special needs are unique and individual. Unfortunately, many of their difficulties are multiple and extremely complex while some are singular and more obvious. The descriptions of Mary and Bill below are given as examples of rather apparent special needs.

Mary

Mary, with seemingly normal intelligence, has difficulty with reading. She squints and stumbles over words during oral reading and complains of headaches and falling asleep when she does her homework. Her teachers and parents both recognized the possible need for glasses. After a competent eye examination, Mary receives a pair of glasses to correct her unique handicap, one unlike that of anyone else in school. To the inexperienced observer, the mystery has been solved and the story is over. However, the physical diagnosis and corrective device are only the beginning. The treatment, though related to the symptoms, has not yet begun to correct the learning difficulty. Unfortunately, peer pressure and/or family reaction may be stronger negative influences in Mary's decision to wear glasses than the positive reward of improving her reading efficiency. Positive adjustment to the glasses may be gradual and may require some consoling moments if others make thoughtless comments about her looking "funny." If all learning problems connected with eye deficiencies could be solved by wearing glasses, there would not be so many students choosing to wear contact lenses. With respect to Mary and the term "special needs," only time will tell whether or not she will experience normal progress after adjusting to her corrective devices.

Bill

Bill represents a more complex learning difficulty. Several years ago he nearly drowned, and being without oxygen during the revival period left him with some brain damage. Since the accident, school has been hard for him, and he has found more in common in terms of friendship with the school's "uncooperative students." Tardiness, absenteeism, suspension, low and failing grades, and dislike for school in general describe his overall achievement, effort, and attitude over the past four years. In terms of special needs, Bill seems a prime target for supplementary assistance from the school system in an attempt to turn him around educationally.

WHAT IS SPECIAL EDUCATION?

In an attempt to provide educational experiences more adequately for those who are having unusual learning difficulties, special education personnel provide assessment, prescription, instruction, and evaluation assistance. Substantial research is being generated to deal more effectively with the exceptional learner. Unfortunately, the term special education is interpreted by many outside the field as being synonomous with mental retardation. Actually special education tends to be much broader and includes handicapping conditions such as emotionally disturbed (ED), mentally retarded (MR), learning disabled (LD), socially disadvantaged (SD), visually handicapped (VH), hearing handicapped (HH), speech handicapped (SH), physically handicapped (PH), and the inefficient gifted (G). To develop a better understanding of these handicapping conditions, learners will be described with names similar to the abbreviations of their disabilities as follows:

Ed is emotionally disturbed.
Lloyd has learning disabilities.
Mark is mentally retarded.
Vera is visually handicapped.
Harry is hearing handicapped.
Steve is speech handicapped.
Phyllis is physically handicapped
Gary is gifted.

Even though few students have single handicaps or disadvantages, these will be described in large part as if they did in order to clarify the terminology, though you will notice some commonality of characteristics among some of the areas.

FIGURE 1-2. ED

Ed

Ed has been referred by several classroom teachers and diagnosed as being emotionally disturbed by the school psychologist and a psychiatrist. He is a high school sophomore from a broken home and lives with his mother, one older sister, and two younger ones. His school record contains numerous disciplinary actions including after-school detention for smoking in the rest room, removal from class for fistfighting in biology lab, one-day suspension for letting the air out of the principal's tires, and a three-day suspension for carving his initials on a seat in the high school auditorium. Although his work in drafting is excellent, he seldom sits at the drawing board for more than five minutes before wanting to leave the room for a drink, go to the bathroom, or punch a "friend" on the shoulder. Often during group instruction he either daydreams or attempts to compete with the teacher for attention. While completing work in drafting he becomes distracted easily by an unusual noise or movement such as a truck passing by the school or a group of girls walking down the hall talking. A few days prior to grade time he becomes depressed and withdrawn because as he says, "I ain't gonna pass anyway!" The sad part is that he really doesn't think that he will. There is little question of Ed's talent, both academically and in his physical ability as evidenced by his understanding of the basic concepts in drafting and the manner of his work, but his thirst for attention, impulsiveness, and aggressiveness tests the patience of his special needs teacher, drafting teacher, and all who are close to him.

In the above, no attempt is being made to present a diagnostic model of emotional disturbance but simply to indicate that one or more of the following characteristics are abnormally apparent in emotionally disturbed students.

Lack of confidence	Withdrawn
Hyperactivity	Aggressiveness
Inattentiveness	Conduct problem
Depression	Impulsivity
Fearfulness	Nonconforming
Low frustration tolerance	Phobias
Distractability	

CARqƎNTƎR Lloyd

FIGURE 1-3. LLOYD

Lloyd has been diagnosed as learning disabled because of the wide discrepancy between his estimated potential and his unusually poor academic performance in high school. Both his parents have advanced degrees and his two older brothers are successfully progressing through college, but Lloyd is struggling in the junior year of high school. His chemistry teacher indicated that he has dropped more test tubes than any previous student, and his English teacher is concerned about his hyperactive behavior in the classroom. Most of his math assignments are started but few are ever completed. He is a handsome, well-dressed young man who is popular with both the boys and girls of his age but not well liked by most of his instructors. His low grades are a result of his inability to read assignments quickly, write summaries of reading assignments, and make oral reports to the class.

Much to his family's dismay his favorite classes are in the manufacturing areas. He has successfully completed a variety of welding and machine tool activities. Lloyd's reading, writing, and speaking difficulties are least noticeable in the welding class, but his handicap is obvious during evaluation periods.

Lloyd is one of many types of students with learning disabilities, and many of them possess traits such as hyperactivity, difficulty with math, reading, writing, and speaking, impulsiveness, and inattention, as well as functioning academically far below their estimated potential.

agiculchur

FIGURE 1-4. MARK

Mark

Mark has been diagnosed by an educational planning and placement committee (EPPC) as mentally retarded. The committee carefully reviewed both his test results and his general behavior. There is some question whether he is borderline retarded or educable mentally retarded because of the inaccuracies and inconsistencies in his measured verbal IQ. There is consistent agreement, however, that he is not trainable mentally retarded or profoundly retarded based on his previous class performance, behavior, and nonverbal IQ measures.

As a preschooler he received a serious skull fracture—the result of a car-bicycle accident—and it is believed the accident may be the main cause of his learning problem. His being born prematurely may also contribute to his condition, as may having had a high fever several times.

Although he has evidenced a developmental lag in reading, writing, and arithmetic, his rural background has provided him numerous mechanical experiences in repairing farm equipment, caring for animals, and helping his father plant and harvest crops. His agriculture teacher indicates that he is likeable with a good attendance record and positive attitude but needs considerable help in math and reading skills. Understanding "parts per million," for example, is difficult for him, whereas actually mixing one cubic centimeter of chemical to a tank of water is done accurately and consistently after the procedure is explained to him. He also maintains neat and complete daily records of plant and animal growth after having the system clarified for him. Part of his motivation for accurate record keeping relates to his excellent reputation in the state and local Future Farmers of America (FFA) club activities.

If given a textbook reading assignment or a series of theoretical math problems he becomes confused, embarrassed, and defensive.

Mentally retarded students are sometimes described as having a developmental lag, limited ability, or low IQ and are frequently described as slow learners, mentally impaired, or late bloomers.

FIGURE 1-5. SADIE

Sadie

Sadie has been identified as disadvantaged. She is the third of five children who are being raised on a poverty-level income by their mother. Sadie's older brother and sister both dropped out of school, partially due to the family moving frequently. She repeated second grade but doesn't seem to have trouble with school when she attends. Last year as a junior she was absent from school an average of one day per week and was tardy numerous times in all her classes except health occupations. Not only has her personal hygiene and appearance improved immensely, but her attitude about neatness, cleanliness, and punctuality has made substantial progress. One of the major turning points in her attitude change occurred during her co-op experience at Community Hospital. Her health occupations teacher is impressed with the improvement she has made in personal appearance and the knowledge she is demonstrating in the health occupations lab, but her progress in other subjects is minimal.

Socially disadvantaged students are commonly plagued with problems such as low family income, often minority race, large families, poor language developments, short attention span, and low motivation for school success.

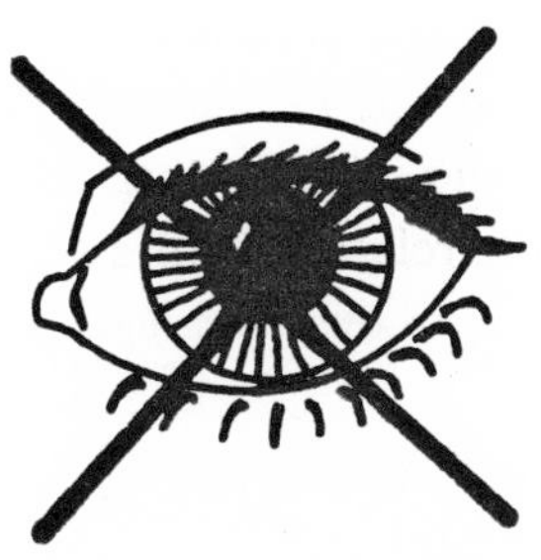
FIGURE 1-6. VERA

Vera

Vera is visually handicapped. When she was five she was declared legally blind. She lives at home with her family and her newly acquired leader dog, Major. She distinguishes between light and dark and is able to read to some extent with enlarged print. She and her family have adjusted psychologically to the handicap. The initial social stigma connected with having a blind child has been replaced with a genuine commitment to provide her with whatever meaningful learning experiences are available.

She spent first and second grades at a residential school where she learned the fundamentals of reading and writing braille, became familiar with large print materials and, most important, became more accepting of her sight problem.

This year typing class is her favorite. Mr. Bob Grande, her typing teacher, has utilized various tape recording devices so that Vera receives the same instruction and performs the same speed and accuracy activities as do her classmates. She types with fewer errors than anyone else in class, her speed is improving normally, and she is an excellent speller. Her typing teacher has very effectively used a buddy system in class by encouraging her peers to provide help when necessary. Fortunately, Vera has learned how to accept help graciously from her friends without losing her pride, and her peers seem pleased to have learned how to offer assistance without being offensive.

The visually handicapped range in vision from total blindness to being partially sighted, with diagnoses such as being severely nearsighted, far-sighted, or having astigmatism. Symptoms that teachers may recognize that are related to common visual handicaps include excessive eye rubbing, squinting, watering eyes, and frequent blinking.

FIGURE 1-7. HARRY

Harry

Harry may have the most serious handicap of all because he has an invisible handicap—deafness. Having hearing loss from birth, he developed little language and at age eight was committed to a state institution as mentally retarded. Due to a concentrated parent-speech and hearing therapist effort, Harry received a thorough hearing evaluation, was fitted with a hearing aid, and began intensive auditory training, speech and language training, and lipreading training during the following several years in a class for hearing impaired children. At age eleven he was integrated into his neighborhood elementary school as a third grader. Intensive speech and language training, parent involvement, regular teacher adjustments, and peer acceptance have been several important events enabling Harry to become fully integrated into a high school program this year. His early diagnosis of mental retardation should probably have been called educational retardation since he is progressing satisfactorily now. Initially, an interpreter was provided for him so that he could keep up with lecture and discussion-type classes, but now that his teachers speak to him so he can lip-read and since several of his buddies help him with his notes, the interpreter is no longer necessary. Printing and running the offset presses are his most popular activities in school, and his teacher is confident that when he graduates in two years he will be employable.

Hearing loss that exists before language development is more handicapping than hearing loss acquired at a later age. Types of loss involve intensity measured in decibels and frequency or pitch measured in cycles per second (HERTZ). Often the slight and mild hearing losses go undetected, whereas the marked, severe, and extreme hearing problems are recognized and diagnosed early.

C·C·CARB·B·BURATOR

FIGURE 1-8. STEVE

Steve

Steve is considered speech handicapped because of his stuttering problem. He is basically a handsome lad with normal intelligence and excellent athletic and musical abilities. His handicap is very apparent during situations where attention is focused upon his speaking abilities, for example, reading in front of his class, being asked to respond to an unexpected question, or responding to an authoritarian adult. His relatively low self-concept is probably related to the snickers, jeers, ridicule, embarrassment, and anxiety that he experienced during his frequent speech blocks in elementary and junior high school. In high school he has established some close friendships and his teachers this year seem to be more patient with him. They have learned to maintain eye contact compassionately during speech blocks and wait for him to finish speaking. Much of his improvement is related to his excellent speech therapist and his automotive teacher. The therapist has visited each of his teachers and made them more aware of how to help Steve extinguish the stuttering. His automotive teacher's class is relaxed and is obviously related more to fixing malfunctioning automobiles than making speeches. The speech therapist and automotive teacher maintain a daily contact and words that initially were expressed as "c-c-c-c-car-bur-a-a-a-tor" are now expressed as "c-carburator" or "carburator." Steve has been given a new and difficult task of meeting customers and making out service orders. The automotive teacher encourages a buddy system, and Steve and his buddy have shared a reasonably successful experience in meeting customers and taking service orders. In addition to working with automotive words and phrases, the speech therapist has helped Steve to eliminate the unpleasant eye-blinking and eye-rolling habits he had.

FIGURE 1-9. PHYLLIS

Phyllis

Phyllis is physically handicapped and has relied on a wheelchair for her mobility since she was seven. She lost the use of both legs as the result of a family automobile accident. Like many handicapped people who have adjusted to their difficulties, Phyllis is a warm and considerate person with a commitment to help others with the problems she has managed to overcome. For example, as a paraplegic, she is in physical therapy to develop her own mobility skills but spends most of her time helping the therapist with the younger children. One of the young children is a monoplegic learning to use various devices on his left leg. Another monoplegic is becoming more skillful with the use of her left arm. Helping is mutual between Phyllis and a twenty-five-year-old adult, a Vietnam veteran who has limited use of both hands and both legs (quadraplegic). His presence and positive attitude serves as an example to all of the students, and he seems to enjoy being in the physical therapy room.

While Phyllis was recouperating from her spinal injuries in the hospital, she developed an unusual skill and interest in stitchery that later developed into knitting and sewing. As a high school freshman she liked best the sewing units in home economics, which were followed by a one-year clothing construction course. She is looking forward to her co-op work experience as an alteration tailor at a local clothing store this year as a junior. She has an excellent academic record in school and has relied on a physical therapist, home economics teacher, and counselor and assistance from several other school personnel while exploring various careers and cultivating healthy peer and social relationships. In recent years, the school has demonstrated a commitment and made a number of facility adjustments such as ramps, cutaway curbs, special bathroom facilities, and wider doors to accommodate Phyllis and other people with special physical problems.

FIGURE 1-10. GARY

Gary

Gary was identified when a sixth grader as being gifted. He is the tallest boy in his class, can run the fastest, is involved in the most extracurricular activities, has read the most books, is the best speller, and has the highest average test scores in math, but he is not well liked by most of his teachers. He often seems to pay little attention to a teacher, seldom completes his homework, and becomes belligerent when forced to do repetitive drills during class time. His nonconforming nature and inability to "sit down and shut up" were the primary reasons given for removal from one of his classes, yet his seventh-grade industrial arts teacher has been overwhelmed by his progress. During a recent mass production activity, Gary was selected as president of the company, which allowed him to manage the personnel and financial arrangements of the enterprise. Gary was also the mechanical engineer for the group and played a major role in the design and construction of several critical jigs and fixtures to control the quality of production. The teachers having the most difficulty with Gary feel that "all he needs is some discipline." Due to the seriousness of the problem, an educational planning and placement committee (EPPC) was established to review the situation and make recommendations. His measured IQ is unusually high, his reading, writing, and mathematical levels are all at least two years above his present grade level, he is much more physically mature than his classmates, and the increased flexibility in high school have led the committee to agree that an accelerated program could offer him the academic challenge and increased variety of subject areas to study. Understanding the seriousness of the decision, his parents are both willing to endorse this recommendation and feel it is the best alternative available.

WHAT ARE MULTIPLE SPECIAL NEEDS?

The preceding examples were provided to explore the underlying characteristics of students who are potentially special needs students. They focused on learners with single special needs or described only the primary learning difficulties.

It is important to note that the description of each of the learners has attempted to clarify the uniqueness of nine categories that are diagnosed in many special education programs.

Unfortunately most students who aren't doing well in school suffer from not just one but several integrated handicaps. The primary handicap is often the most serious, but one or more secondary handicaps may be equally devastating to their educational progress.

Commonly, students with a specific primary handicap, such as a serious hearing loss, may develop secondary emotional problems and may appear to the uninformed person to be mentally impaired. Some of these multiple handicaps exist at birth—congenital blindness, for example—while others are the result of accidents, heredity, or serious illness. The complex problems faced, as well as presented, by multiple handicapped persons can be recognized in the following descriptions of Sara and Paul.

FIGURE 1-11. SARA

Sara

Sara has cerebral palsy. Her crippling condition is most obvious where controlled muscular movement is essential. In addition to prosthetic aids used in walking, she wears glasses to correct her nearsightedness, relies on a hearing aid to increase sound intensity, speaks very slowly with some articulation problems, and has experienced consistent difficulties with reading and writing. Being an only child and born after her parents were well established, she received excellent attention and reinforcement as a youngster. School, in general, has been extremely difficult for her, including the academic subjects, physical education, industrial arts, music, art, and home economics except for child care. As a high school freshman she has been participating in a nursery school program in the home economics department and reflects unusual satisfaction when working with the preschoolers. They realize she has physical problems, but she develops rapport easily with them and they seem to enjoy being with her. Sara spends considerable time helping the teacher and becomes actively involved in the nursery school's play time, snack time, and individual activities.

Even though Sara's coordination, visual, and hearing handicaps seem almost insurmountable, her home economics teacher intends to recommend her for the child care program next year and is seeking advice from other teachers relating to what type of assistance might be made available.

Paul

Paul is epileptic, educable mentally retarded, emotionally disturbed, as well as being socially and culturally disadvantaged.

As a first grader, he had unusual difficulty with language development and reading skills and was identified by an educational planning and place-

FIGURE 1-12. PAUL

ment committee (EPPC) as being educable mentally retarded. With the help of the special education teacher, he made reasonable progress through the early elementary grades but was described as a loner. Several of his seventh grade teachers witnessed petit mal seizures (short periods of unconsciousness) with concern. One was in the industrial arts lab when he thrashed his arms around aimlessly for a few seconds and another was in the gym when he walked around in a daze making sucking noises. Several teachers noticed his twitching eyelids as he daydreamed in class and appeared to be gasping for air.

Although his widowed mother was made aware of the potential problems, nothing medically was done until he had his first grand mal seizure in the school cafeteria. Everyone but the school nurse was caught off guard as he uttered a shrill cry, slumped to the floor, and began making spasmodic movements. Paul was breathing intensively, gnashing his teeth and salivating profusely, and his face turned deep red to purple in color.

The nurse very calmly asked several students to move the tables and chairs away from him so he wouldn't bump into them and placed several clean towels from the kitchen under his head. Although most of the students and some of the teachers were horrified, the nurse calmly explained that he would be OK in a few minutes and there was no cause for alarm. She also mentioned that is was important for everyone to accept Paul and to show concern and kindness to him.

During the next several months, Paul experienced several more seizures, but by the end of the school year Paul's doctor believed that his medication would control future problems.

HOW DO TEACHERS REACT TO LEARNERS WITH SPECIAL NEEDS?

It is not uncommon for occupational teachers to say, "Don't tell me what is wrong with the kids until I work with them for a while." Since the nature of many occupational programs provides a wide variety of learning experiences including hands-on activities, many teachers see a successful integration of special needs students with the "regular students" because of the practical and concrete nature of the learning in their subject area. In some cases the special needs learner will fit into a program successfully, but in other cases, when communications and learning become minimal, the teacher may need information about a specific student's learning difficulties Where does the occupational teacher turn for help? The special education teacher, speech therapist, school psychologist, resource room teacher and others are specialists in school and know much about both the causes of learning difficulty and the occupational interests and potential of the special needs student. Through effective utilization of the educational planning and placement committee (EPPC), teachers are provided this information about a student's past experiences of their learning difficulties, and their learning strengths can be passed along in an attempt to better meet the learner's needs.

What kind of information should occupational teachers be provided and when should it be made available? Occupational teachers should definitely be kept constantly aware of the special needs of each student who has sight, hearing, or physical handicaps or who may experience epileptic seizures. Many other types of background information about a special student's IQ, attendance record, and social status in school may or may not be as meaningful or accurate in occupational experiences. Each situation will require careful handling by the special education and occupational education personnel. Sharing information about a learner's interests, strengths, weaknesses, and personal characteristics is a delicate subject but may shed light on alternative ways of dealing with one who is experiencing unusual difficulties in a classroom or laboratory environment.

Most teachers are sensitive and inquisitive about abnormalities in achievement, effort, and attitudes and are never really content until normal progress for an individual is being achieved. An impressive poster has been observed above a teacher's desk which states, "If a student can't learn the way we teach, then we should teach the way he can learn."

SUMMARY

The selected references at the end of this chapter have been carefully grouped to be consistent with the special needs learner illustrations in this chapter. These references are intended to provide a greater depth of understanding in each of the disability areas. Some teachers will communicate very effectively with certain kinds of special needs learner because of a natural gift, special training, or numerous experiences and yet may experience great difficulty with others. It is hoped that, by developing a deeper understanding of the characteristics of special needs learners through additional study, teachers can experience a broader range of success in being effective with special needs learners.

As indicated by the examples of special needs learners in this chapter, each situation is unique, requiring a delicate implementation of carefully planned activities by sensitive and experienced teachers. The effect that dedicated teachers have on the lives of "students who are difficult to teach" relies heavily upon their enthusiasm, ingenuity, creativity, and a degree of tenacity in continuing to utilize effective techniques and to search for new ones to replace ineffective ones. Since many teachers have a wealth of experience to share with others about what may or may not be effective, it seems essential to emphasize the importance of teachers coordinating their efforts, working cooperatively, and sharing ideas in an attempt to maximize the positive impact that can be made on the special needs learner. The major goal then is being more successful in teaching the "difficult to teach."

REFERENCES

SPECIAL EDUCATION–GENERAL

Birnbrauer, J., Bijou, S., Wolf, M., and Kidder, J. Programmed instruction in the classroom. In L. Krasner and L. Ullmann (Eds.), *Case studies in behavior modification.* New York: Holt, Rinehart, & Winston, 1965.

California State Department of Education. *A master plan for special education in California.* Sacramento: The Department, 1973.

Dunn, L. M. (ed). *Exceptional Children in the Schools.* (2nd ed.). New York: Holt, Rinehart, & Winston, 1973.

Hewett, F. M. *Education of exceptional learners.* Boston: Allyn and Bacon, 1974.

Jones, R. L. Labels and stigma in special education. *Exceptional Children,* 1972, 38, 553-564.

Kirk, S. A. *Educating exceptional children* (2nd ed.). Boston: Houghton Mifflin, 1972.

Rhodes, W. C. The disturbing child: A problem of ecological management. *Exceptional Children,* 1967, 33, 449-455.

Schwitzgebel, R. The science of learning and the art of teaching. Paper presented at the First Annual Educational Engineering Conference, University of California, Los Angeles, 1965.

Webb, Lesley. *Children with special needs.* London: Colin Smythe, 1967.

Wickman E. *Children's behavior and teachers' attitudes.* New York: Commonwealth Fund, 1928.

EMOTIONALLY DISTURBED–ED

Bettelheim, B. *Truants from life: The rehabilitation of emotionally disturbed children.* Glencoe, Ill.: Free Press, 1955.

Bruno, F. Life values, manifest needs, and vocational interests as factors influencing professional career satisfaction among teachers of emotionally disturbed children. *Dissertation Abstracts,* 1969.

Hewett, F. M. *The emotionally disturbed child in the classroom.* Boston: Allyn and Bacon, 1968.

Morse, W. C. The crisis teacher. In N. Long, W. Morse, and R. Newman (Eds.), *Conflict in the classroom: The education of emotionally disturbed children.* Belmont, Calif.: Wadsworth, 1965.

LEARNING DISABLED–LLOYD

Bateman, B. Learning disabilities—yesterday, today, and tomorrow. *Exceptional Children,* 1964, 31, 167.

Gearheart, B. R. *Learning disabilities: Educational strategies.* St. Louis: Mosby, 1973.

McCarthy, J. J., and McCarthy, J. F. *Learning disabilities.* Boston: Allyn and Bacon, 1969.

MENTALLY RETARDED–MARK

Baller, W. R., Charles, D., and Miller, E. Mid-life attainment of the mentally retarded: A longitudinal study. *Genetic Psychology Monographs,* 1967, 75, 235-329.

Edgerton, R. B. *The cloak of competence: Stigma in the lives of the mentally retarded.* Berkeley: University of California Press, 1967.

Heiss, W. E., and Mischio, G. S. Designing curriculum for the educable mentally retarded. *Focus on Exceptional Children,* 1971, 3, 1–10.

President's Committee on Mental Retardation. *Report to the president: A proposed program for national action to combat mental retardation.* Superintendent of Documents, U.S. Government Printing Office, Washington, D.C., October, 1962.

SOCIALLY AND CULTURALLY DISADVANTAGED–SADIE

Morlan, J. Multisensory learning. In S. W. Tiedt (Ed.), *Teaching the disadvantaged child.* New York: Oxford University Press, 1968.

Parker, W. Science activities. In S. W. Tiedt (Ed.), *Teaching the disadvantaged child.* New York: Oxford University Press, 1968.

Reissman, F. *The culturally deprived child.* New York: Harper & Row, 1962.

VISUALLY HANDICAPPED–VERA

American Foundation for the Blind. *A teacher education program for those who serve blind children and youth.* New York: American Foundation for the Blind, 1961.

Ashcroft, S. Blind and partially seeing children. In L. Dunn (Ed.), *Exceptional children in the schools.* New York: Holt, Rinehart, & Winston, 1963.

HEARING HANDICAPPED–HARRY

Groht, M. *Natural language for deaf children.* Washington, D.C.: The Volta Bureau, 1958.

Myklebust, H. R. *Psychology for deafness: Sensory deprivation, learning, and adjustment.* New York: Grune and Stratton, 1960.

SPEECH HANDICAPPED–STEVE

Bloodstein, O., Jaeger, W., and Tureen, J. A study of the diagnosis of stuttering by parents of stutterers and nonstutterers. *Journal of Speech and Hearing Disorders,* 1952, 17, 308–315.

Van Riper, C. *Speech correction: Principles and methods.* Englewood Cliffs, N. J.: Prentice-Hall, 1954.

PHYSICALLY HANDICAPPED–PHYLLIS

Connor, F. P., Rusalem, H., and Cruickshank, W. M. Psychological considerations of crippled children. In W. Cruickshank (Ed.), *Psychology of exceptional children and youth.* Englewood Cliffs, N. J.: Prentice-Hall, 1971.

Friedman, R. J., and MacQueen, J. C. Psychoeducative considerations of physical handicapping conditions in children. *Exceptional Children,* 1971, 37, 538–539.

GIFTED–GARY

Gallagher, J. J. *Teaching the gifted child.* Boston: Allyn and Bacon, 1964.

Terman, L. M., and Oden, M. H. *The gifted group at mid-life.* Stanford, Calif.: Stanford University Press, 1959.

MULTIPLE HANDICAPPED–SARA

Hopkins, T.W., Bice, H. V., and Colton, K. C. *Evaluation and education of the cerebral palsied child.* Washington, D.C.: International Council for Exceptional Children, 1954.

Moed, M., and Litwin, D. The employability of the cerebral palsied. *Rehabilitation Literature,* 1963, 24, 266–277.

MULTIPLE HANDICAPPED–PAUL

Bagley, C. R. The educational performance of children with epilepsy. *The British Journal of Educational Psychology,* 1970, 40, 82–83.

Dennerll, R. D., Rodin, E. A., Gonzales, S., Schwartz, M. L., and Lin, Y. Neurological and psychological factors related to employability of persons with epilepsy. *Epilepsia,* 1966, 1, 318–329.

CAREER EXPLORATION AND PREPARATION

Often it is difficult to identify a personal teaching relationship with a general concept such as career education because of its many interpretations and even more difficult to see how other teachers fit into the same general concept. If communication relating to career education for learners with special needs is to be frequent and productive, a certain amount of common understanding must be established in terms of a teacher's own perception of the concept of career education and that teacher's personal contributions to it. This is especially true when communication is to be intensified within an occupational field, among different occupational areas, and between occupational and typically nonoccupational disciplines. ∾ The primary

intent of this chapter is to provide a common explanation of career education and to break down the concept into the awareness, exploration, and preparation phases. By having a basic understanding of career education in general and by recognizing the relationship to each phase, it is expected that 1) communication among teachers from similar occupational areas at the junior and senior high school will be more productive, 2) communication between teachers of different occupational fields will be more productive and, most important, 3) communication between occupational and special education teachers will be more productive to the benefit of the special needs learner.

CAREER EDUCATION DEFINED

Career education is interpreted by many people as simply being a new name for such occupational programs as home economics, industrial education, and business education; however, a much broader meaning is intended. In 1972, Hoyt et al. defined career education as

> *the total effort of public education and the community aimed at helping all individuals to become familiar with the work values of a work-oriented society, to integrate these values into their personal value system, and to implement these values into their personal lives in such a way that work becomes possible, meaningful, and satisfying to each individual.*

Several features of the definition need emphasis. The first is the broad spectrum of "public education," which includes not only vocational education programs but also the college preparatory programs. Second is the involvement of the community as a source of curriculum planning advice and supplying work experience opportunities. Third, the word "individual" is essential if we recognize that one of our students needs a curriculum focused toward becoming a medical doctor while another will be preparing for a more immediate occupation as an X-ray technician. The fourth is the awareness that the "work values" of certain occupations include working conditions, life styles, and expected monetary compensation. The fifth relates to the "Who am I?" question we all face as we cultivate a "personal value system" for use in the decision-making process. Obviously, we must ask ourselves how important is money and status, but possibly more important, what do we enjoy doing, what can we do well, and what might we contribute to our society. Sixth, the definition involves the blending of personal values and work values. This blending process implies the efforts of parents, academic teachers, practical arts teachers, special education teachers, administrators, and counselors in helping students make appropriate career choices and prepare for them. This theme of cooperation and group planning will be woven throughout this text.

FUNDAMENTAL CONCEPTS OF CAREER EDUCATION

Early in the 1970s the personal commitment and driving force of the Commissioner of the U.S. Office of Education, Sidney P. Marland, Jr. was responsible for drawing national attention and resources to the career education movement. The booklet, *Career Education, A Handbook for Implementation,* and succeeding publications by the same writing team, formalized the basic ideas and accelerated progress toward establishing career education as a stable educational thrust. The basic concepts are stated as follows:

1. Preparation for successful working careers shall be a key objective to all education.
2. Every teacher in every course will emphasize the contribution that subject matter can make to a successful career.
3. "Hands-on occupational experiences" will be used as a method of teaching and motivating the learning of abstract or academic content.
4. Preparation for careers will be recognized as the mutual interaction of work attitudes, human relations skills, orientation to the nature of the workaday world, exposure to alternative career choices, and the acquisition of actual job skills.
5. Learning will not be reserved for the classroom, but learning environments for career education will also be identified in the home and the community and in employing establishments.
6. Beginning in early childhood and continuing through the regular school years, career education will seek to extend its time horizons

from "womb to tomb." It will provide the flexibility for a youth to leave for experience and return to school for further education (including not only opportunity for upgrading and continued refurbishing for adult workers but also productive use of leisure time and the retirement years).

7. Career education is a basic and pervasive approach to all education, but it in no way conflicts with other legitimate educational objectives related to citizenship, to culture, to family responsibility, and to basic education.

In 1972 Hoyt et al. added an eighth underlying principle to the list:

8. The school cannot shed responsibility for the individual just because he or she has been handed a diploma or has dropped out. While it may not perform the actual placement function, the school has the responsibility to stick with youth until they have their feet firmly on the next step of a career ladder, help them get back on the ladder if their feet slip, and be available to help them onto a new ladder at any point in the future when the old one proves to be too short or unsteady.

CAREER EDUCATION MODEL

The preceeding eight concepts and related basic components supplied the foundation for the development of numerous career education models and a multitude of definitions of career education.

The original model, presented in *Career Education: A Handbook For Implementation* (1972), represents career education with respect to vocational education, the educational community, and the educational system.

The model illustrated in Figure 2-1 (Career Education's Place in Education) subdivides the career education portion into three phases for discussion purposes.

PHASES OF CAREER EDUCATION

Career education has been divided into three phases. Phase I provides a foundation for the focal point of this text and is the elementary career

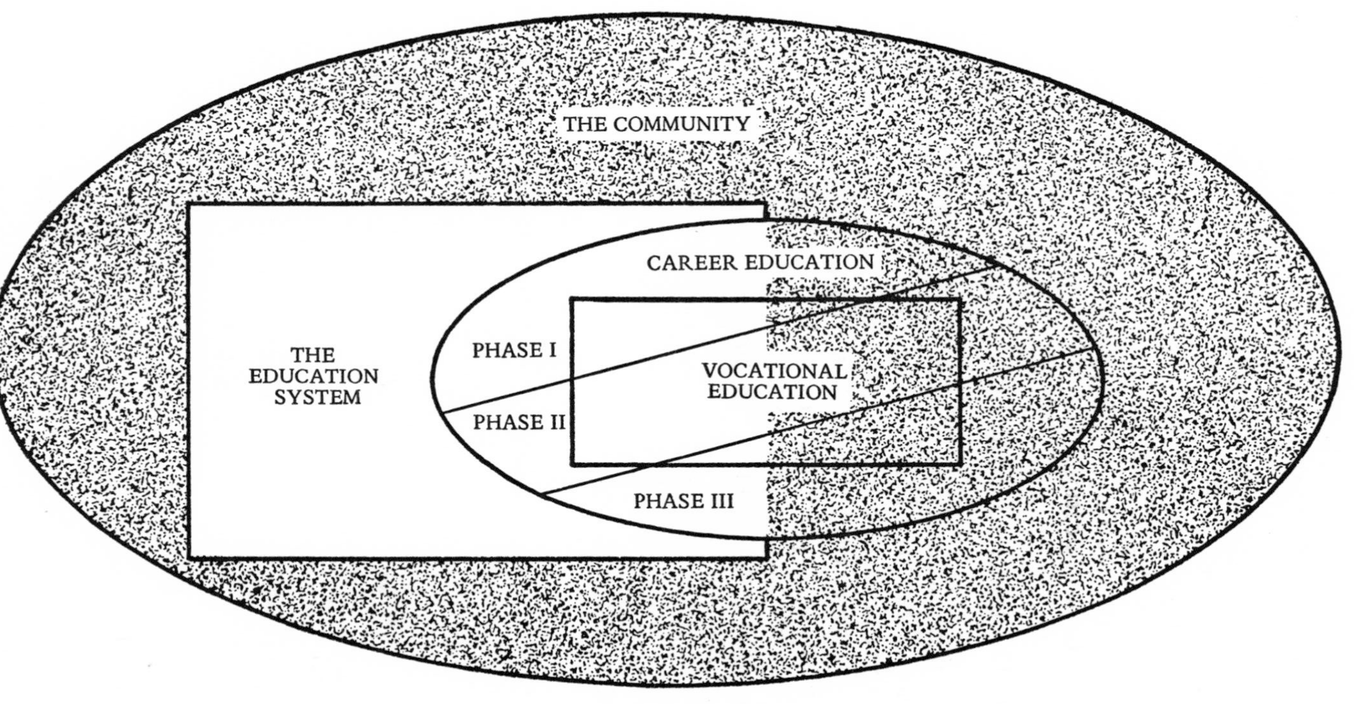

FIGURE 2–1. CAREER EDUCATION'S PLACE IN EDUCATION

awareness phase. Career awareness focuses upon making individuals familiar with all kinds of careers and helps them to recognize various levels within each career. For example, at an early age when many boys want to become either policemen or firemen and many girls want to become nurses and actresses, teachers should provide learning experiences that expose all youngsters to a wide range of public service careers involving various levels of training, degrees of responsibilities, and associated work values. The Technology for Children program developed in New Jersey provides examples of educational experiences to provide learners with an awareness of a broad spectrum of occupations. As implied in the Awareness-Exploration-Preparation Model, Figure 2-2, while the awareness phase relies heavily upon the educational system for the basic reading, writing, and arithmetic skills, it is also a part of vocational education and of community involvement. Although self-awareness seems to fall within the awareness phase of career education, a closer look makes it obvious that self-awareness and career awareness surface continually throughout one's life.

The remainder of this book will focus upon concepts relating to the career *exploration* and career *preparation* sections of the model.

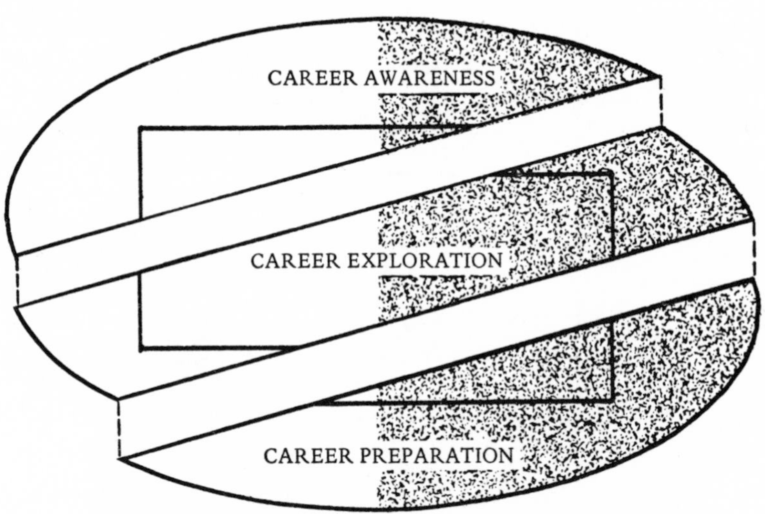

FIGURE 2-2. THREE PHASES OF CAREER EDUCATION

CAREER EXPLORATION

In the junior high or middle school, individuals are provided opportunities to explore the world of work with simulated and hands-on experiences involving materials, tools, processes, and personal relationships consistent with career opportunities. By exploring work values and personal values through these hands-on experiences with materials, tools, processes, and people, an individual will establish more realistic career goals to pursue in the career preparation phase. A few examples of nationally recognized career exploration programs that concentrate on hands-on exploration include American Industry, The World of Manufacturing, The World of Construction, Partnership in Vocational Education, Richmond Plan, and Project Feast (food, education, and service technology). Cochran (1970) identifies and describes the major curriculum innovations in the field of industrial education developed through the 1950's and 1960's. Spin-off programs with an occupational exploration flavor developed during this period at the local level and are evidenced in national and state convention programs in educational journals in the industrial education, home economics, and business education fields.

Thousands of teachers have taken advantage of the research and development involved in these and other curriculum materials and have localized and implemented the programs as they are provided. Other teachers

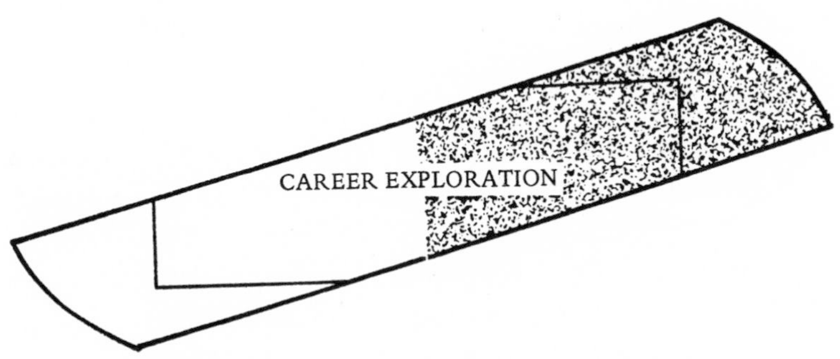

FIGURE 2-3. PHASE II CAREER EXPLORATION

have either blended their materials with the nationally recognized programs or have chosen to develop their own career exploration curriculum. Essential to the career exploration phase is a set of hands-on exploratory experiences that help each individual answer the "Who am I?" question and develop work values.

With respect to the career exploration model (Figure 2-4) four basic elements appear. First, Area A reflects a career education-educational system relationship. A continued development of language and communication, mathematics and science, social studies and socialization, and health and physical education provides the student with the background for additional formal education.

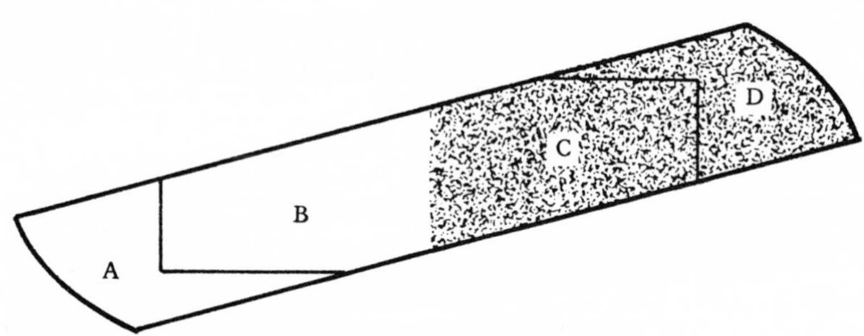

FIGURE 2–4. CAREER EXPLORATION

Area B is the prevocational hands-on exploration in industrial arts, home economics, general business, and the fine arts. Obviously applications of language and communication, mathematics and science, and socialization saturate the learning experiences. Students learn to identify materials, tools, and processes, discover physical properties of materials, measure sizes and quantities, compute costs, and develop social skills as part of the practical arts exploratory program.

Area C is that involving vocational education and the community. Work experiences such as Junior Achievement, simulated work in fine and practical arts classes, and observing workers in the community during field experiences characterize vocational-community exploration. Numerous professional journal articles and the nationally recognized curriculum materials mentioned earlier, provide a wealth of ideas and programs.

Area D is the career education-community relationship and relates to experiences such as community youth activities, including Scouts, church organizations, music groups, and part-time jobs. Often leadership-followership qualities, punctuality, responsibility, dependability, and trustworthiness are developed as youth become involved in community activities. Numerous after-school jobs such as paperboy or waitress help learners to establish values, discover interests, and develop talents.

CAREER PREPARATION

The senior high schools, area vocational or career centers, trade schools, community colleges, and universities are examples of learning environments for people preparing for a career.

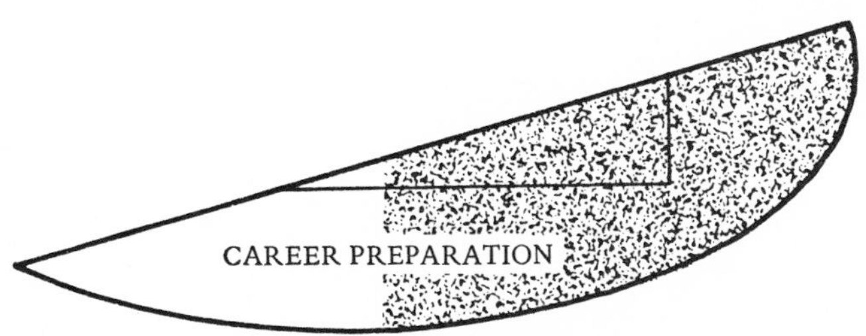

FIGURE 2-5. PHASE III CAREER PREPARATION

Effective career preparation programs do not attempt to establish general goals for all students such as "everyone going to college," but instead they simulate activities and real occupational experience to help individuals develop their own career options.

Some careers require two, four, six, or more years of college preparation as in health, medicine, education, agriculture, engineering, business, economics, science, arts, or humanities. On the other hand, numerous careers in manufacturing, construction, food preparation, agriculture, health, office occupations—to mention a few—may require no college preparation.

The Career Preparation portion of the Career Education Model in Figure 2-6 implies four important features. Area E relates to a continued emphasis on communication, language, computations, and socialization. Area F blends the vocational specialization aspects with the academic areas. This relationship suggests cooperative curriculum planning and team teaching.

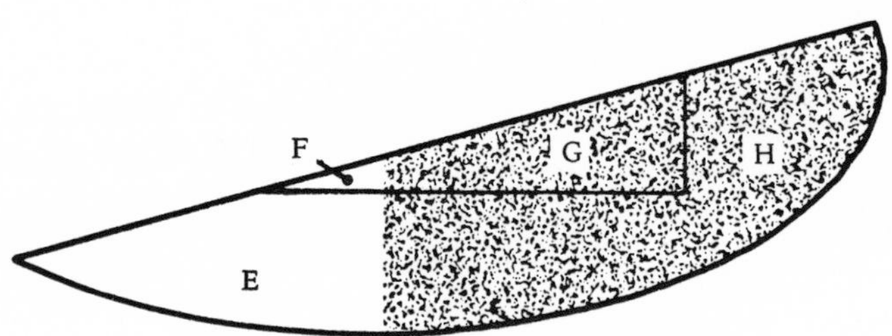

FIGURE 2-6. CAREER PREPARATION

As an example, a manufacturing activity in a welding program may involve the cooperative efforts of mathematics teachers, art instructors, English teachers, science teachers, and so on to broaden the experiences for the learners. This integrated teaching approach, which focuses upon practical experiences, often helps a "turned off" learner to recognize the importance of improving reading, writing, and mathematical skills.

The involvement of advisory groups in career-vocational education is suggested in Area G. Many students establish realistic career goals early in life by carefully planning a cooperative educational experience with an employer, serving an internship, entering an on-the-job training program, or choosing a part-time or full-time employment as a hands-on application of the formal education process.

Area H represents the successful integration of a student into the community as an independent productive citizen. This goal tends to be the target that students search for in elementary grades, aim at during middle/

junior high school, and stick to as they graduate from the public school system.

Some students put up a new target during the preparation phase. Open entrance-open exit policies will allow a student to step into employment with the opportunity of stepping back for further training for advancement or to provide the opportunity to try another occupational area.

Many adults will recycle the awareness, exploration, and preparation phases when their occupation no longer proves satisfying or meaningful.

CLUSTERS

Occupations that are similar are often referred to as clusters of occupations. These job families may relate to broad categories such as health occupations or may relate to a more specific group of jobs such as nursing occupations. The main theme of the cluster concept does not necessarily require teachers to establish career ladders for students to select, but instead to match job opportunity with student interests and abilities and especially to help persons to build their own career ladders within a cluster of occupations.

For example, the U.S. Office of Education designated fifteen occupational clusters for the development of a career awareness program. These clusters included:

Agri-business and natural resources
Business and office
Communication and media
Consumer and homemaking education
Construction
Environment
Fine arts and humanities
Health
Hospitality and recreation
Manufacturing
Marine science
Marketing and distribution

Personal services
Public services
Transportation occupations

These broad clusters serve career awareness, career exploration, and career preparation programs as a guide for identifying state, regional, and/or local occupational clusters. For example, a three-year Vocational Education-Special Education Curriculum Development project at Central Michigan University identified ten clusters of occupations as reflecting Michigan's manpower needs without regard to any handicapping conditions of employees. The ten clusters included:

Agriculture and natural resources
Automotive and power services
Clothing and textile services
Construction
Distribution
Food preparation and services
Graphics and communication media
Health
Manufacturing
Office and business occupations

During the inservice phase of this project hundreds of teachers, consultants, and administrators were observed developing regional and local clusters and subclusters representing differences in occupational potential in Detroit suburbs and the rural, recreational areas of northern Michigan.

The career exploration/preparation figure (Figure 2-7) illustrates a variety of clustered opportunities for the special needs learner as he or she moves from the security of a special education program through a series of career exploration and preparation experiences. The focal point is the availability of special needs services as provided by special education teachers, various consultants, and therapists. These services enhance and support each learner's career exploration and career preparation program. Career exploration experiences occur in general agriculture, industrial arts, home economics, and general business in the figure, as well as, in many fine arts,

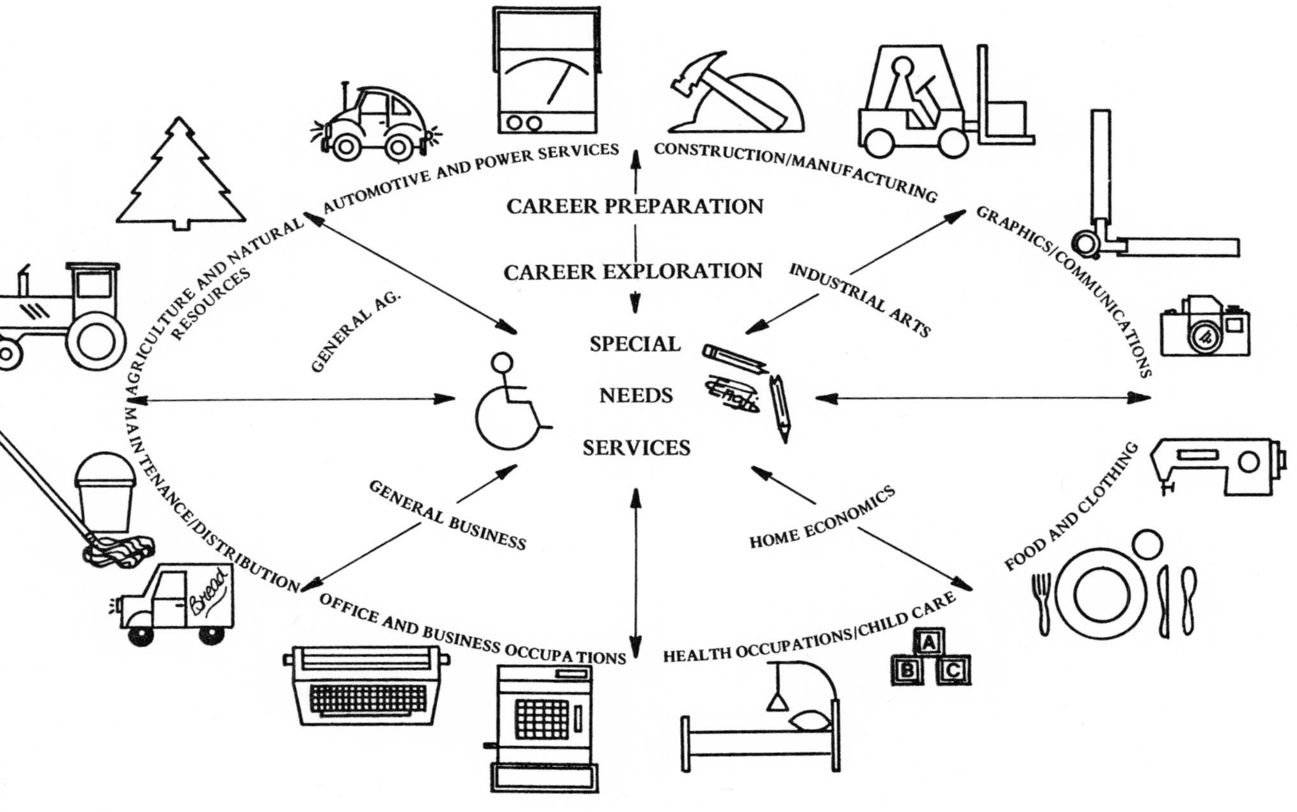

FIGURE 2-7. CAREER EXPLORATION AND PREPARATION

athletic, and academic offerings. Most learners with special needs will attend these classes with their nondisabled peers but will require periodic reinforcement and therapy from the special education staff. This support may be necessary in reading for many individuals, mathematics for others, or speech therapy for another, and almost all will need their self-confidence and social skills bolstered periodically. Through an integrated teaching/counseling approach, successful and unsuccessful experiences during the exploring activities will help the learner center in on the most appropriate career preparation cluster.

Similar special education support is necessary for the learner as he enters and becomes involved in a career preparation program. Many of these programs will prepare the learner for employment upon graduation from high school, while others will require additional technical preparation or college work. The availability of a unified, coordinated effort on the part of special education, vocational and practical arts instructors, academic teachers, and so forth allows the learner with special needs to move through educational experiences in a meaningful way.

Clustering provides administrators and teachers with an organizational strategy for developing career exploration programs with middle school students and in providing relevant career preparation programs for young adults. The cluster concept will be thoroughly analyzed in Chapter 8 with an emphasis on how to localize and personalize clusters for learners with special needs.

CAREER LADDERS

For many teachers, the term career ladder relates to the established job families that have basic entry occupations on the first rung and the most sophisticated occupations near the top rung. Career lattice is also used frequently to represent horizontal relationships between work experience and training from one career ladder to another. For example, Mark (our mentally retarded example in Chapter 1), studies agricultural mechanics in high school, completes his co-op work experience as a student ag mechanic, and after graduating from high school selects an occupation as a mechanic at a farm equipment dealership. Instead of attending company training programs to improve his technical competence, he has an opportunity to move laterally in the same company as a farm equipment salesman. His mechanic experience and training provide an excellent background for his new salesman position.

In many schools the college prep programs have become a part of the multi-faceted development of occupational programs that will provide people with numerous stepping-off points from various career ladders. Let us examine a college program from a traditional and contemporary point of view. Some who decide in high school to become medical doctors actually become doctors, and a few of them return to their career ladder for further study to become neurosurgeons. Traditionally, we may have felt, "Well, some make it and some don't." Contemporary teachers are deliberately providing experiences for students who may find the entry step on their career ladder as a health service support person such as X-ray technician, inhalation therapist, or a physical therapist. Due to personal drive, talent, and financial assistance, some will chose to return to colleges for advanced levels of training needed for personal advancement.

Evidently, far too little effort is being expended nationally on the identification and cultivation of career goals and career ladders for the learner with special needs. Barone (1973) indicates that only 21 to 25 percent of the handicapped students leaving school between 1972 and 1976 will be fully employed or engaged in higher education. Although a small percentage of the severely and multiply handicapped persons will find their highest level of achievement in sheltered family or institutional settings, approximately two-thirds of the handicapped are projected as being either underemployed or unemployed. Without a coordinated local, state, and national effort these projections indicate that thousands of special needs persons will not successfully complete school nor enter gainful employment because of some physical, mental, emotional, socioeconomic and/or cultural difficulty. Traditional efforts have been neither financially responsible or morally prudent.

Since the learner with special needs may not have the necessary personal drive, talent, or financial assistance, career ladders are obviously more complex to create than for his nonhandicapped peers. Helping one who needs help by providing broad career exploration and preparation experiences and taking the time to discuss one's personal abilities and career possibilities must be recognized and respected as being complex and absolutely essential.

Career ladders obviously have a technical component but, even more important, they have a human interaction component. It seems possible that, when students are given proper career awareness and career exploration opportunities, each student in school will chart her or his own career ladder and be prepared to revise it periodically.

CAREER DECISION MAKING

For exceptional teachers, career decision making is a familiar and pleasant concept because they have always developed a meaningful rationale and explained to each student how concepts to be learned may be applied to their future life.

Those in the K–6 career awareness phase of career education have an opportunity to provide a valuable and creative component to a child's future as he or she thinks, "Who am I and what am I becoming?"

For teachers in the middle school or junior high school (7–9), the career exploration phase provides hands-on experiences involving materials, tools, processes, and people involved in a variety of occupations in our society. Each of these experiences can help to clarify strengths, weaknesses, likes, and dislikes, which will make the career decision-making process more realistic.

Teachers in the senior high school, area vocational centers, or any programs of 9–12 career preparation will focus upon learning experiences that simulate and replicate tasks expected by employers and by customers.

Since most Americans value making a living and most students are looking forward to being independent someday, the relationship between school learning and potential employment provides a logical and meaningful vehicle for the teacher in making learning experiences relevant for the student. This feature is utilized at all levels of education by good teachers, who constantly struggle to teach their students to identify, discuss, explore, and prepare for future occupations. This teaching concept is fundamental in career education; therefore, the teachers' work experiences are an essential part of their preparation for teaching. For example, to have sold papers on the corner, worked on a farm, in a factory, at a restaurant, or as a hospital aide, or to have built houses helps teachers understand what students face as they search for a place as a worker in our society. The insight, compassion, patience, and concern that teachers provide young people making important career decisions is essential, especially for the special needs learner. It has been said that some students will make appropriate decisions without much help, but the handicapped and disadvantaged need optimistic and creative teachers to help them recognize their potentials and make realistic career decisions.

SUMMARY

During the early 1900's parents were doing much of the career education because their children's help was needed at home. Career awareness, exploration, and preparation were experienced in much of rural America as young people learned how to raise animals and crops, build buildings, design and repair machines, prepare food, make clothing, care for children, buy and sell goods, and provide basic first aid. The one-room school house was designated as the place where reading, writing, and arithmetic would be taught.

Both the home environment and school programs have undergone drastic change. The eighty-acre farm has become an acre lot with a modern, attractive home equipped with educational TV programs, educational toys, encyclopedias, books, magazines, newspapers, and numerous other school-related materials. The one-room school has become a series of neighborhood elementary schools, middle schools, consolidated high schools, and skill centers. Reading, writing, and arithmetic continue to be important, as in the one-room school house, and contemporary schools recognize the need for expanded programs in these areas.

The family still provides an important influence on the future employment of students. However, the school system is expanding its role by providing experiences that will make the students aware of thousands of occupations on hundreds of career ladders and preparing them for a career ladder that will provide not only employment but also insight as to requirements for advancement and for job satisfaction.

The concepts, components, and definitions of career education may not seem new, but since the 1960's the movement has become a more common and deliberate theme for formal education because of the increasing need for educational experiences that are meaningful for more individuals.

A refreshing and challenging characteristic of the career education movement of the 1970's is the attempt to coordinate the efforts of all teachers for the sake of the individual student. This career education movement has caused many teachers to write curriculum in a different way, to add and modify facilities, and to change from teaching "what everyone should know" to preparing materials for "individuals." No longer can society afford to educate only those most easily educated and allow those who find learning difficult to drop out, be pushed out, or graduate without having established personal career goals.

REFERENCES

Bailey, J. A. Career development concepts: Significance and utility. *Personnel and Guidance Journal,* 1968, 47, 24–28.

Bailey, Larry J. Clarifying some misconceptions: A look at what constitutes career education. *Illinois Career Education Journal,* 1972, 29, 8–13. (Illinois Board of Vocational Education.)

Banta, Trudy W., and Marshall, Patricia. Bringing schools and industry together. *Manpower,* 1970, 2, 24–41.

Barone, C. Samuel. Paper presented to a forum of national organizations sponsored by the Vocational Evaluation and Work Adjustment Association, The National Rehabilitation Association, and The President's Committee on Employment of the Handicapped, October, 1973.

Career education: A handbook for implementation. U.S. Department of Health, Education and Welfare, Office of Education, 1972.

Career education: A national priority. Mimeograph available from the Maryland State Department of Education, James L. Reid, Assistant State Superintendent in Vocational-Technical Education.

Center for Vocational and Technical Education. *A comprehensive career education model.* Columbus: Ohio State University, 1971.

Cochran, Leslie H. *Innovative programs in industrial education.* Bloomington, Ill.: McKnight and McKnight, 1970.

ERIC Abstracts. *Developing vocational education programs in the public schools.* Washington, D.C.: AASA, March 1971.

Evans, Rupert N. *Foundations of vocational education.* Columbus, Ohio: Charles E. Merrill, 1971.

Evans, Rupert N., Mangum, Garth L., and Pragan, Otto. *Education for employment: The background and potential of the vocational education amendments of 1968.* Ann Arbor: Institute of Labor and Industrial Relations, University of Michigan, 1969.

Feldman, Marvin. *Making education relevant.* New York: Ford Foundation, 1966.

Frank, Alan R., et al. Developing a work skills inventory. *Teaching Exceptional Children,* 1971, 3, 82–86.

Hoyt, Kenneth B., et al. *Career education: What it is and how to do it.* Salt Lake City: Olympus, 1972.

Hoyt, Kenneth B. Career education and the handicapped person. Unpublished paper presented at the American Vocational Association Convention, 1975.

Lux, Donald G., Ray, Willis E., and Towers, Edward R. *A rationale and structure for industrial arts subject matter.* (Industrial Arts Curriculum Project 1966.) Columbus, Ohio: Council of Graduate Students in Industrial Technology Education, 1912 Neil Avenue. ED 013955, VT 003203.

Mangum, Garth L. *Reorienting vocational education.* Ann Arbor: Institute of Labor and Industrial Relations, University of Michigan, 1968.

McMurrin, Sterling M. (Ed.). *Functional education for disadvantaged youth.* New York: Committee for Economic Development, 1971.

Reynolds, M. L., Lutz, Ronald J., Phelps, L. Allen, and Johnson, Cleo B. *Cluster guides.* Mt. Pleasant: Central Michigan University, 1973.

Reynolds, M. L., Lutz, Ronald J., Phelps, L. Allen, and Johnson, Cleo B. *Program guide.* Mt. Pleasant: Central Michigan University, 1973.

A VIEW OF TEACHERS WORKING WITH SPECIAL NEEDS LEARNERS

As indicated throughout the text, it is believed that maximum success in working effectively with special needs students commonly requires the co-operative involvement of a team, both professionals and others. A few of the team members include vocational and practical arts teachers, special education teachers, administrators, counselors, parents, siblings, peers, and employers. In this chapter particularly—and in the rest of the book as well—reference will be made to various instructors, to specific special needs students from Chapter 1

who are variously handicapped, and to a special-help team working cooperatively within a model school system. Figure 3–1 will help the reader keep track of the instructors and learners by name, identifying information, and page numbers where they are originally introduced.

Effective involvement as a team member may require mutual understanding of backgrounds in education and work experiences in addition to understanding the types of facilities and experiences that are provided for learners. In Chapter 2 the focus was on the learners described, but here the focus is upon the teachers' backgrounds and their involvement in cooperative planning, instructing, and evaluation.

Sometimes special educators are unclear as to the background and education of practical arts teachers, for example, business education, general agriculture, home economics, and industrial arts. They may also need some clarification on the backgrounds of vocational teachers in commercial foods, welding, or data processing. Similarly, many practical arts teachers and vocational instructors may need a clearer understanding of the role and background of a junior and senior high school special education teacher. The intent of this Chapter is to provide typical examples of vocational, practical arts, and special educators who are cooperatively working with special needs learners.

EPISODES

The following descriptions point up the importance of the cooperative philosophy and illustrate the involvement of occupational and special needs teachers in career exploration and preparation programs. Each occupational teacher has at least two special needs learners mainstreamed with his or her regular students. The special needs teacher attempts to work on an individual basis with each special needs learner, and the learning activities focus directly upon concepts being learned in their vocational classes.

The cooperative teaching model (Figure 3–2) will be analyzed in detail with respect to each teacher and the learning activities being provided for each learner. Beginning with the agriculture instructor the descriptions will follow in a clockwise direction and conclude with the special needs teacher.

The cooperative teaching model graphically represents the activities of a public school system that integrates learners with special needs into regular

FIGURE 3-1. INSTRUCTIONAL STAFF AND LEARNERS WITH SPECIAL NEEDS

PAGE	INSTRUCTORS	LEARNERS	PAGE
51	Al Reese (agriculture mechanics and vocational agriculture)	Mark (mentally retarded)	13
53	Tom Powers (industrial arts and vocational automotive)	Steve (speech handicapped)	16
54	Mike Cary (construction)	Bill (brain damaged) Gary (gifted)	10 18
55	Matt Forbes (industrial arts and vocational welding)	Lloyd (learning disabled)	12
56	Greg Atwood (vocational drafting)	Ed (emotionally disturbed)	11
56	Connie Casha (graphic communications)	Harry (hearing handicapped)	16
57	Chauncy Burger (commercial food preparation) Jan Craig (home economics)	Mary (visually impaired)	9
58	Sue Loth (clothing construction)	Phyllis (physically handicapped)	17
59	Hilda Moore (child care)	Sara (multiply handicapped)	20
60	Alice Healy (health occupations)	Sadie (disadvantaged)	14
62	Betty Ness (business and office occupations)	Vera (visually handicapped)	15
62	Bob Grande (typing)		
63	Theopolis Jackson (building maintenance)	Paul (multiply handicapped)	20
64	Candy Jenkins (special education)	All special needs learners	9–21
	ADDITIONAL SUPPORTIVE PERSONNEL		
53	Carolyn Olsen (speech therapist)		
59	Pat Porta (physical therapist)		
62	Cleo Ester (visually handicapped)		
66	Ted Johnson (general mathematics)		
66	Rhonda Smith (basic English)		
66	Gordon Ramsey (reading specialist)		
59	Lori Richards (placement coordinator)		
66	Norm Ely (work-study coordinator)		
58	Merle Francis (special needs coordinator)		
57	George Edmund (principal)		

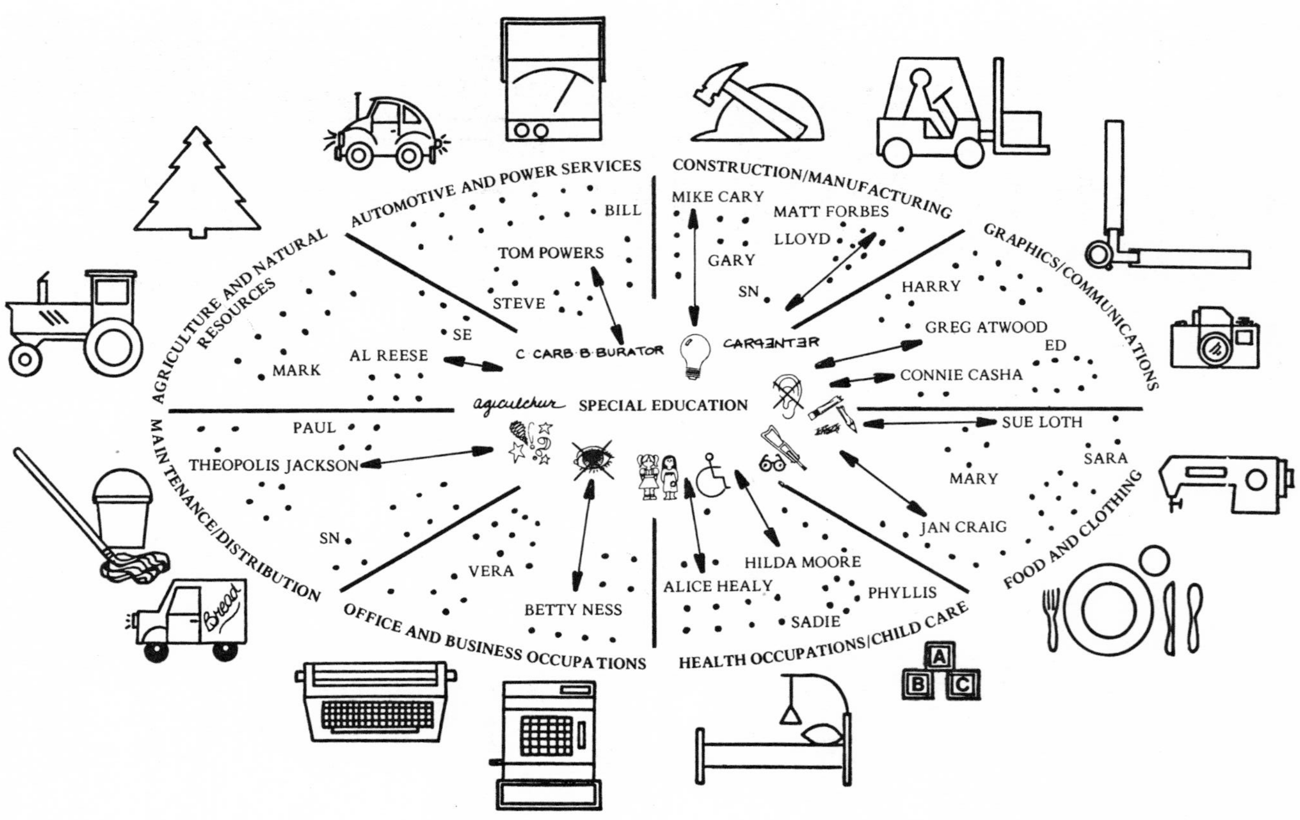

FIGURE 3–2. COOPERATIVE TEACHING MODEL

practical arts and vocational classes. The arrows suggest a cooperative planning and teaching relationship between the special education staff and the practical arts and vocational personnel with regard to the learners with special needs. This cooperative effort focuses upon the assessment, instruction, and evaluation of each learner. All three of these components occur frequently to keep the learner actively involved in meaningful and appropriate experiences.

Each dot symbolizes a learner at a work station within the classroom and laboratory settings. Each learner with special needs, as described in Chapter 1, is integrated into the cluster most suited to his or her interests and abilities. The practical arts and vocational teachers involve them with the regular students in a buddy system. For example, Mark is working with a regular student in agriculture mechanics overhauling an engine. Phyllis is working with five other students with a group of children in the child care program, and Vera is one of nine students working on improving typing skills in the business cluster.

The absence of a line or barrier between Ms. Candy Jenkins, special education teacher, and the other teachers in the practical arts and vocational areas is intended to imply that teachers are welcome and feel comfortable in each other's facilities. Sometimes Ms. Jenkins spends time in the classrooms and laboratories to observe students and discuss their progress. Teachers in occupational areas also feel comfortable visiting the special education staff to find ways to improve the learning situation for students having difficulty.

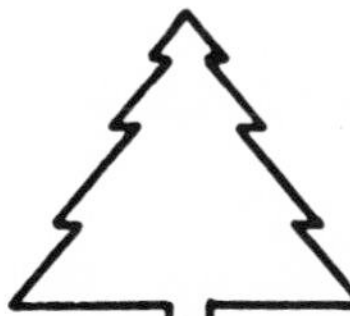

FIGURE 3-3. AGRICULTURE AND NATURAL RESOURCES

Mr. Reese with Mark in Agriculture

Mr. Al Reese, vocational agriculture instructor, was born and raised on a dairy farm and graduated from a state land grant university where he was educated in "on the farm" and "off the farm" occupations in agriculture. He is recognized locally as an excellent teacher, which is reflected in his classroom organization, student interest in agriculture mechanics, the productivity of the experimental plots, and the attractiveness of the school greenhouse and landscaping. Each year the Future Farmers of America (FFA) club competes successfully in state competition, which provides an added incentive for students to do well.

Although Mr. Reese has had students in the past who experienced difficulty with reading, Mark (described in Chapter 1) has been the first to be identified as educable mentally retarded. As expected, the major difficulties Mark experiences are in reading, writing, and arithmetic. He is now in the agriculture mechanics area with nine other students. His farm background and close working relationship with his father have provided a compensatory effect on his learning difficulty.

Additionally, the experiences in agriculture mechanics that Mr. Reese has organized are all completed in a buddy system where two students work together on each job.

A second special education student in vocational agriculture class has been working in the greenhouse with the other students. They raised and sold several hundred poinsettias at Christmas, Easter lilies at Easter, and are now concentrating on the tomatoes, peppers, and other garden vegetables for the spring season.

Mr. Reese feels encouraged by the informal curriculum planning that he and Ms. Jenkins work on during their common planning period. This communication helps to maintain a consistent set of learning activities for Mark. For example, Mark and his buddy have been overhauling an engine. During this time Ms. Jenkins has been helping him compute volume problems with cylinders so he better understands cubic inch and cubic centimeter displacement. She has also helped him with reading assignments from the textbook and with reading technical information from technical manuals.

Mark's father, who is also the counselor, and the vocational director visit the vocational agriculture class routinely, thus providing reinforcement for Mark, Mr. Reese, and Ms. Jenkins.

One of Mr. Reese's advisory committee members operates a John Deere dealership and Mark is enthusiastic about the co-op experience being planned for him and is hoping to work there after graduation.

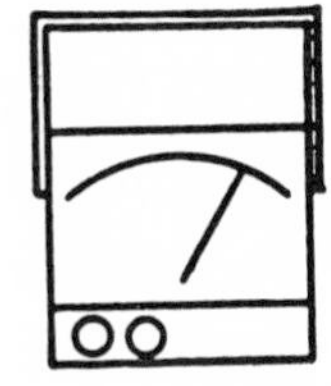

FIGURE 3-4. AUTOMOTIVE AND POWER SERVICES

Mr. Powers with Steve in Automotive

Mr. Tom Powers, the automotive and power instructor, received his undergraduate and graduate education in industrial education where he concentrated on a power and energy cluster. Due to his work experiences in automotive mechanics, he graduated as a vocationally certified automotive teacher and now has a split assignment as an industrial arts teacher in power and energy during the morning and a vocational automotive instructor in the afternoon.

Bill, who has some brain damage, is in Mr. Powers' first-hour industrial arts class and, although Bill is not doing well in some of his other classes, he finds the introduction to power and energy exciting and challenging. Bill and his classmates may use Mr. Powers' class for several purposes. Some may someday find employment in the automotive, small engines, or power and energy fields due to their exploratory experiences. Some others will use the class for vocational purposes, and most will apply their knowledge and skill to do their own minor automotive and small engine maintenance work as a leisure time activity. A few students may find that automotive and power services is not a field they want to pursue, and this actually helps them narrow down the possible career choices.

On the other hand, Steve, our speech handicapped student, is in Mr. Powers' vocational automotive class. His exploratory experiences in using basic hand tools and developing a basic understanding of the operation of small (lawn mower type) engines and automotive engines were his favorite experiences in junior high school.

Since Steve's technical competence is improving extremely well, Ms. Jenkins (special education teacher), Ms. Carolyn Olsen (speech therapist), and Mr. Powers have planned to have Steve handle the customer service responsibilities with two other students for the next few weeks. The three teachers are convinced that he can handle the job and that it will help him control his stuttering problems. Ms. Jenkins, Ms. Olsen, and Mr. Powers eat lunch during the same period and much of their planning occurs then.

Steve understands the importance of controlling his speech in his new role as service manager, and all three teachers are eager to help him successfully overcome his handicap.

FIGURE 3-5. CONSTRUCTION

Mr. Cary with Gary in Construction

Mr. Mike Cary completed an apprenticeship as a carpenter, and has had his own residential contracting business for a number of years. Since he has always been interested in teaching, he utilized his GI Bill provisions several years ago and entered a four-year teacher education program. He began teaching as a vocationally certified, nondegree teacher and completed his university work at the end of his first year of teaching.

Mr. Cary works with two "crews" of students in building trades. The first-year crew spends most of its time at the school developing basic hand tool and power tool skills necessary in the building of a home. These skills range from identifying and knowing where to use common building materials to actually performing basic carpentry, electrical, plumbing, heating, and/or masonary skills in simulated activities. His second crew builds a house, starting with locating the building site and ending when the house is sold.

Gary, our gifted learner, is in the first crew that is learning what goes into building a house. He was an extremely productive student in industrial arts last year, simulated building trades this year, and may continue next year as a house is being built. Mr. Cary has spent considerable time talking with Ms. Jenkins—primarily on the phone—about ways to handle Gary. Basically, Gary is an extremely bright, energetic, independent thinker. When he is in the mood, he completes the reading and written work in record time, but he is often reluctant to complete the skill development activities. When he is not in the mood, the phone rings regularly in the special needs room. Nothing works all the time with Gary, but having leadership responsibilities such as being cleanup foreman, showing another classmate how to wire a three-way switch, and preparing orders for supplies usually keeps him on the right track. Ms. Jenkins has helped to channel Gary's spare time into productive work by locating and keeping available the current issues of magazines related to designing, building, and remodeling houses.

FIGURE 3–6. MANUFACTURING

Mr. Forbes with Lloyd in Manufacturing

Similar to Tom Powers, Mr. Matt Forbes completed his undergraduate work in industrial education at a four-year university but also completed an apprenticeship as a welder. He teaches one two-hour block of vocational welding and several sections in the manufacturing, construction, and power exploratory courses. Within these courses students explore six-week units in twelve different areas, from which some students may make career choices.

Lloyd, who is learning disabled, experienced unusual success and satisfaction during the unit of "manufacturing wood products." Mr. Forbes organized the class into a factory setting, and the learners actually designed, sketched, planned, produced, and sold a large number of products. Lloyd's class chose to mass produce a wren house in kit form. Each student had a labor-type job as well as a management position to get the "feel" of both kinds of work. Lloyd's management position was in the engineering department as a jigs and fixture designer, and his labor job was drilling the hole in the front piece for the bird to enter the house. Ms. Jenkins worked with him frequently on readings, related textbook units, newspapers, and magazine articles that she and Mr. Forbes had identified.

Next year Mr. Forbes plans to involve Lloyd in a number of custom welding jobs in vocational welding, where meeting a customer, estimating costs, determining time required, and doing the job satisfactorily are some of the learning experiences. Mr. Forbes's students are now in the process of manufacturing pairs of automotive jack stands. They have fifty sets sold so far and are anticipating additional orders. Since each student has at least one shift at each job in the production process, Ms. Jenkins has been kept especially busy helping the special needs learners with the math and writing needed to complete order forms for materials, balancing the budget, and doing the inventory.

Due to the close relationship between Mr. Forbes and Lloyd, Lloyd is anticipating employment in the welding field after he graduates. His first year in the welding class, followed by a co-op experience the following year, will certainly help him in making that career choice.

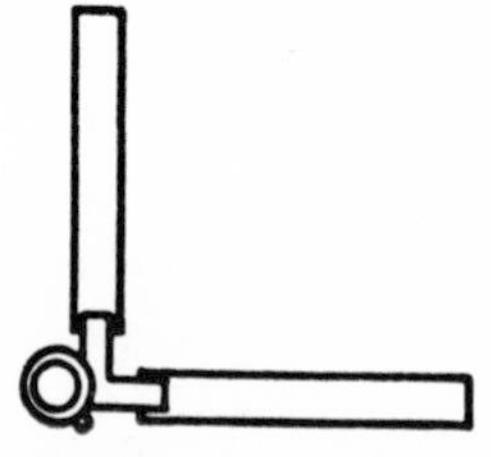

FIGURE 3–7. GRAPHICS

Mr. Atwood with Ed in Drafting

Mr. Greg Atwood is the vocational drafting instructor and has had a variety of experiences related to his teaching position. During his undergraduate studies he completed a six-month internship as a junior process engineer for a large automotive manufacturer. Although his degree is in industrial education, after graduation he returned to industry for two years to work in the engineering field. In an attempt to move into a rural setting to raise a family, he then accepted an industrial arts position that included exploratory experiences for seventh graders in manufacturing and construction and a choice for eight and ninth graders from the general areas of drawing, metalworking, woodworking, graphic arts, and power/energy. In junior high school where he taught, all students had industrial arts, and he worked closely with the special education teacher, basic academic teachers, and counselors to maximize the classes for those who were identified and some who could have been identified as special needs students.

Mr. Atwood began his tenth year of teaching as a vocational drafting instructor. Although many students in his previous classes had learning difficulties, Ed was the first with serious emotional problems. Ms. Jenkins, being very aware of his difficulties, provided a mjaor role in modifying Ed's behavior by using the learning experiences in vocational drafting as a vehicle for communicating with him. Mr. Atwood and Ms. Jenkins often spend time before school discussing and analyzing unusual situations that Ed has experienced and attempting to anticipate his next moves and programming for him.

FIGURE 3–8. COMMUNICATIONS MEDIA

Ms. Casha with Harry in Printing

Ms. Connie Casha is teaching graphic communications in high school and concentrates her instruction in the areas of sketching, drawing, typesetting, photography, and offset printing. She worked in a small home town printing establishment for several years after graduating from high school and had a position in the university Quick Copy Center while completing her undergraduate degree in industrial education. After teaching two years in the junior high school she transferred to the high school where she is in her sixth year of teaching. In junior high school she worked with all the students. Some liked school, some did not; some learned easily, some had difficulty learning, but this year she has her first deaf student–Harry.

Ms. Casha relies heavily upon the consultant for help with the hearing impaired. As she learns signing and finger spelling, Harry improves his lip-reading and signing techniques, and together they practice communication related to the printing occupations. Ms. Casha's genuine interest in learning this new technique of communication has had an impressively positive effect on most of Harry's classmates. Harry is no longer perceived by his peers as "different" but, instead, most realize that learning to talk with Harry would add a new dimension to their own lives.

FIGURE 3-9. FOOD PREPARATION AND SERVICE

Mr. Burger and Ms. Craig with Mary in Food Service

Mr. Chauncy Burger is the commercial foods instructor and does all of his teaching in the large foods lab (kitchen) with his paraprofessional, and he is visited often by the high school home economics teacher, Ms. Jan Craig. She completed a Bachelor of Science degree and worked several years in the waiter-waitress field before she began teaching. Mr. Burger developed most of his technical competence as an Air Force cook and later as a restaurant manager of a national motel chain. One might well ask: "Why would anyone leave a well-paying, stable position to become a nondegreed commercial foods teacher?" Many ingredients are blended into such a decision, but the strongest one seems to be related to one's life goals. The personal rewards related to sharing valuable knowledge and skill with learners who want to be independent, self-sufficient citizens are difficult to match.

Another critical ingredient in the decision was the work of a couple of insightful and sensitive administrators, the principal, Dr. Edmond, and the special needs coordinator, Mr. Francis, who discovered Mr. Burger's talent and were able to plant the seed of his becoming a teacher and then developing a sense of security, confidence, and support after he accepted the position. These administrators personally visit each classroom and laboratory in the school to complement instructors for the things that are impressive and to offer personal suggestions where improvement seems necessary. Their presence is rewarding to both the instructors and the students because it indicates that they care and think of themselves as an integral part of the team.

Since Mr. Burger is most challenged by the special needs students, he has his fair share of those students who have found school difficult. With the help of a paraprofessional to handle many of the daily routine duties connected with preparing food for a cafeteria line and a restaurant menu, Mr. Burger has a better opportunity to work individually with the students who are preparing the food and to develop learning materials for the special education teacher, for example, learning the proper names of cooking utensils, being able to measure accurately both by weight (pounds and ounces or grams and kilograms) and by volume (teaspoonsful and gallons or cubic centimeters and liters), being able to recognize such words in a recipe as shortening, and knowing the types of containers and locations of the items in the kitchen.

Mary, who needs her vision corrected, is in the high school home economics course and has so far enjoyed the unit in waiter-waitressing the most. Ms. Craig provides a variety of exploratory experiences that apply to living independently, pursuing leisure time activities, and choosing an occupational goal. Mary has learned a great deal with regard to knowing herself better, caring for her personal needs, and exploring many career possibilities. Unfortunately, she absolutely refuses to wear glasses during school because as she says, "I look funny," so several agencies are being contacted about getting contact lenses for her. She needs them and her parents cannot provide them.

FIGURE 3-10. CLOTHING SERVICES

Ms. Loth with Phyllis in Clothing

Ms. Sue Loth teaches clothing construction and received her undergraduate and graduate degrees from the department of home economics of a state university. She worked several summers in a drapery shop and one year as a seamstress to balance out her academic and work experience.

Phyllis, our physically handicapped learner, is one of the many handicapped and disadvantaged students that Ms. Loth has worked with during the past ten years. Her master's degree option in vocational education-special education provided an excellent background for preparing instructional materials and, more important, a better understanding of the learner in both home economics at the junior high school level and in her present high school position.

This semester Ms. Loth, Ms. Jenkins, Mr. Pat Porta (physical therapist), and Ms. Lori Richards (placement coordinator) have identified and secured a co-op position for Phyllis as an alteration tailor at a large department store. Ms. Loth has developed a curriculum that is divided up into modules or tasks that are sorted out and matched with the interests and abilities of each student. Phyllis has completed an average of one task every week, and these task modules have been helpful for Phyllis and Ms. Loth during the daily teaching-learning process. They have also been of help to Ms. Jenkins in preparing related materials and Mr. Porta as he talked with Phyllis's employer about the competencies she has developed. Much of the student's success is related to her stable, helpful personality, which says a lot for her loving parents, dedicated teachers, and conscientious therapists and counselors.

FIGURE 3-11. CHILD CARE

Ms. Moore with Sara in Child Care

Ms. Hilda Moore is the child care teacher who graduated from college with an undergraduate major in home economics and a graduate degree in a combination of child development and special education. She taught in the junior high school for six years as a home economics teacher, where the career exploration areas of food handling and preparation, textiles and clothing construction, consumer economics, and family life were provided for all students, both boys and girls, as a required course. This year Ms. Moore is in her third year as the child care instructor in a miniature world of preschool-sized tables, chairs, stoves, refrigerators, and a variety of child development toys, games, and pets. The eighteen youngsters range in age from three and one-half to five and spend two and one-half hours a day in the day care center. The high school students working with these youngsters spend two hours, either morning or afternoon, learning how to work with them.

Sara, our model for cerebral palsy, is one of Ms. Moore's afternoon students. She shows genuine interest in the little ones and demonstrates an ability to communicate with them. Ms. Jenkins (special needs), the physical therapist, and the counselor have spent considerable time with Sara helping her adjust to situations in the day care center. Sara's interest in child care seemed to blossom during her junior high school home economics class and it is hoped that, with the cooperative involvement of the team at school and her parents at home, she will have a co-op position next year. One of Ms. Moore's advisory committee members owns a nursery school and has visited class to see Sara in action with the thought of providing her a co-op position. Although Sara has mobility problems, her ability to attract the interest and attention of the youngsters almost makes the problem unimportant. Recently, one of the hinges of her leg brace needed adjusting, so she had several of the youngsters "help" her tighten an allen screw. As Ms. Moore has indicated, the youngsters don't seem to notice her handicap.

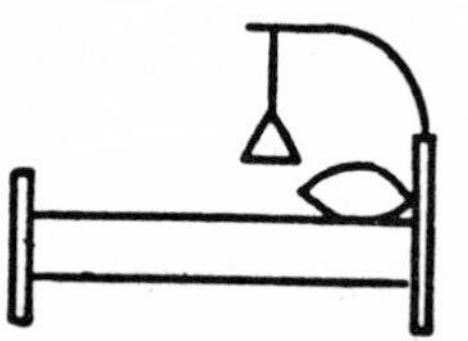

FIGURE 3-12. HEALTH OCCUPATIONS

Ms. Healy with Sadie in Health

Ms. Alice Healy is a registered nurse who worked in several hospitals for five years before accepting a position as a health occupations teacher two years ago. She will be completing her undergraduate teaching degree this year. Working with enthusiasm in the simulated hospital environment, she and the paraprofessional deal on an individual basis with each student as they learn how to feed, bathe, and care for patients' personal needs, perform basic procedures such as taking temperature, pulse, and respiration, and completing essential housekeeping tasks including bed making, dusting, and cleaning.

Sadie is our example of a learner who is disadvantaged and Ms. Jenkins and Ms. Healy have been concentrating on her employability skills including her ability to speak clearly, establish eye contact, listen intently, and work efficiently. One of the techniques they employ is to have Sadie—as well as the other students—keep track of the number of people she greets, makes eye contact with, and smiles at in the hallway during the time she is going to and coming from school and going from class to class. Another activity that takes place in the health lab is an attempt to encourage every student to talk to other students. The utilization of the buddy system in performing the basic health procedures of taking temperature, pulse, and respiration is helping to bring Sadie out of her low self-concept shell.

The close personal relationship that exists between Ms. Healy, a paraprofessional, and each student is one of the secrets of success in this situation. Each student has been carefully assessed as to interests, abilities, and attitudes in the health field, and the students are each on their own track leading to an occupation of their choice. For some teachers that may seem impossible but Ms. Healy and Ms. Jenkins (special education teacher) have worked out a modularized curriculum that allows each student to complete tasks that are necessary for their entry occupation.

Sadie, for example, is leaning toward hospital housekeeping as the first step of her career ladder, so modules in making beds, cleaning walls, and cleaning floors, are three of the many tasks she will be learning during the time she is in the health occupations program. Since Ms. Healy and Ms. Jenkins work in different buildings, they are in telephone communication at least twice a week about Sadie's progress and problems, and they hold brainstorming sessions as to methods and techniques to try. Fortunately, the task module system provides a communication link between Ms. Healy and several other professionals who work with Sadie. Both Sadie and her teachers are aware of what is to be learned and are kept abreast on a daily or weekly basis of progress being made. In her folder Sadie has eleven tasks to be accomplished reflecting the duties that community hospitals require in hospital housekeeping. Additionally, there are seven tasks related to hospital conditions that she did not have when she entered the program and that the hospital employers will expect. These include using the telephone and communicating with peers.

Ms. Healy has twenty-five students—five having special needs—and she believes that realistically all students must be programmed individually in terms of their interests, abilities, and attitudes instead of being taught as a class. Their individuality and uniqueness provide a real challenge and personal satisfaction when success is achieved.

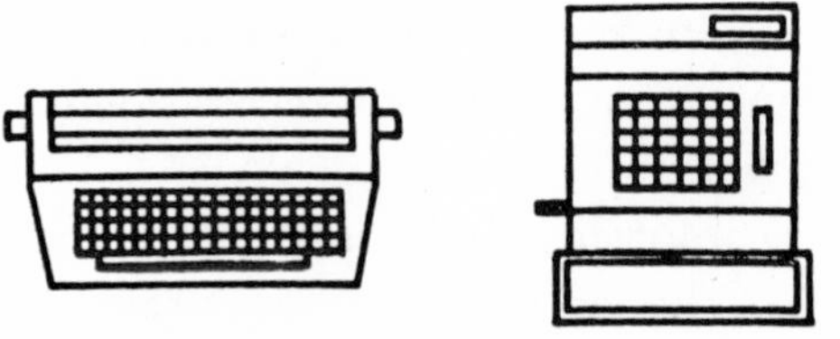

FIGURE 3-13. OFFICE AND BUSINESS OCCUPATIONS

Ms. Ness with Vera in Business and Office

Ms. Betty Ness completed a two-year business program after graduating from high school and worked as a typist, bookkeeper, receptionist, and secretary over a period of five years before graduating from a four-year business education program. Due to her work experience and formal education, she has organized the office and business occupations room into a variety of learning environments. For basic skill development there are eight individual learning carrels supplied with audio-visual materials programmed for basic typewriting, shorthand, bookkeeping, data processing, and marketing. For other students developing basic skills, Ms. Ness organized a small group with a demonstration and handout assignment procedure. Another group of students work individually on class assignments taken from the textbook and check periodically with Ms. Ness for suggestions, evaluations, and ideas for additional work. Several model offices are also used to simulate actual work positions in applying the basic knowledges, skills, and attitudes learned.

Vera, who is legally blind, has been enrolled in the typing class with Mr. Grande but, at the suggestion of her educational planning and placement committee, she is being passed into Ms. Ness's office and business occupations class due to the progress she has made. Sight therapist Ms. Cleo Ester helps her on a routine basis with her homework. They utilize the large print machine and braille textbooks and work informally on personal health, dress, and employability skills. Since Ms. Ester travels between schools for other students with sight handicaps, Ms. Jenkins provides instruction in her absence.

Mr. Jackson with Paul in Building Maintenance

FIGURE 3-14. MAINTENANCE

Mr. Theopolis Jackson teaches building maintenance at the area occupational center. Over a twenty-year period he developed a very successful family business in janitorial service that the family still owns and manages. Several years ago he recognized that the number of people interested in learning the trade was dwindling and that there was a growing need for skillful people for this service. He applied for a teaching position as a building maintenance instructor at a local center and was employed as a nondegreed teacher. Five years later he had accumulated approximately two years of past college course work, a healthy amount of trade competency credit, and a series of off-campus and summer school course work to complete his degree.

A confident man, he accepted the challenge and commitment to teaching a class of building maintenance to multiply handicapped children only. His ability to draw out obscured talent is matched by few master teachers. He carefully dismantles each job into bite-sized steps for a specific student or a group of students, sequences the steps so the job can be completed efficiently, and then starts a trial-and-error search for what turns each student on, what makes him want to learn. Sometimes it is a pat on the back, sometimes charting student successes on the wall, sometimes peer recognition—the list is almost endless and his search is always intense and thorough. Paul was one of fifteen students who were all multiply handicapped, i.e., epilepsy, mental retardation, cerebral palsy. He is not only learning to perform jobs such as how to strip and wax a floor but also developing a pride in doing a job well and gaining the ability to get along with peers and an employer.

Shaking hands with a multiply handicapped person who knows that he has something to offer our society is a deeply moving experience.

FIGURE 3-15. SPECIAL EDUCATION

Ms. Jenkins with Special Needs Learners in a Resource Room

Ms. Jenkins received her special education preparation in a variety of settings. As a high school graduate she worked in a summer church program with under-privileged youngsters and found the experience both challenging and rewarding. During her undergraduate studies she worked one summer at a camp for emotionally disturbed boys and another summer at a state institution for retarded adults to satisfy a practicum requirement on her degree program. Her first two years of teaching experience were in the elementary school as a "type A" teacher in a self-contained classroom designed for educable mentally retarded students. Rather than concentrating on the regular, academic college preparation classes, she substituted a more practical set of language, reading, and arithmetic skills. For the past five years she has been teaching in a resource room at the high school and has nearly completed her Master of Arts degree in special education-vocational education.

The resource room is divided into three areas. The largest area contains several small tables, two dozen chairs, a portable chalkboard, and so on and is used for large- and small-group instruction as well as for general announcements.

The second largest area contains a series of individual study carrels. Several of the carrels are equipped with audio and visual playback equipment, whereas several others have tool panels containing basic tools used in vocational and prevocational classes. This area is used by students working independently or in a buddy system while being supervised by the teacher. The third area is subdivided into a series of spaces used by the speech therapist, physical therapist, psychologist, and consultants for the hearing and impaired-sight school.

Two of her students spend all day in the resource room, fourteen others are taking vocational and prevocational classes in addition to one or more classes outside the resource room each day, and several students will stop in the resource room for an hour a day to receive help in reading, writing, and/or arithmetic.

Ms. Jenkins is often asked how she has time to work with so many students individually and her reply remains, "The only way I can function is to work with unique individuals; group instruction is usually much less effective." To help keep track of what the students are doing, she and several teachers have developed a system that maximizes teacher interaction and individualizes content and instruction. The basic ingredient of this cooperative teaching system is the task sheet (developed fully in Chapter 7). Each task sheet contains information to be learned by the student in his classroom-laboratory instruction, plus related knowledge to be learned from the resource room teacher. Progress is recorded on each task sheet as is a summary of progress made on a series of task sheets on a learning profile. The learning profile is developed and reviewed by members of the educational planning and placement committee (EPPC) and modified by the classroom teachers. The learning profile becomes the student's record of progress and may be used by teachers in a variety of ways including the establishment of work experiences with employers.

Ms. Jenkins has an unusual talent for finding work stations in the community for most, if not all, of her juniors and seniors. This experience is often the student's first work experience and becomes the major motivation for staying in school. Employers also review and modify task sheets so a close-knit communication exists between the vocational teacher, employer, and Ms. Jenkins with respect to the interests, goals, and progress of each student.

Ms. Jenkins' position is a complex, challenging, and rewarding one because it includes daily relationships with twelve to twenty students on an individual basis, routine communication with their other instructors, and follow-up visits to employers who offer work stations. Her primary commitment is to search constantly for talents and abilities in her students and to blend these with appropriate classroom and work experiences so that each student will become an independent, self-sufficient citizen.

Additional Supportive Personnel

Many people have an opportunity to affect the special needs learner in the public school system. As mentioned earlier, the occupational instructors have daily involvement with them as they are mainstreamed into classrooms and laboratories with regular students. Special education teachers also have daily contact with each special needs learner in either the resource room or in other classrooms where special supportive instruction is needed.

The special education staff also includes various therapists and consultants as determined by the needs of the learners. Examples are Carolyn Olsen (speech therapist), Pat Porta (physical therapist), and Cleo Ester (consultant for visually handicapped). Often therapists are consultants who travel to several schools on a routine basis to provide specialized services.

The basic academic teachers—Ted Johnson (general math), Rhonda Smith (basic English), and Gordon Ramsey (reading specialist)—work with Candy Jenkins and the occupational instructors to correlate instruction for a special needs learner wherever possible.

The administrative personnel such as Lori Richards (placement coordinator), Norm Ely (work-study coordinator), Merle Francis, (special needs coordinator), and Dr. George Edmund (principal) develop the necessary community relations, encourage curriculum development, reward staff productivity, and provide adequate financial support.

SUMMARY

Each person described in the chapter represents a real individual who has been a peer of the authors or has been observed teaching learners with special needs. Because of their individualism and character, some of their characteristics are not generalizable, whereas others can be easily recognized and personalized by the reader. The reader is encouraged to develop an in-depth understanding of the technical and philosophical foundations of the vocational and special educational areas described in the chapter by developing more personal acquaintances and working professional relationships with others who help to prepare special needs learners for life.

To accomplish such a goal that is relatively complex, all must cooperate. Each person has a contribution to make and each is as important as the next. Although no rule is hard and fast, one's awareness of other professionals and an understanding of their roles enhances communications in helping people—special people—find their place.

REFERENCES

Byram, Harold M., and Wenrich, Ralph C. *Vocational education and practical arts in the community school.* New York: Macmillan, 1956.

Evans, Rupert N. *Foundations of vocational education.* Columbus, Ohio: Charles E. Merrill, 1971.

Jones, Reginald L. *Problems and issues in the education of exceptional children.* Boston: Houghton Mifflin, 1971.

Krebs, Alfred H. *The individual and his education.* Washington, D.C.: American Vocational Association, 1972.

Long, Nicholas J., Morse, William C., and Newman, Ruth G. *Conflict in the classroom: The education of emotionally disturbed children.* Belmont, Calif.: Wadsworth, 1976.

Marland, Sidney P. *Career education.* New York: McGraw-Hill, 1974.

Neff, Herbert, and Pilch, Judith. *Teaching handicapped children easily.* Springfield, Ill.: Charles C Thomas, 1975.

Pucel, David J., and Knaak, William C. *Individualizing vocational and technical instruction.* Columbus, Ohio: Charles E. Merrill, 1975.

Strain, Phillips, Cooke, Thomas P., and Apollni, Tony. *Teaching exceptional children.* New York: Academic Press, 1976.

TEACHING COOPERATIVELY

Few teachers have been prepared in special education with a strong emphasis in vocational/practical arts education and, conversely, few teachers in occupationally related disciplines have received a strong emphasis in teaching learners with special needs. It may not be possible or even advisable for one teacher to become an expert in both disciplines but, instead, to become competent in one discipline with enough information to understand the role of teachers in the other. In an attempt to bridge the gap for persons in teacher preparation programs, cross-discipline experiences between vocational-practical arts and special education departments in methods classes, prestudent teaching, and student teaching can be provided. Inservice experiences including cross-discipline seminars, practicums, and internships may be implemented for teachers attempting to improve their effectiveness in cooperatively planning, teaching, and evaluating learning activities for learners with special needs. ∾ Self-initiative may be most

common for teachers who recognize the need to share the responsibility of teaching special needs learners and do not require additional motivation in terms of administrative directives or university credit.

Teaching is basically communicating ideas and concepts with people. Too often teachers see themselves only as teachers for students. Obviously, teaching student learners is of primary importance but also important is teaching and learning from other teachers. It is essential that teachers develop and maintain their own teaching style and establish their own identity as being good teachers, but the personal gratification received after having been successful with a difficult-to-teach learner through a sharing of ideas and strategies with other teachers is difficult to match.

When communication flows, the difficult teacher-learning problems are identified honestly and openly between teachers, and solutions are investigated mutually and cooperatively. This chapter will lead the reader through a series of ideas related to teaching cooperatively and will suggest some advantages of further developing cooperative relationships with other teachers.

WHAT IS COOPERATIVE TEACHING?

Similar to "team teaching," "individualized instruction," and other teaching designs, "cooperative teaching" has numerous definitions and implications. You may see cooperative teaching as simply being friendly with other teachers and interested in the learning activities they provide for their students. We all know how good it feels to receive a warm smile or friendly greeting and to have someone else genuinely interested in what we are doing.

Cooperative teaching may infer a frank and enthusiastic sharing of ideas and pooling of information related to student's goals, objectives, and alternative learning activities. Being intensively involved with students, working to solve their "learning mysteries," and sharing this energy with other teachers are the most exciting facets of the teaching profession. Frustrated, disgusted, sarcastic teachers will sometimes become enthusiastic over a period of time, and most of their "rebirth" is often attributed to professional conversations with peers. The change from "What a lousy day it is" to "Do you think Mary will make it as a dietician?" or "How do you think Mary will respond to planning a menu today?" seems to be well worth the cooperative teaching effort.

It may suggest the development of trust, respect, and recognition of peers. Essential to any concentrated effort in cooperative instruction is the need for honest and open communication among those who share the teaching responsibilities. Although teaching cooperatively and sharing ideas may be perceived as being risky, it has been stated, "If you have a good teaching idea, give it away, and you will get a better one." Few bits of advice can be more influential in improving my teaching effectiveness! It works like this: As an idea that has been found to be effective in a given situation is shared with other teachers they react to the idea, and before the conversation shifts to another topic several other innovations are given back. Teachers do not go back to their classrooms and copy ideas, as many would suspect, nor do individual teachers lose their "trade secrets." The contrary is true in both cases. Teachers become identified by their peers for their unique

FIGURE 4-1. COOPERATIVE TEACHING AND PLANNING

teaching characteristics as professionals and they in turn become identified for their uniqueness.

The most productive cooperative teaching will include frequent, routine planning periods with several other teachers requiring the careful scheduling of common planning periods and the establishment of an acceptable system of recording ideas and progress. The administrators contribute a major role in fostering these cooperative teaching relationships. Scheduling of the common planning periods, providing adequate planning facilities, and making secretarial and duplication services available are some of the most obvious, but knowing that the principal cares seems to be the most critical.

WHY TEACHERS SHOULD COORDINATE THEIR EFFORTS

Before charging headlong into a discussion of how to develop and maintain cooperative teaching relationships, let us address the question, "Should teachers coordinate their efforts?" In some instances, teachers may find security behind closed classroom doors with a class of bright, normal, or difficult-to-teach youngsters. On the other hand, there is usually frustration connected with one individual attempting to provide the necessary stimulation for each of the youngsters and to keep them interested in the concepts to be learned.

The major justification for developing cooperative teaching relationships with other teachers is to share ideas and insights for creating effective learning experiences for individual students, especially for those who are difficult to teach. As traditionally successful teaching methods and techniques generate blank stares or disruptive behavior in a classroom, the sensitive teacher begins an exhaustive search for effective teaching-learning alternatives. Effective teachers are constantly searching for better ways to meet the needs of their students, and another teacher who works with a student can often help to solve the communication difficulties.

When instruction tends to become structured in content and inflexible to the unique needs and characteristics of students it will likely be ineffective. Our rapidly changing technology and society make "sacred content" an unstable foundation on which to build. Unless the interests and characteristics of the learner are blended with current instructional content, making it relevant and meaningful, the difficult-to-teach students will find school uninteresting and not worth continuing.

It is during this constant blending process that students experience a multiple reinforcement for learning provided by two or more cooperating teachers. Not only does the student become highly motivated by more meaningful content, but teachers themselves become excited because 1) the students are more receptive and therefore undertake and complete activities more successfully and 2) other cooperating teachers recognize an improvement in student productivity and attribute this success to their own unique teaching contributions as team members. This contagious excitement of working with other cooperative teachers tends to sooth the pain during difficult times when progress seems minimal or nonexistent. These honest exchanges among teachers often spark creative, individualized teaching strategies, whereas the traditional "do it by yourself" philosophy often generates despair and loss of teaching confidence or, worse yet, the tendency to say "they can't learn."

DEGREES OF COOPERATIVE TEACHING INVOLVEMENT

The extent to which teachers become involved in a productive, cooperative teaching relationship ranges on a broad continuum. It encompasses everything from a mother hen/one-man show teaching philosophy to the integrated team teaching process where teachers develop instruction collectively, teach cooperatively, and share in the evaluation of student progress as it applies to the students' career goals.

Vocational and practical arts teachers who accept the challenge of working with special needs students need the cooperative efforts of additional academic and special or basic education teachers. In many situations, fostering this cooperative involvement simply requires the expansion of an already healthy exchange between two or more teachers.

The lunch periods, common planning periods, or a few minutes before or after school are appropriate for teachers to discuss positive and negative aspects of the specific day. "Ed was higher than a kite today in my class. I wonder what's bugging him!" is a common example of lunch room conversation that can be guided into a productive situation for Ed and the teachers who have him in class. "You know, Ed craves for attention. I find that giving him responsibilities in the classroom, such as taking attendance, calling clean up, and so forth helps to calm him down" are comments that feed ideas to other teachers. Spontaneous conversations and brainstorming situations in lunchrooms, prep-rooms, and other areas related to the children in general have satisfying consequences when teachers discover that others are also searching for seemingly impossible answers and, more important, when successful solutions are discovered through the collective process.

As teachers become identified and recognized in their instructional areas, the conversations about students may take on an interdisciplinary flavor. A vocational automotive teacher may remark, "The special needs students seem to be doing much better in my class since *you* have been working with them." Or a special education teacher may say, "My students certainly like *your* automotive class."

As this teaching relationship between a vocational and supportive teacher becomes more frequent and organized, comments become more specific and meaningful. For example, the automotive teacher may say to the special education teacher "Since *you* have helped Steve with the related automotive reading materials, he has successfully completed the task of oil changing and lubrication." Or a special education teacher may remark to a vocational automotive teacher, "Steve wants to learn to read the manual relating to tuning up cars in *your* automotive class."

Sharing these challenges with other faculty members often alleviates difficult situations. Special education teachers may concentrate on helping youngsters develop a general knowledge and awareness of occupations in their field of interest (including safety precautions) as well as the importance of employee attitudes and personal relationships. In addition to special education teachers, the basic mathematics and basic English teachers may provide activities which emphasize the specific practical job as it relates to arithmetic and language skills.

At least three basic ingredients are required to maintain productive planning periods. First, we must have recognized which learners are having unusual difficulty and be concerned about their progress. Second, we must be willing to share ideas with others and ask for help in exchange. Third, we must establish a mutually understood system of writing curriculum and conducting evaluation.

TYPES OF COOPERATIVE TEACHING

Various types of cooperative teaching exist within school systems. It is not uncommon to find curriculum being developed and instruction being shared among faculty members of a single department or cluster. Less common are cooperative teaching relationships faculty members between similar departments such as home economics and industrial arts. Seldom do exchanges take place between teachers in departments such as home economics and special education that relate to philosophy, content, and instructional methods.

Fundamental to cooperative teaching are several essential human characteristics which include:

A desire to be successful with all learners
A willingness to share teaching responsibilities with others
A recognized need to organize curriculum materials
An ability to develop a mutually understood record-keeping system
A commitment to maintain cooperative teaching relationships

COOPERATIVE TEACHING WITHIN A SINGLE CLUSTER AND BETWEEN CLUSTERS

How often do teachers providing the general career exploration experiences such as in industrial arts maintain close communication about problems and curriculum with career preparation teachers in automotive servicing, construction, manufacturing, and graphics areas? In situations when the junior and senior high school teachers dovetail their instructional efforts, it is understandable why learners pass from the general to the occupational courses smoothly and logically. Correlated courses help the learner to make wise career decisions and to accumulate occupational skills from instructor to instructor instead of being faced with learning the same things over again because of duplication of teaching effort. As the learners move along through correlated sets of relevant experiences, less time needs to be spent in correcting deviant behavioral problems.

The amount of success that Bill and his classmates experience in the general power and energy course with their industrial arts teacher, Mr. Powers, will affect their career decision. Those who choose to follow into an automotive servicing career such as Steve should expect to move smoothly from the general concepts into a series of more specific tasks related to diagnosing and servicing automobiles. In this case, Mr. Powers is a half-time industrial arts teacher and half-time vocational automotive instructor, so cooperation should be unusually efficient.

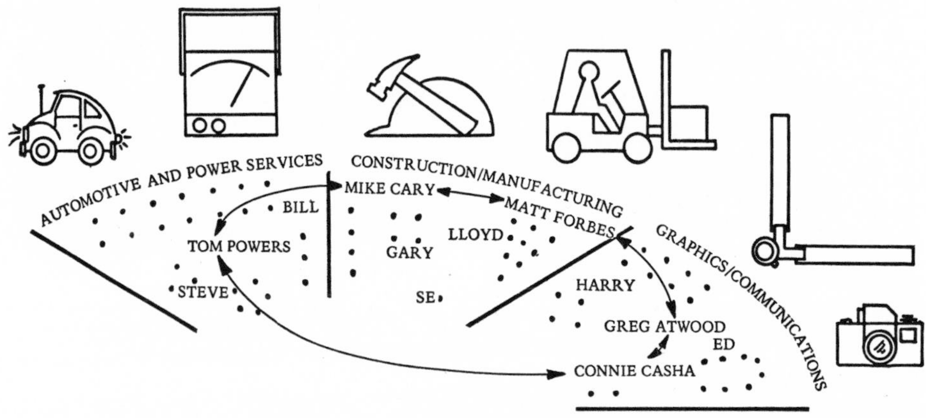

FIGURE 4–2. COOPERATIVE TEACHING IN INDUSTRIAL EDUCATION

In the construction cluster, Gary's success relates somewhat to the teaching relationship that his building trades instructor, Mr. Cary, has with his former industrial arts teacher, both in terms of course content and in handling Gary's behavior effectively. Mr. Forbes, Lloyd's instructor in manufacturing, may find that sharing methods and instructional materials and visiting the industrial arts teacher's facilities is a worthwhile use of time for blending the exploration and preparation activities.

Since sketching and graphics experiences are commonly provided in industrial arts classes, Mr. Atwood and Ms. Casha will probably be able to provide more sequential instruction for Ed and Harry if they maintain a close relationship with their previous teachers with regard to curriculum and instructional methods.

Sometimes, for a variety of reasons, learners' interests change substantially and they choose a different occupational area. What seemed to be career preparation becomes another career exploration experience. Communication between Mr. Powers, Mr. Cary, Mr. Forbes, Mr. Atwood, and Ms. Casha and a common curriculum design will help to facilitate these changes without causing major problems for the instructors or the learner who is changing areas.

How often do home economics teachers in the career exploration phase maintain close working relationships with occupational instructors in the career preparation phase such as clothing construction, food preparation and services, child care, and health occupations?

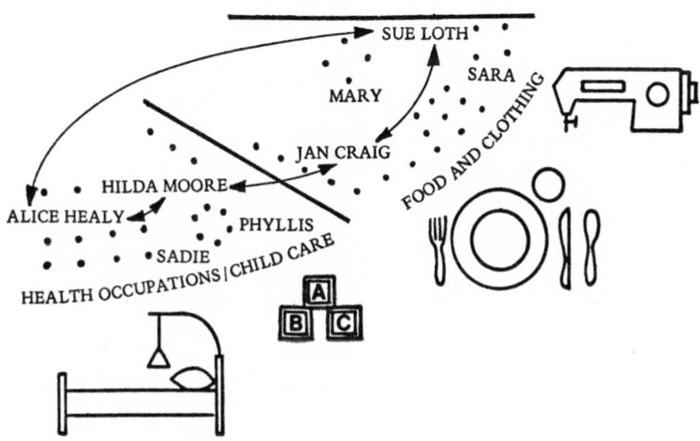

FIGURE 4–3. COOPERATIVE TEACHING IN HOME ECONOMICS

As Sara moves toward an occupation as an alteration tailor, the accumulated efforts of her junior high school home economics teacher and Ms. Loth, her clothing construction instructor, have positively affected her career. Carefully prepared curriculum by these teachers working together allows Sara to move along through a series of appropriate experiences without the frustration of duplication or skipping essential concepts.

Mary's success in waiter-waitress preparation relies on her exploratory experiences in home economics for making a reasonable career choice, and the flow of tasks from exploration in junior high to Ms. Craig's waiter-waitress program in high school relies upon a correlated effort between the teachers. Although this curriculum writing effort can be time consuming, watching a learner move through a program involving several teachers makes the time spent seem worthwhile.

Communications between the general home economics teachers in junior and senior high school and occupational teachers such as Ms. Moore and Ms. Healy make the educational transitions for Phyllis and Sadie in child care and health occupations more realistic. Shifts in curriculum emphasis in the occupational classes based upon employment trends should be mutually understood by all involved instructors. Similarly, when innovative activities are initiated during the career exploration classes, the occupational instructors need to be kept informed.

The home economics field provides a series of alternative objectives for learners including the preparation for adulthood, parenthood, and personal care as well as a variety of potential areas of employment. Curriculum designed with a simple and uniform format for all teachers allows for frequent and dramatic changes in content or with learners without causing any major communication problems.

Do exploratory experiences in general business and general agriculture dovetail with occupational opportunities provided by high school instructors? The degree of success that special needs learners such as Vera, Paul, and Mark experience in their junior and senior high school programs may rely heavily upon a close working relationship between their teachers.

There are several advantages of having a uniform curriculum format for all career exploration and career preparation teachers. One of the strongest is to allow and encourage teachers to understand the goals and objectives of each other's classes. When mutual understanding exists, teachers can help by sharing instructional materials, methods, and evaluation techniques. Another advantage of the uniform curriculum design is the convenience of being able to record learner progress uniformally in each area. A mutually developed system allows teachers and the learner to observe continuous progress rather than relying on the traditional A, B, C, D, E method. Progress can be described in terms of improving one's knowledge, skill, and attitude on an individual basis instead of comparing learner to learner in the grading method.

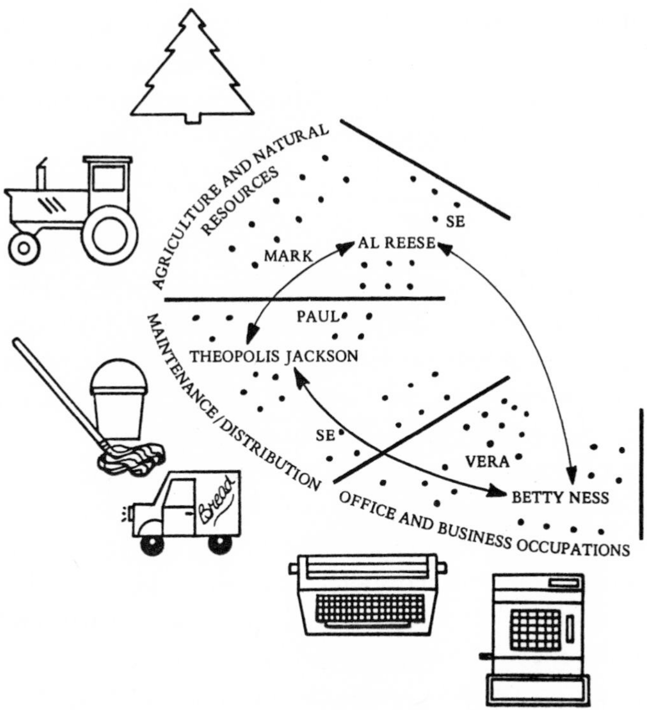

FIGURE 4-4. COOPERATIVE TEACHING IN GENERAL BUSINESS AND AGRICULTURE

COOPERATIVE TEACHING BETWEEN VOCATIONAL-PRACTICAL ARTS AND SPECIAL EDUCATION TEACHERS

Since vocational/practical arts instructors and special education teachers have different undergraduate preparation, work in different educational environments, and have not traditionally been expected to work together, some would argue that cooperative relationships in planning curriculum, correlating instruction, and establishing learner progress are nearly impossible tasks to expect. One simple fact makes the cooperative effort possible and worthwhile—the teachers share many of the same learners with special needs. These learners, who often find traditional course offerings difficult, find vocational and practical arts programs more relevant due to the more pragmatic philosophy and practical nature of the learning experiences.

In many situations if teachers do not work together, they become confused and frustrated because the learner is unable to tie together the bits and pieces of "general education" into anything meaningful. The correlated effort is an attempt to tie learning experiences together into a worthwhile package for the learner. For the non-special needs learner the isolated curriculum approach to general education may be valuable as long as parents, siblings, and counselors help bring potential occupational goals into focus.

Cooperative relationships become imperative for special needs learners as they attempt to weave together the exploratory and preparation experiences into a logical and practical pattern. When these relationships are established and practiced by teachers, it is anticipated that the learner will be better able to recognize occupational opportunities stemming from exploration experiences and, therefore, make wise career decisions followed by an appropriate career preparation.

The most productive cooperative teaching may exist between the vocational/practical arts teachers and the special education teachers. These relationships, which are represented by solid lines with arrows on each end in Figure 3–2 (see page 50), may generate a better mutual understanding of the contributions the special education teachers and the occupational teachers have to offer each special needs learner. As the learners move successfully through career exploration and preparation programs, many features of their education may be analyzed. First, their vocational and practical arts instructors have probably been extremely effective in teaching the prevocational entry-level skills. Second, the special education teachers are probably helping to improve the learner's self-image and to adjust to their disability or handicapping condition(s). Third, various teaching personnel (occupational, special and regular education) are probably communicating regularly on what teaching techniques have worked and what might work in the future as they help their learners prepare for occupations of their choice.

Eventually, a close professional working relationship will exist between the special education teacher, Ms. Jenkins, and each teacher who teaches special needs students. Ms. Jenkins and Ms. Ness will establish a series of tasks related to Vera's abilities and interests. Together with the placement counselor they will coordinate her program to maximize her employment potential in the office and business field. They have included a counselor from vocational rehabilitation services to add support to their effort. Mr. Jackson is working with Ms. Jenkins in developing clearer understandings of Paul's potential in the building maintenance field. They also discuss and plan instructional materials that will be most appropriate for Paul, and they evaluate his progress during their regularly scheduled planning period. Mark's knowledge, skill, and attitude development is directly attributed to the positive correlation of effort between Ms. Jenkins and Mr. Reese. Ms. Jenkins helps Mark on a daily basis with his reading and writing skills. The activities that Mark completes usually relate to the agriculture mechanics field and are also evaluated by Mr. Reese. The special needs teacher concentrates on reinforcing the concepts which the students are learning in their occupational classes as illustrated in the special needs room of the cooperative teaching model (see page 50).

COOPERATIVE TEACHING—PLANNING CONSIDERATIONS

Above all, the reason we are teachers is to promote student learning. Those students who are highly motivated and academically talented learn with the least amount of teaching effort, but such students may be in rather short supply. Since many students have varying degrees of difficulty—physically, mentally, or emotionally—student learning provides a daily, thought-provoking challenge for teachers who expect *all* students to learn. Many teachers develop an integrated curriculum with other professionals to increase their effectiveness, whereas some choose to remain isolated from other teachers with regard to their curriculum and teaching/learning activities. Figure 4–5 illustrates various features of cooperative teaching in terms of person involvement and events.

A careful review of the ideas given in the figure reflects two polarized philosophies. The middle column provides for, accepts, and actually expects failure along with success, whereas the right column anticipates success for all learners in an atmosphere of mutual sharing.

The actual teaching takes place in the occupational labs, special classroom libraries, learning resource centers, regular classrooms, and other areas. Some involves teachers in various situations including teaching indepen-

FIGURE 4-5. COOPERATIVE TEACHING CONSIDERATIONS

	NO COOPERATIVE INVOLVEMENT	INTENSIVE INVOLVEMENT
Teaching style	Self-contained classroom	Changeable lab or classroom
	Mass information giving (lecture)	Individualized instruction
	Class and large-group-centered activities	Student and small-group-centered activities
	Teacher-teacher isolation	Teacher-teacher unity
	One teacher to thirty students	Differentiated staffing
Learning style	Peer competition	Student cooperation
	Class assignments	Independent studies
	Teacher domination	Self-responsibility
	Minimum alternatives	Various methods and media
Curriculum	Stable content over time	Constant analysis and updating
	Divergent movement	Convergent movement
	"One best way for all"	Individualized
	Fifty-minute periods	Flexible scheduling
	Year long courses	Open entry/open exit
Administrative involvement	Establish "bell curve" grading	Encourage individual evaluation
	Random planning periods	Common planning periods
	Teacher offices diffused	Common office complex
	Bus schedules and lunchroom first priority	Student learning and teacher cooperation first priority

dently, teaching as a team member in a single lab, and teaching knowledges and skills that have been mutually planned and correlated in more than one lab or special room.

Currently, far too little cooperation exists in the public schools, especially in special occupational education where teachers need to be constantly searching for appropriate methods and materials that will lead to successful learning experiences for the special needs student. The intent here is to nurture and develop whatever cooperative teaching relationships already exists and to encourage and provide direction for potential cooperative teaching relationships.

SUMMARY

Often a discussion and illustration of cooperative teaching and planning without a practical system for implementation leaves teachers inadequately prepared to implement the ideas. A practical system of developing and monitoring curriculum for individual special needs students can be implemented by utilizing a separate file folder for each learner.

The educational planning and record keeping for each special needs learner is provided in his and her learning record folder, which is cooperatively developed, monitored, and evaluated by the cooperating teachers. In expanded form, this folder may contain the most essential data for job placement and successful work experiences for the learner and provide the basic communication vehicle for cooperating teachers as they plan for, teach, and evaluate the learner.

The intent of the text is to make a real and positive impact upon a teacher who will in turn do a more effective job with the occupational preparation of a student, especially a difficult-to-teach student who probably will not succeed unless something more effective is done.

To this point we have touched some of the concepts related to teaching cooperatively. The following chapters will outline and describe a series of techniques and strategies which organize instructional planning so that youngsters' needs can be discussed and planned for efficiently.

So long as teachers remain open about successes, near successes, and temporary failures in our classrooms and maintain a healthy, positive communication with other empathetic teachers, the ultimate goal in education will be reached. That goal may be described as "preparing each youngster in the school system to become a productive, healthy, happy, and independent human being."

REFERENCES

Gallagher, James J. Vocational education, special education, and vocational rehabilitation: A marriage of professionals needed for handicapped children. In Stanley J. Urban and Tsuji Thomas (Eds.), *The Speical Needs Student in Vocational Education.* New York: MSS Information, 1974.

Hanslovsky, Glenda, Moyer, Sue, and Wagner, Helen. *Why team teaching.* Columbus, Ohio: Charles E. Merrill, 1969.

Johnson, Robert H. *Rx for team teaching.* Minneapolis: Burgess, 1968.

Polos, Nicholas C. *The dynamics of team teaching.* Dubuque, Iowa: W. C. Brown, 1965.

Shaplin, Judson, and Olds, Harry F., Jr. *Team teaching.* New York: Harper & Row, 1964.

Stanford, Gene, and Roark, Albert. *Human interaction in education.* Boston: Allyn and Bacon, 1974.

Warwick, David W. *Team teaching.* London: University of London Press, 1971.

Weisgerber, Robert A. *Prospectives in individualized learning.* Itaska, Ill.: F. E. Peacock, 1971.

DEVELOPING AND MANAGING INSTRUCTION FOR SPECIAL NEEDS LEARNERS

PART TWO

This section of the text focuses on a set of activities that can be used to develop and effectively manage individualized career instruction for special needs learners. Building upon the general concepts introduced in Part I relating to special needs learners, career education, and the nature of cooperative teaching, this section highlights an operational system for planning, implementing, and evaluating instructional programs. The basic system components presented here have been used successfully in a number of secondary school programs across the country with differing types of special needs learners. ∾ Chapter 5 presents a brief overview and introduction to the System for Developing and Managing Instruction for Special Needs Learners. ∾ The first component of the system is presented in Chapter 6—Identifying and Assessing Learner Needs. Prior to developing instructional plans and arrangements, it is important that the specific needs of the individual learner be reviewed and analyzed. The chapter discusses the development of learner profiles and learning prescriptions that characterize the specific instructional needs of the learner. ∾ Chapter 7 focuses on the process of identifying the school and community resources that can provide key supportive services for the career-related instructional program. These resources include both those for the special needs learner and his or her teacher. ∾ Chapter 8 describes the tasks of identifying and analyzing clusters of occupations for the purpose of determining curriculum and specific instructional content. Job and task analysis techniques that generate information appropriate for teaching special needs learners are included. ∾ Chapter 9 presents a process by which occupational and special educators can cooperatively design and manage the instruction and supportive services to be provided for each learner on an individual basis. ∾ Chapter 10 addresses the task of cooperative instructional planning for the special needs learners. Occupational and special educators can effectively plan instruction by identifying, sequencing, and planning a series of instructional modules. The module format for the special needs learner includes identification of performance objectives, basic skills and basic skill content, teacher activities, learner activities, and instructional resource materials.

Techniques for planning and coordinating work experience programs for special needs learners are discussed in Chapter 11.

Chapter 12 focuses on the considerations that are essential in implementing career-related instruction for special needs learners. Evaluating and modifying instructional materials, providing reinforcement and feedback, and adjusting facilities and equipment are among the major considerations when implementing instructional plans.

Finally, Chapter 13 describes several techniques for monitoring, assessing, and reporting learner progress or achievement in career-related instructional programs. Special considerations for evaluating special needs learners are extensively discussed.

A number of forms that can be used by classroom personnel are presented and discussed throughout this section. (The forms are provided with filled-in, illustrative examples.) They are designed to aid occupational and special educators with the tasks of instructional development and management. It is intended that readers review and adapt or modify those instructional development forms that are appropriate for their programs and students.

DEVELOPING AND MANAGING INSTRUCTION: AN OVERVIEW

This chapter will provide an overview of a System for Developing and Managing Instruction for Special Needs Learners (Figure 5-1). It is hoped that this overview will give the reader several insights and suggestions for using the information presented in later chapters. ∾ In recent years, especially since the passage of the 1968 Amendments to the Vocational Education Act of 1963, there has been an increasing interest in serving special needs students in all types of occupational education programs. While numerous project and workshop reports have been prepared in this area, relatively little information has been disseminated with the specific intent of describing for others "how to do it." Chapters 6 through 13 will

focus on eight key how-to-do-it activities in developing and managing instructional programs for special needs learners.

The use of a "system" for describing the instructional development activities in Part II *does not imply that these activities have to be completed in the sequence the system suggests.* Experienced educators will, undoubtedly, already be using several of the activities in working with special needs learners. For these individuals, the systems approach used here will help clarify the relationships between certain activities and assist in identifying instructional development activities that perhaps need to be expanded. For those preparing to teach, as well as for those educators inexperienced in working with special needs students, the system presents a logical approach that is helpful in establishing or modifying programs for special needs learners and in suggesting a sequence in which critical activities can be initiated.

It is also essential to recognize that not all activities in the system are of equal importance. In essence, all of them move toward the activity of "implementing instruction" or "teaching." Depending upon the nature and severity of the learner's special needs, certain of the activities will be of greater importance in planning his or her program. However, all of the system's activities can only be considered as "effective" if they contribute to "effective teaching."

A SYSTEM FOR DEVELOPING AND MANAGING INSTRUCTION

The System (as it will be referred to hereafter) presented in Figure 5-1 represents a functional approach to designing, implementing, and evaluating both learning experiences and total instructional programs that are specifically appropriate for special needs learners. The System is intended to be a flexible, conceptual framework that enables occupational and special educators to visualize the activities or processes that need to be undertaken in providing a comprehensive program and supportive services. To some extent, the eight major activities identified in the system are similar to instructional development processes in most educational programs. However, each of the activities here contributes to developing individualized, prescriptive educational plans for students with special needs.

FIGURE 5-1. A SYSTEM FOR DEVELOPING AND MANAGING INSTRUCTION FOR SPECIAL NEEDS LEARNERS

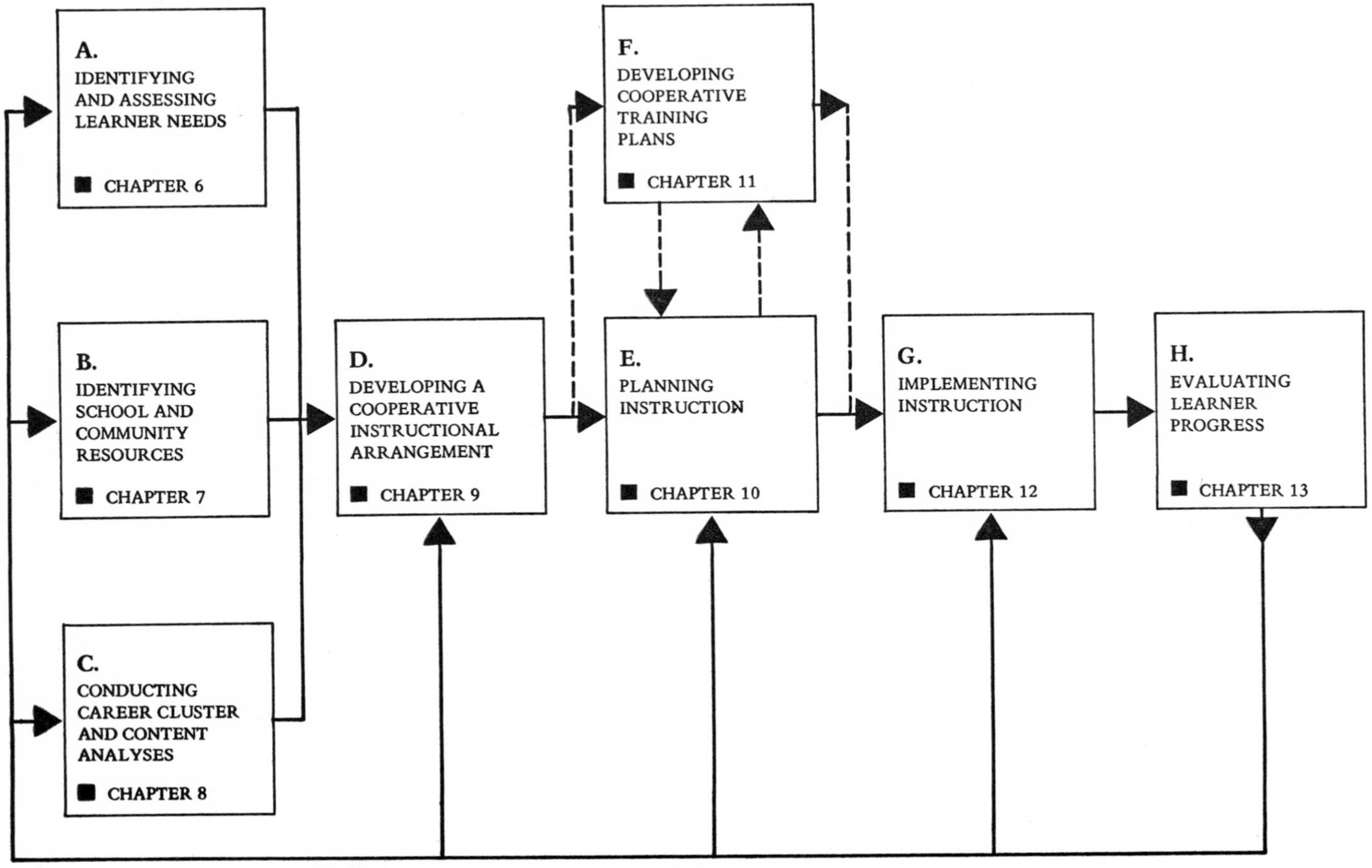

IN WHAT WAYS CAN THE SYSTEM BE HELPFUL?

Implementation of the activities and processes represented in the System can benefit teachers, counselors, coordinators, administrators, and students in both occupational and special education programs in several ways. It enables the teachers and/or administrators involved in programming for special needs students to:

1. Communicate effectively regarding individual learner needs and, thereby, coordinate their instructional and supportive efforts.
2. Identify and effectively use the available school and community resources.
3. Base instructional content on the competencies needed to explore and prepare for the world of work.
4. Utilize student needs assessment information, available resources, and occupational demand information in developing and implementing individualized instructional plans.
5. Systematically evaluate the performance and achievement of special needs learners and use the resulting information to expand and improve the instructional program.

The System also provides several secondary benefits. It enables administrators and teachers to visualize the critical elements of a *total* program and enables them to pinpoint strengths, weaknesses, or shortcomings in their present programs. Adopting an operational system similar to this one greatly facilitates communication among instructional staff and between staff and administrative personnel. Staff responsibilities and cooperative working arrangements can be readily identified once the System is adapted to a specific, local educational program.

HOW CAN THE SYSTEM BE USED?

First, it is important to point out that in many local educational agencies, instructional and administrative staff are already involved in several of the activities presented in the System. Some readers may only be interested in specific activities or selected chapters, which they foresee as being helpful in expanding their existing programs and services for special needs learners. The authors strongly encourage practicing teachers to take this approach and use the text as a resource guide rather than a procedural cookbook.

A number of suggestions and implications for using the System have been mentioned. First, however, in order for it to be useful to practitioners in a specific educational setting, the System must be viewed as a flexible working model. It is not intended to be a specific, direct procedure to be followed as an exact blueprint with equal attention and effort given to each activity. Depending upon the types of special needs students to be served, the local employment trends, the availability of instructional resources, and other similar considerations, certain activities may be more critical than others.

It should also be noted that occupational and special educators each contribute a special expertise to each of the activities. Special educators with their in-depth understanding of diagnosis, assessment, and treatment of learning and behavioral problems can provide leadership in the activities related to assessing learner needs. Occupational educators, on the other hand, are adept at job and occupational task analysis and can specifically identify the competencies individuals will need as they prepare for the occupational aspects of an independent, adult life role.

WHAT ARE THE MAJOR ACTIVITIES IN THE SYSTEM?

There are eight major activities included in the System for Developing and Managing Instruction for Special Needs Learners. Each of these are activities that should involve both occupational and special educators in a cooperative effort. Figure 5-2 provides a summary overview of each of the activities and their purpose and outcomes.

The first three activities—identifying and assessing learner needs, identifying school and community resources, and conducting career cluster and content analyses—can be viewed as preliminary or input tasks. That is, the information generated from these activities are necessary inputs for designing and implementing individualized, prescriptive plans for the learner.

The other five activities (D, E, F, G, and H) represent the general sequential process for formally designing and implementing individual educa-

FIGURE 5-2. INSTRUCTIONAL DEVELOPMENT ACTIVITIES

ACTIVITY AND CHAPTER	PURPOSE	OUTCOMES
Identifying and Assessing Learner Needs (Chapter 6)	To identify special needs learners and determine their specific learning needs	Accurate learner identification information Learner Profiles illustrating learning strengths, weakness, and needs Learning prescriptions describing instructional strategies and materials appropriate for the learner
Identifying School and Community Resources	To identify and inventory the school and community resources available to assist special needs learners and instructional staff	An inventory of school resources An inventory of community resources Advisory committee involvement in identification of community resources
Conducting Career Cluster and Content Analyses	To identify and analyze a cluster(s) of occupation(s) and the pertinent specific instructional content for career exploration and preparation programs	Identification of clusters and included occupational titles Identification of the occupational and basic competencies needed for employment Specification of relevant instructional content for exploration and/or preparation for an occupational cluster
Developing a Cooperative Instructional Arrangement (Chapter 9)	To formally designate a special needs learner's instructional team	Identification of team members and instructional programs and/or services to be provided by each
Planning Instruction (Chapter 10)	To develop an individualized, prescriptive instructional plan for a special needs learner	Instructional modules

FIGURE 5-2 *(Continued)*

ACTIVITY AND CHAPTER	PURPOSE	OUTCOMES
Developing Cooperative Training Plans (Chapter 11)	To develop a plan for using out-of-school and in-school work experiences as part of the special needs learner's instructional program	Cooperative career exploration or work experience plans
Implementing Instruction (Chapter 12)	To deliver planned instructional programs and services to special needs learners	Instructional sequence plans Analysis of instructional materials Behavioral management strategies Learning environment management strategies
Evaluating Learner Progress (Chapter 13)	To assess the progress and achievement made by special needs learners during and following instruction	Learner performance profiles

tional plans. The fourth activity—developing a cooperative instructional arrangement—requires that the specific professionals (occupational education, special education, work experience coordinators, and supportive agency personnel) involved in working with a special needs learner be formally identified as members of the cooperative team. Once the cooperative instructional arrangement is identified, they assume responsibility for planning, implementing, and evaluating the individual prescriptive plan (activities E, F, G, and H) for a special needs learner.

Perhaps an effective means of further describing each of the activities in the System is to use one of the special needs learner examples from Chapter 1. The paragraphs that follow will describe each of the activities as they might be undertaken by the individuals responsible for Mark's educational program.

A. Identifying and Assessing Learner Needs

You will recall that several specific special needs were identified by Mark's educational planning and placement committee. In assessing Mark's specific learning needs, the committee, which in Mark's case is composed of his special education teacher, agriculture teacher, the school psychologist, his parents, and the director of special education, has identified the following on his learning profile as needing special attention:

Reading (two and one-half grade levels below norm approximately)
Math (three grade levels below norm approximately)
Written communication skills

Also identified on the learner profile are some of the learning strengths Mark has exhibited:

General school social behavior is good
Excellent mechanical aptitudes
Excellent school attendance and attitude
Can handle basic "applied" math problems
An intense interest in agriculture mechanics

An initial analysis of learning strengths and weaknesses, when portrayed in a graphic profile, can provide insight into the unique learning styles exhibited by different special needs learners. It must be remembered, however, that to be useful, Mark's learner profile (learning needs) will have to be reassessed frequently and regularly.

B. Identifying School and Community Resources

Two basic types of resources can be identified to assist Mark's teachers in implementing his individualized prescriptive program: school resources and community resources. In order that the resources inventory compiled by Mark's teachers might be useful in planning instruction for other special needs learners enrolled in the agriculture and agribusiness courses, the resource inventory to be developed will focus on this particular set of occupational courses. Working as a team, and utilizing the school's agricultural occupations advisory committee, the agriculture teachers and Mark's special education teacher have identified and described a number of services available to special needs learners from the following community resources and agencies:

Mental health agency
Vocational rehabilitation service agency
State employment service office
County agricultural extension office
Chamber of Commerce
Specific civic groups (e.g., the Lions)
Local greenhouses and other agribusiness establishments willing to provide career speakers or tours

In addition to individuals and agencies from the community, several key resource personnel within the school have been identified who might be helpful:

Reading specialist (Mr. Gordon Ramsey)
General mathematics instructor (Mr. Ted Johnson)
Cooperative work-study coordinator (Mr. Norm Ely)
Placement coordinator (Ms. Lori Richards)

One can readily see that Mark's teachers will benefit from being familiar with the multitude of community and school resources that are available to assist them with special and supportive services for Mark.

C. Conducting Career Cluster and Content Analyses

Prior to formulating a specific education plan for Mark, his teachers have expressed a desire to look closely at the different career clusters and options in which Mark appears interested. Since Mark is entering the eleventh grade and has expressed and demonstrated a specific interest in agricultural mechanics, his teachers decide to analyze closely that particular cluster of occupations with the expectation that Mark would seriously pursue a career in this field. His grade reports indicate that since junior high school he has had a continuing interest and positive performances in industrial arts and general agriculture.

After reviewing *Dictionary of Occupational Titles* and talking with several members of the agriculture occupations advisory committee who own and operate businesses in this field, a list of potential entry occupations is generated for Mark. Although some occupations are listed that might be considered particularly appropriate for lower ability individuals, the majority of entry occupations identified are those jobs open to any graduate of the agricultural mechanics program at Mark's high school.

After the list of potential entry occupations is assembled, a list of the major tasks (for example, reading a micrometer or replacing wheel bearings) performed in these occupations is identified. The tasks which are common to several of the entry occupations previously identified will be further analyzed and will form the basic instructional content for much of Mark's educational program in both agricultural mechanics and special education.

D. Developing a Cooperative Instructional Arrangement

With a clearer understanding of Mark's learning needs, the available instructional resources, and the occupational cluster Mark hopes to enter, his teachers are now ready to formulate a cooperative instructional arrangement. In Mark's case the development of such an arrangement was greatly facilitated by the existence of the educational planning and placement committee. The cooperative instructional arrangement will formally identify those teachers and special services personnel who will be responsible for designing and implementing Mark's individual prescriptive plan. After Mark's school schedule and placement is finalized, we find that the following individuals will be involved in the cooperative instructional arrangement:

Mr. Reese	Agriculture mechanics
Ms. Jenkins	Special education
Mr. Johnson	General mathematics

Mr. Ely	Cooperative work-study coordinator, agriculture occupations

Since it is anticipated that Mark will be ready for a cooperative work placement sometime during the second semester, Mr. Ely is added to the cooperative instructional arrangement to provide input that will·be helpful in preparing Mark for his work station next semester at one of the agricultural equipment businesses in town. To facilitate implementing this cooperative instructional arrangement for Mark, copies of it have been forwarded to the directors of occupational and special education and the building principal for their endorsement.

E. Planning Instruction

During the early part of the fall semester the cooperating team meets formally several times and informally on a regular basis during their common planning period to develop Mark's plan. As a beginning point they develop each of the instructional tasks identified from their earlier analysis of the agricultural mechanics cluster into an instructional unit. It takes considerable time and discussion to determine an appropriate initial sequence of units and to develop a set of terminal performance objectives for each unit. Mark's learner profile and prescription is consulted frequently when the learning experiences, instructional methods, and instructional materials are selected for each unit. For each set of terminal performance objectives, the team attempts to identify the basic skills required in the performance. "Measuring parts per million" is a basic skill involved in the task of "preparing tank mixes." Mark's special education teacher (Ms. Jenkins) and general mathematics teacher (Mr. Johnson) attempt to work closely in developing Mark's math skills in this area, which they realize is critical to the successful performance of tasks in the agricultural mechanics cluster.

In summary, each unit that is developed for Mark focuses on one of the occupational tasks he will be required to perform upon entering employment in the agricultural mechanics cluster. Mark's individual prescriptive plan consists of a series of these units which includes: performance objectives, identification of the basic skills needed to successfully complete the performance objectives, and a description of the learning experiences, teaching strategies, and instructional materials to be used by the cooperative teams in implementing Mark's instruction.

An important feature of the team's cooperative planning meeting is their evaluation sessions. At each meeting they discuss Mark's performance from a diagnostic perspective and refine the content of their upcoming units and teaching strategies to more accurately focus on Mark's special learning problems.

F. Developing Cooperative Training Plans

Using the work environment for instructional purposes has proved to be vitally important in educating most special needs as well as nonspecial students. During the first semester, Mr. Ely, the cooperative work-study coordinator for the agriculture programs, will attempt to locate an appropriate part-time work station in the community. In developing the cooperative training plan, he works closely with Mark's teachers, parents, and prospective job supervisor to insure that Mark's work experience will be consistent with his career interests and aptitudes.

G. Implementing Instruction

When each of the units is about to be or is in the process of being implemented, several specific aspects of the overall instructional plan have to be closely monitored. How and when to provide the appropriate reinforcement and feedback and adjusting the classroom facilities and equipment to minimize the effects of Mark's learning difficulties are typical considerations discussed by the cooperative team when implementing instruction. Here again, you will note that each of the implementation considerations is based on evaluative feedback and team discussions of Mark's performance.

H. Evaluating Learner Progress

As pointed out in describing several of the preceding System activities, continuous evaluation of Mark's performance during and following instruction is an important feature in individualizing his educational plan. When the cooperative team meets to review and discuss Mark's progress they exchange two basic types of evaluative information: formative and summative. The formative information is used for adjusting and refining the individual prescriptive plan so that it more closely addresses Mark's learning problems. More specifically, this diagnostic information could be used to adjust Mark's learning prescription, modify the sequence of instructional units, or select more appropriate teaching strategies and materials. The summative information exchanged by the team is intended to summarize the progress Mark has made to date. Summative information, which is recorded on Mark's learner performance record, is used for purposes such as communicating his achievements and level of competency attainment to his parents, prospective employers, or perhaps his second semester teachers.

Evaluating Mark's performance is also likely to involve the cooperative team in follow-up activities after Mark has completed his school experiences. Follow-up contacts for surveys are an important part of evaluation and of the System for Developing and Managing Instruction because they provide: 1) a means for continuous communication between Mark and his former teachers that helps to insure his successful transition from school to work and independent adult living and 2) a vehicle for incorporating information from graduates, nongraduates, and employers to justify revision of course content or the expansion of supportive and special services provided for special needs learners such as Mark.

WHO CONDUCTS THE VARIOUS ACTIVITIES IN THE SYSTEM?

This System is not intended to imply any specific role responsibilities for occupational or special educators. Determination of who should "identify the school and community resources," for example, will depend upon the local school situation. It may be the industrial arts teacher, the resource room teacher, or a supervisor or administrator. In a given program it may be any individual who is most familiar with, has the time available for, or is in a unique position to identify and inventory the available school and community resources appropriate for special needs learners. The primary purpose in using a systems model is to describe the activities or elements of a comprehensive program and not to suggest that any one professional is responsible for any one activity in the System.

Ideally, the responsibility for carrying out each of the eight activities should be shared among occupational and special education staff. Chapter 3 provided a rationale indicating *why* cooperative teaching and similar involvements are critical and outlined a model for cooperative teaching (see Figure 3-2). The System for Developing and Managing Instruction outlines the specific activities that are involved in the cooperative teaching model. Whenever possible, occupational and special education staff should jointly share in the leadership and responsibility for implementing the System activities. Such cooperation facilitates a greater awareness and understanding of individual student needs and problems and leads to professional efforts that minimize the special needs and problems encountered by students.

IS THE SYSTEM ADAPTABLE TO DIFFERENT EDUCATIONAL SETTINGS?

Since the System is only designed as a general conceptual framework, the answer is "Yes." It has been utilized in various types of educational programs serving special needs learners. Junior high and middle school teachers have found it helpful in designing programs and instructional experiences that are focused on the exploration of career clusters as well as careers within a given cluster. At the senior high level, it has been used to guide the development and management of career preparation programs and instruction. Obviously, the activities in the System vary in their importance depending upon the educational setting, since the educational goals in each setting are different. Yet they are—or should be—articulated with the goals of previous settings or future programs in which the learner might enroll. The authors have found that the activity, "conducting career cluster and content analyses," creates the widest range of discrepancy in this area of concern. Junior high school teachers have not been trained to use occupational analysis techniques as a procedure for deriving instructional content; however, occupational personnel at the high school level are usually more familiar and comfortable with this approach. It is important for both groups to realize that the intent of this approach is not to change that particular arrangement, but rather to point out the importance of deriving instructional content from some form of systematic, comprehensive analysis. It is vitally important that the instruction provided for special needs learners be chiefly relevant for independent adult living and occupational competence. Thus, justifiable course content can be based on an analysis of the *general and specific career competencies* one needs in a chosen career or career cluster in the world of work.

The System has also been used to facilitate instructional development in institutional programs serving the occupational education needs of adolescents and young adults with special needs. Institutions such as state schools for the blind and deaf have readily been able to adapt this system to their staff arrangements and special needs learners.

HOW DOES THE SYSTEM BENEFIT THE SPECIAL NEEDS LEARNER?

A systems-oriented approach directly benefits the special needs learner by improving the instructional programs and services available to him or her. Each activity undertaken is designed to provide instructional, administrative, and special services staff with a clear and concise description of each learner's unique and individual needs. The principal outcome of this approach is the development and implementation of an individual prescriptive plan for each special needs learner, with occupational and special educators sharing the primary responsibility for delivering at the secondary school level.

HOW CAN IT HELP IN "MANAGING" PROGRAMS AND INSTRUCTION?

Managing has to do with the day-to-day operations of an instructional program or class. Probably the most important factor in effective management is a mechanism for continuous evaluation. Evaluation and assessment done by occupational and special education personnel on a regular (sometimes daily) basis is the key to modifying instructional content for a specific learner to accommodate a new occupational interest or updating his or her learning prescription. In the System, evaluative information, which should be collected both during and at the end of instruction, is cycled back to each of the other seven activities through feedback loops to improve the overall programs. The feedback information also permits teachers to modify and adjust the individual programs of special needs learners at various points in the instructional period.

SUMMARY

This chapter has introduced a flexible conceptual System for Developing and Managing Instruction for Special Needs Learners who are enrolled in career exploration or preparation programs. The System presented in Figure 5–1, involves occupational and special educators in cooperative efforts to design, implement, and evaluate individual prescriptive programs for special needs learners. A total of eight activities are included in the System. Three activities, focused on assessing learner needs, identifying school and community resources, and conducting career or job cluster analyses, are the initial steps in this approach. Other activities included in the system emphasize developing cooperative arrangements among all instructional personnel, developing job training plans, and planning specific instructional units. The final two activities involve implementation of the planned instruction and evaluation of learner progress. The eight chapters that follow in Part Two describe each of the System activities in detail.

Like all systematic approaches, this one is based on several key assumptions regarding the nature of special needs students and their teachers. The assumptions most crucial to the successful implementation of this system in *any* educational setting are:

1. Special needs learners require individually guided instructional experiences.
2. Occupational and special educators are willing and capable of working together in effectively designing and implementing these experiences.
3. The continuing support and endorsement of administrators is critical to the long-range effectiveness of programs designed to serve special needs learners.

REFERENCES

Altfest, Myra (Ed.). *Vocational education for special needs students: A teacher's handbook.* Fort Collins: Department of Vocational Education, Colorado State University, 1975.

Suggested utilization of resources and guide for expenditures: guidelines for identifying, classifying, and serving the disadvantaged and handicapped under the vocational education amendments of 1968 (Rev. ed.). Washington, D.C.: U.S. Department of Health, Education, and Welfare, Office of Education, Division of Vocational and Technical Education, 1973.

Szoke, Clarie Olson. *To serve those who are handicapped: Procedures and format to implement a model career education program for the handicapped.* Champaign, Ill.: Technical Education Research Centers/Midwest, 1973.

Thiagarajan, Swasailam, Semmel, Dorothy S., and Semmel, Melvyn I. *Instructional development for training teachers of exceptional children: A sourcebook.* Bloomington, Ind.: Center for Innovation in Teaching the Handicapped, Indiana University, 1974.

Vocational Education-Special Education Project. *Program guide.* Mt. Pleasant, Mich.: Central Michigan University, 1973.

Young, Earl B. *Vocational education for handicapped persons: Handbook for program implementation.* Washington, D.C.: U.S. Office of Education, 1969.

IDENTIFYING AND ASSESSING LEARNER NEEDS

One of the major considerations in curriculum or instructional development is the target population for which the curriculum or instruction is intended. The learner's level of educational, psychological, physiological, psychomotor, cognitive, and social development represents a critical area of consideration for the instructional team of occupational and special educators. Recognition of unique learner characteristics and developmental patterns is essential in determining specific content and sequencing instruction. ∾ Three basic steps or processes are included in identifying and analyzing the educational needs of the special learner. First, some basic problem identification information is usually reported by the regular class teacher. Often this information is reported by means of a "referral," which briefly describes the student's problem, and tells "why" he or she is in need of special services.

While such information is usually collected for administrative purposes, it can also be helpful to the instructional development team as well.

Once a prospective special needs learner is identified through the accumulation of basic referral information, a more detailed analysis of the student's learning strengths, weaknesses, and special problems is undertaken. Here, this process will be referred to as learner analysis. A learner analysis profile is based on information from documented sources such as teacher observations and portrays the learner's unique characteristics in a variety of different performance areas.

The third basic process is the development of a learning prescription. Based on available diagnostic information and the learner analysis profile, a prescriptive statement is prepared providing information on the individual's learning style. More specifically, the instructional techniques and materials that are most appropriate for the student in question are specified.

It should be pointed out that identifying and analyzing learner needs is a continuous, ongoing process, rather than solely a preinstructional assessment activity. Frequently, teachers, psychologists, and diagnosticians refer to this activity as a "staffing." Traditionally, staffings have involved reviewing test data and medical and school achievement records with only limited amounts of time actually being spent on planning an instructional program for the student. To be effectively utilized, learner profiles and learning prescriptions must be reviewed and updated at least every two months. The instructional team should periodically review the learner's progress relative to gains and improvements made in each of the profile areas (for example, social skills, perceptual skills, and occupational interests). The ultimate goal is to remediate and minimize the student's special needs to a level where he or she can be productively employed and economically independent.

This chapter will review and discuss each of the three basic processes in greater detail: identification, developing a learner profile, and writing a learning prescription.

IDENTIFICATION OF SPECIAL NEEDS LEARNERS

Various definitions have been used to identify students with different types of handicaps and disadvantages in the field of special education.

Chapter 1 provided a narrative description of students exhibiting various types of handicaps and disadvantages. Definitions describing the causes of a handicap—brain damage, for instance—are seldom useful in providing information that describes the learning or behavioral problems a student might be encountering in school. In beginning to identify and analyze the educational needs of special students, it may be more helpful to define these students by the situations or difficulties they encounter in school. The authors of the Education Amendments of 1976 chose to define handicapped and disadvantaged students in a manner similar to the definitions provided in earlier vocational education legislation.

> *Disadvantaged and handicapped persons means persons who have academic or economic handicaps . . . or who are mentally retarded, hard of hearing, deaf, speech impaired, visually handicapped, seriously emotionally disturbed, crippled, or other health impaired persons who by reason thereof require special services and assistance or special education and related services to enable them to succeed in regular vocational education programs or who require a modified vocational education program.*

Lilly (1970) has developed a definition for describing "exceptional situations" rather than "exceptional children."

> *An exceptional school situation is one in which interaction between a student and his teacher has been limited to such an extent that external intervention is deemed necessary by the teacher to cope with the problem.*

In applying these definitions in practice, the starting point for identification of a special needs learner is a teacher referral. Nearly all teacher referrals are based on the existence of one or both of two types of problems: 1) a student is having difficulty learning skills of an academic nature or 2) a student is having problems with social behavior, either acting out or not interacting sufficiently with the teacher and/or other children (Lilly 1975).

Most school districts have established a process that is used to identify students in need of special services. In the past, when teachers or other professionals have felt that a student is having problems that require special attention, the student has frequently been "referred" and, in many instances, subsequently taken out of the regular instructional program. In some cases the resulting placement in special classes will prove to be productive, while in others it has been shown to do little for the mildly or moderately handicapped student. In either case, the referral-identification process often removes the student and dangerously labels him or her among the peer group and the instructional staff.

The current trend in providing special services is to decrease the number of referrals "out" of regular programs. The aim instead is to minimize the stigmatization by keeping the student in the mainstream, while providing special help for both the regular class teacher and special student. When managed appropriately, this arrangement can provide an optimum and more productive learning environment for the student. For those students who cannot be served totally in regular, mainstream classes, the current trend is to determine and use the least restrictive placement. This placement concept has emerged in recent federal legislation pertaining to education of the handicapped. The basic notion is that students must be educated in environments where the opportunities for their educational and social development are as close to normal as possible.

The identification process usually begins when a teacher or parent, or perhaps a group of teachers, feels it necessary to bring to the attention of other teachers, specialists, coordinators, and administrators, a particular student who is having difficulty. The first step in this process involves collecting some basic information to verify that the student is indeed having such difficulty and that further professional attention is needed.

Suggestions for the Identification Process

A number of specific suggestions are offered here to assist individual teachers or members of the instructional team to collect and report student information systematically for the purpose of making an identification.

1. Initially, you should review and become familiar with any existing identification criteria, procedures, and/or forms used for the referral of special students in the district. It is important to be familiar with any existing process used in your school district so that the identifi-

cation utilized here does not result in a duplication of effort. It may also be that some of the identification information has already been compiled on the special needs students in your class.

2. A second activity involves deciding what specific identification information it is important and essential to collect. Most student identification information forms include the following:
   a) Name, age, birthdate, sex, school, and grade placement of student
   b) Name, address, and phone numbers of parents or guardians
   c) Date on which the information is submitted for review
   d) Name of referring teacher, teachers, or, in some instances, parents
   e) Reason for the referral (usually a detailed description of the specific problems the student is encountering)
   f) Special services the student is already receiving
   g) Type of action the referring teacher or professional suggests as being appropriate
   h) Name and title of the individual to whom the identification information is submitted. This is usually the building principal or director of special education.

   All of this information may or may not be specifically appropriate for your student identification needs. A sample student information form provided in Figure 6-1 illustrates one that is currently used for this purpose. After reviewing this form you should carefully consider the exact information you feel is needed in the initial identification process in your situation. You can then modify the form or expand the referral form used in your district to include the essential information.

3. Careful consideration also has to be given to how the student identification information will be collected. Questions of *who* should compile the information and *which information sources* are to be used will also influence the identification-referral process. In some instances parents will point out the specific problems to individual teachers or counselors and request that a referral be initiated. In most cases, however, teachers or other school personnel will initiate the referral and utilize their written observation reports as an information base when compiling the necessary information. Parent and student interviews, school records, and numerous other references can and should be also consulted for background information.

FIGURE 6-1. SPECIAL NEEDS PROGRAM – STUDENT INFORMATION FORM

Instructions: Please complete as much of the information below as possible. Sources of information to be used in completing the form include: pupil school records, classroom observations, and individual counseling with the student.

Student name ______________________ Grade ______ Referral date ______

Address ______________________ Sex ___ Age ____ Birthdate ______

Reason for referral action ______________________

____

____

____

PARENTS: Father's name ______________________

Address ______________________ Telephone ______

Mother's name ______________________

Address ______________________ Telephone ______

Guardian's name ______________________ Relationship ______

Address ______________________ Telephone ______

EMPLOYMENT: Father ______________________

(occupation and place of employment) Mother ______________________

Guardian ______________________

Have parents been contacted? ________ yes ________ no

Student employment goals ______________________

____

Special services being received ______________________

____

Received by ______________________ Title ______________ Date ______

Action taken ______________________

____

4. Once the basic student identification information is collected and summarized, it must be submitted to the appropriate person for action. As suggested earlier this will usually be the building principal or director of special education. Whoever this individual is, he or she must have the responsibility and authority for seeing that the referral-identification is acted upon.
5. Depending upon the special services and personnel available and the nature of the student's special need, a variety of actions may then be undertaken by the principal or director of special services. In some cases it may be appropriate to call a meeting of the student's teachers to determine what special considerations or modifications are needed in the student's instructional program. In other cases it may be necessary to have the student's hearing or vision tested or to have some additional educational assessments done to determine more specifically the student's learning or behavioral problem(s).
6. The identification-referral process can easily become bogged down in paperwork and exhaustive procedures. It is best to keep it as simple and as efficient as possible. Collect and report only the basic information needed to establish the student's eligibility to receive the special services he or she will need to succeed in an educational program.

DEVELOPING A LEARNER PROFILE

Once each student has been formally identified, it then becomes the responsibility of the occupational-special education team to design and implement an effective instructional program. One of the tasks that will greatly facilitate instructional planning is a functional analysis of the learning problem or problems the student is encountering.

The learner profile is designed to provide the instructional team with a general overview of the student's learning strengths and weaknesses, which will, in turn, provide a basis for developing a learning prescription for the student. It is important to note here that *both* strengths and weaknesses can provide important diagnostic information for teachers, counselors, and other personnel who have contact with the student. Traditionally, assessment and testing have focused almost exclusively on weaknesses, deficiencies, or problems in need of attention. Educators have typically examined only the "problems" of special students and attempted to provide special remediation according to discrete disability labels, such as educable mentally retarded. Oftentimes, however, we have found that certain individuals have overcome their handicaps by compensation. For example, many individuals have developed their intellectual skills to a level where they are no longer vocationally handicapped by their inability to walk. Thus, it is important to keep in mind the learner's strengths as well as his weaker areas when developing a learner profile.

Causes, Effects, and Learner Analysis

The relationship between cause and effect of handicapping and disadvantaging situations is frequently unclear when a special needs learner is identified through referral. In order to provide useful information, an analysis of learning difficulties must focus on the *effects* and not the causes of educational situations that require special attention. Simply because individuals are identified as mentally retarded, neglected, or a member of a minority group does not mean that they can automatically be classified as special needs learners, nor can effective instruction and supportive services be formulated on the basis that a person is mentally retarded, learning disabled, black, Spanish, poor, a migrant, or for any other internal or situational *cause.* Instruction must be designed or modified to overcome specific *effects,* such as limited reading ability, motivational or behavioral problems, limited computational skills, and so on (Kay, Kemp, and Saunders 1973). It reasonably follows then that a learner profile should focus upon specific academic, behavioral or social, perceptual, or physical competencies, instead of simply indicating that the learner is mentally retarded or culturally disadvantaged. To be of maximum benefit, a learner profile must provide information that is useful for instructional planning.

Assessing Learner Needs through Instruction

The relationship between instruction and analysis of learner needs is a continuing and dynamic one. As teachers engage in their daily teaching activities, they are continuously observing and evaluating the performance of their students. It is important that accurate evaluative information on the performance of special needs learners be shared regularly among instructional team members, administrative personnel, and parents. Information can be shared through the development of a learner profile and subsequently using the profile for such purposes as improving instructional practices, adjusting the learner's program placement as needed, providing effective and appropriate supportive placement as needed, and providing effective and appropriate supportive services.

It is important that teachers recognize the importance of obtaining information on learner needs primarily through instruction. Regular class teachers have been apprehensive in the past about taking identified special needs students into their classes without knowing specifically what to expect in the way of performance from the student. In most instances, this apprehension is expressed as a genuine concern for wanting to provide a positive, initial experience for the learner. Most frequently, the only way to provide this preinstructional information is to make the student's file available to the teacher since, as suggested earlier, the test scores and other data contained in the file are seldom very useful in planning for instruction. Consequently, a more realistic and less restrictive approach to learner needs analysis must be found. An alternative, more functional approach is to work with the student in an educational setting and record observations from his or her performance. Regular class teachers should plan to spend a minimum of two weeks in daily contact, interaction, and observation before meeting with other members of the instructional team to develop a learner profile. This approach enables the teacher to consider carefully the learner's special needs through observation and personal interaction. The following section will describe a process of obtaining reliable observation data and developing a learner profile.

The Learner Profile

Figure 6-2 gives a suggested format for developing a learner profile for an identified special needs learner. This form is similar to several different behavioral or developmental checklists that are commercially available and

FIGURE 6-2. LEARNER PROFILE

LEARNER PROFILE

Learner *Lloyd*
School *Johnstown H. S.*
Date *9-15-78*

Assessment/
Appraisal Team
Mr. Forbes, Welding
Ms. Jenkins, Spec. Ed.

Special Needs Indicators	Learning (Strength / Difficulty)	Documentation/Observed Behavior
Quantitative/Numerical Skills		
Count and record		*Math teacher reports below average performance in basic math (+, −, ×, ÷)*
Add/subtract		
Multiply/divide		
Measure		*Has little difficulty reading a rule in welding class*
General number use		} *No observations made in these areas*
Money		
Other quantitative/numerical skills:		
Verbal Skills		
Read		*Has difficulty reading simplified project worksheets*
Spell		
Record information		
Verbal communication		*Stutters occasionally*
Written communication		*Has difficulty writing a project procedure*
Other verbal skills: *Reading rate*		*Takes considerable additional time to read worksheets*
Cognitive Skills		
Retention		
Sequence		
Attentiveness		*Completes only very short tasks*
Planning ability		
Mechanical aptitude		*Excellent "sense" for using hand tools in welding*
Transfer		
Other cognitive skills:		

FIGURE 6-2. *(Continued)*

LEARNER PROFILE

Special Needs Indicators	Learning	Documentation/Observed Behavior
	Strength / Difficulty	
Perceptual Skills		
Auditory discrimination		Often requests that directions be repeated
Form perception		
Form discrimination		
Space perception		
Color perception		Recognizes safety colors in the lab (shop) with no problem
Touch discrimination		
Other perceptual skills:		
Language Skills		
Listening		
Nonverbal expression		
Technical vocabulary		
Grammatical expression		
Other language skills:		
Psychomotor/Physical Skills		
Physical strength		Has difficulty holding on to small objects when involved in activities
Hand-eye coordination		
Manual dexterity		
Mobility		
Other physical skills:		

FIGURE 6-2. *(Continued)*

LEARNER PROFILE

Special Needs Indicators	Learning (Strength / Difficulty)	Documentation/Observed Behavior
Social Skills		
Sociability		Popular with classmates
Cooperativeness		
Conformity		
Loyalty		
Safety		
Responsibility		
Sensitivity		
Other social skills: Hyperactive		Several teachers find him difficult to keep on task
Occupational Interests		
Agriculture/Natural Resources		Always interested in working on his minibike
Automotive and Power Services		Welding and machine tool classes requested
Construction/Manufacturing		
Graphics/Communications		
Food/Clothing/Child Care		
Health		
Office/Business		
Other or specific occupational interests: Welding		Has requested a work observation experience at a welding shop for next semester

commonly used by special educators. This profile, however, focuses upon identification criteria that are especially pertinent for adolescents and young adults—the primary target group for occupational education. A section of the profile is devoted to determining the student's occupational preferences, and this makes it especially appropriate for use by occupational educators. The specific format used for the learner profile should provide a comprehensive behavioral description of the learner's special needs. This is its central and critical purpose.

Assessment-Appraisal Team. The members of the instructional team should be the professionals primarily involved in developing the learner profile. These individuals are identified as the assessment-appraisal team. Diagnosticians, psychologists, and other ancillary personnel can provide interpretations of test data and other supplementary information as needed. Parents should also be contacted, informed, and invited to attend the learner analysis-appraisal meetings where their son's or daughter's program is being discussed. In some states it is possible to utilize occupational evaluators who have assessed the learner's aptitudes with a series of work samples.

It is *essential* that members of the instructional team be directly involved in developing the learner's profile from available diagnostic/prescriptive information, observation reports, and other information and data. Their involvement will make the resulting profile and learning prescription of maximum utility.

Special Need Indicators. The left column of the Learner Profile form (Figure 6-2) identifies eight broad categories of special need. These categories represent the major areas in which the observable effects of handicaps or disadvantages tend to occur. The categories of educational effects, which are of concern here, include: 1) quantitative-numerical skills, 2) verbal skills, 3) cognitive skills, 4) perceptual skills, 5) language skills, and 6) psychomotor-physical skills, 7) social skills, and 8) occupational interests. General definitions for each of the categories are provided in Figure 6-3. Within each of the eight categories a number of specific indicators are listed. In the category of social skills, for instance, the specific indicators of special need could include analysis of the student's cooperativeness, sociability, loyalty, responsibility, or any number of behavioral characteristics. Detailed definitions for each of these specific indicators are provided in Figure 10-9 in Chapter 10.

FIGURE 6-3. SPECIAL NEED INDICATOR CATEGORIES

SPECIAL NEED INDICATOR CATEGORIES	DEFINITION
Quantitative-numerical skills	Involves the ability to count, record, perform basic arithmetic processes, measure and otherwise use or manipulate numerical information
Verbal skills	Involves the ability to communicate in written and spoken forms
Cognitive skills	Involves the ability to follow instructions, remember, sequence information, plan, organize, and make decisions
Perceptual skills	Involves the ability to perceive accurately colors, forms, space, sounds, and odors
Language skills	Involves the ability to listen, understand, and express oneself using written and oral forms of language
Psychomotor-physical skills	Involves the ability to coordinate and perform physical movements
Social skills	Involves the ability to interact with others and act independently in an acceptable manner
Occupational interests	Identifies the learner's major cluster of occupational interest or preference

For each special need indicator category, space has been left on the profile to permit teachers to add additional indicators that are appropriate for individual students. Providing an exhaustive list of indicators would make the profile form several pages in length, and the majority of indicators on a lengthy list would likely be rated as neither strengths nor weaknesses.

Profile Ratings. The center column of the learner profile form provides an area for rating the learner's level of disability for each of the special need indicators. As the examples presented later in this chapter will reflect, this format for assessment clearly indicates both the problems encountered and the strengths demonstrated by the student in school situations. In most cases it provides a comprehensive profile of the learner and optimistically conveys the notion that the individual has several strong areas of performance in addition to his more readily recognized disability or disabilities.

For each of the special need indicators, it is possible for the team to review and discuss their perception of the learner's performance level. Through a discussion in which previous observation and behavior of the student can be noted, consensus ratings for each special need indicator can be derived. These ratings are made on a five-step scale ranging from "learning difficulty" to "learning strength." The specific levels of "difficulty-strength" will be somewhat arbitrarily defined as the discussions of the appraisal-assessment team progress. Students who do not exhibit particular disabilities or strengths with regard to the "indicator" should be rated near the middle of the five-point scale.

It is also possible that teachers may not have collected observational information for all of the special need indicators. In situations where this is the case, the rating should be omitted. It should also be noted that other indicators, in addition to those listed on the form, will be important for certain students. These can be added in the space following each section of indicators.

Dots or checks can be used in marking the profile form. When the rating process is completed, these marks can be connected to provide a graphic portrayal of the learner.

Documentation. Documentation for each assessment or rating made on the learner profile is critical. In order to make sound and unbiased professional judgments, it is important that both the special and occupational educators (who are familiar with the student) document their perceptions of the learning problems involved. Although this type of information collection is somewhat inefficient compared to using tests, the validity and reliability of decisions made in this way are likely to be more accurate and effective over time.

A number of different information sources can be used for documentation of strengths, weaknesses, or perceived learning problems. Possible sources are given in Figure 6–4.

In a given school district these information sources may or may not be available. This is only a suggested list of "legitimate" sources; there will be others that the assessment-appraisal team will find useful.

FIGURE 6-4. SOURCES OF DOCUMENTATION OF SPECIAL NEED INDICATORS

Teacher report and referral
Diagnostic-prescriptive assessment
Social service agency referral
Parent communication
Employer-supervisor communication
Work sample evaluation report and profile
Medical examination
School achievement and attendance records
Visual or hearing exam

Diagnostic information obtained from or through these sources should be carefully reviewed before it is used as documenting evidence for a particular learning problem or special need. Questions such as the following should be raised:

How current is the information?
Does it provide directions or suggestions useful for classroom teaching?
Does it provide information that is specific to the problem?

Most readers will probably note that test data are not suggested as a source of documenting evidence. Specific test data found in the student's file will likely be of only limited value in developing a learner analysis profile. In recent years formal testing of the paper and pencil variety has come under severe criticism when used with special needs learners. Intelligence, aptitude, and achievement tests have been criticized for their cultural bias, lack of content validity for the situations in which the results are used, and lack of appropriate norms or reference groups. Another limitation is the testing medium itself. When students have difficulty reading arithmetic problems on an aptitude test, the test is essentially providing indicators of reading ability rather than numerical aptitudes. Also, as suggested previously, the most significant criticism of most testing programs is inadequacy of the results in terms of suggesting appropriate teaching methods or materials. Few test profiles are readily translated into useful information that can be used by the teacher in planning or sequencing instructional experiences.

Observable Behaviors. The need for teachers to work closely with students and observe their behavior was expressed earlier. Several authors have suggested that the ability of teachers to describe the learning and behavioral problems of students by specifying observable behaviors the learner exhibits is a highly important skill. By carefully observing the classroom behavior of their students, teachers simplify the process of learner needs analysis, and the specific learning problem can be more readily understood. For instance, observing that Lloyd "tends to repeat phrases when describing problems with his welding project" provides more useful information then describing the behavior as "perseveration."

Describing the process of behavioral management, Wallace and Kauffman (1973) define behavior as observable, countable, and repeatable action of the learner. Behavior is "observed" by seeing and/or hearing it. Behavior is "countable" when it can be recorded accurately and reliably by any competent observer. A "repeatable" behavior must be able to occur more than once. Behaviors that are not repeatable are those that only occur once, such as "disrupting the annual student art fair."

Many of the behavioral management tests—several of which are given in the references at the end of the chapter—suggest that it is appropriate to monitor single behaviors over time using graphs and other similar reporting forms. For any given behavior it is possible to monitor, for example: 1) the percentage of correct responses on a math test, 2) the rate of behavior, e.g., speed of computing selected math problems, 3) duration of behavior, or amount of time taken to complete the computation, or 4) percentage of intervals during which the behavior was observed, e.g., percentage of times student was involved in computation when observed at regular intervals (Wallace and Kauffman 1973). Systematic observation of behavior using any of these criteria would be useful in noting behaviors to support the learning difficulty-learning strength ratings given to students on the learner profile.

Using the Information from the Learner Profile

There are a number of specific uses for the information reported in the special needs student's learner profile. These different uses will become more apparent in later chapters. An immediate and direct use of the information can be found in the following section which focuses on the development of a learning prescription. If, for a specific student, the learner profile indicates poor listening skills or auditory discrimination problems, this would suggest that the learning prescription not include the use of audio tapes as an instructional medium to be used by the student. If the learner profile were to reflect strengths in such areas as planning ability and responsibility, this may suggest that student is capable of working on specific learning tasks on an independent basis and be so reflected in the prescription.

In later chapters, the learner profile information will be used for such instructional development activities as: 1) identifying staff to provide needed special or supportive services, 2) selecting specific instructional methods and materials, and 3) modifying or adjusting the learning environment for the student.

Lloyd's Profile

Lloyd's learner profile was shown in Figure 6–2. You will recall that in Chapter 1 he was diagnosed as being learning disabled because of the wide discrepancy between his estimated potential and his unusually poor academic performance in high school.

All of the eight areas of Lloyd's profile are shown in the illustration. His welding teacher, Mr. Forbes, and his special education teacher, Ms. Jenkins, developed the profile after the first four weeks of school. It appears that Lloyd's learning strengths rest with his strong interest in welding and his mechanical aptitude. His tests indicate that he should be performing better in his academic subjects, but he continues to have trouble with written and verbal communication in the welding class as well as in his regular academic subjects. He appears to have some difficulty in discriminating certain sounds and speech patterns, although his hearing acuity appears normal. Mr. Forbes has noted that he has above average mechanical aptitudes when he uses the hand tools and equipment in the welding lab.

At the end of the first month, nearly all of Lloyd's teachers had observed problems in reading comprehension, reading rate, hyperactivity, and in verbal and written communication. After discussing and compiling the total profile in a team meeting, the teachers felt they better understood some of Lloyd's learning difficulties, and felt more comfortable in identifying some of the special services and adjustments needed for Lloyd.

DEVELOPING A LEARNING PRESCRIPTION

The learner profile will be of little benefit unless the results or judgments derived from it are systematically incorporated into instructional planning. As suggested throughout this chapter, one of the long recognized faults of preinstructional testing and assessment programs is that they typically reflect only marginally useful information for the teachers. One way in which to partly overcome this problem is to develop a learning prescription for each student. The use of learning prescriptions has been developed by Dunn and Dunn (1975) and other researchers interested in individualized instruction.

The Learning Prescription

The educational or learning prescription (we will use the latter designation) involves a student-based description of:

1. Which media will be most effective for the student?
2. What types of learning situations and interaction experiences are most appropriate?
3. What are the most effective media in which the student can respond for purposes of expression and evaluation?

A sample learning prescription is illustrated in Figure 6–5. The prescription has three sections which are intended to describe the ways in which the student can learn most effectively: 1) most appropriate learning mode for the individual student, 2) most conducive interaction mode for learning, and 3) additional learning style considerations.

Learning prescriptions have not received wide acceptance to date. This is due primarily to the lack of diagnostic procedures and tests that

FIGURE 6–5. LEARNING PRESCRIPTION

Name Lloyd *School* Johnstown H.S. *Date* 9-15

A. Appropriate Learning Mode
Directions: Indicate by a check (√), the most appropriate learning modes for this student.

- √ Audio/visual presentation
- √ Observation of goal behavior
- √ Interview/conference with knowledgeable person
- __ Experiment/laboratory experience/ project
- __ Programmed instruction
- __ Simulation/games
- __ Field experience(s)
- __ Role playing
- √ Reading
- __ Audio recording
- __ Others (describe):

B. Interaction Mode
Directions: Indicate below (√) the situations in which the student will work most productively.

- __ Independently (alone)
- √ Peer/partner
- √ Small group
- __ Large group
- √ Individually with teacher or aide

C. Additional Learning Style Considerations Tasks and activities should be short in duration (less than 10 minutes), or practice on larger tasks should be broken up into shorter intervals.

would give teachers clues as to how individual students learn. Although some research has been completed on cognitive mapping of learning styles, much of it is focused on adults in the community college setting. The vast majority of the research focuses exclusively on cognitive (knowledge-oriented) learning styles.

In all probability, precise learning style information is not obtainable prior to instruction. However, it is likely that some helpful information can be obtained by interacting with other instructional staff in the process of developing a learning prescription. Another benefit associated with the use of the learning prescription is the fostering of awareness regarding teaching alternatives. It may be that a teacher had not considered using a variety of instructional modes but had traditionally used just two or three. Through the development of a learning prescription, it is possible to suggest to other teachers that they should consider expanding and adapting their teaching style to suit the unique learning styles of different special needs learners.

Learning Modes. A number of learning modes are identified on the prescription form which enable the instructional team to identify the media through which the special needs learner appears to learn most efficiently. Learning modes represent a number of broad types of instructional experiences that might be provided for special needs learners in occupational and special education programs. In most instances, there will be two to four different modes or media which, when used in an appropriate combination, can provide optimum instruction.

Frequent reference should be made to the learner profile when selecting or identifying the appropriate learning modes. The special need indicators can provide useful clues for teachers in describing learning modes. Reading would probably not be identified as an appropriate mode for our example student Lloyd because of the difficulty he has encountered with conventional reading to date. This assumes to some degree, however, that the material he will be reading is the same material other students are reading in the welding class. If it is possible to modify the reading material through the use of simplified illustrations or some other means, it may be that reading would be an appropriate mode for Lloyd. However, it is more likely that reading, combined with audio and visual reinforcement via slides, filmstrips, and audio tapes, would be considered initially by the instructional team.

Obviously, the use of the prescription, based as it is on the learner profile, will guard against the use of totally inappropriate media. If a student is deaf or has a severe hearing loss, audio recordings would not be used unless sufficient amplification could be provided.

Interaction Modes. In addition to the instructional media, consideration should be given to what social environment would be most appropriate for the learner. Some special needs students will be capable of working alone, while others will require one-to-one instruction. Large group, small group, or working in teams are other interaction modes that may be appropriate.

Here again, the learner profile should be reviewed to identify the social and emotional characteristics of the learner. If the learner has learning strengths reflecting cooperativeness or responsibility, these would serve to indicate that team or independent learning arrangements may be appropriate.

Additional Learning Style Considerations. This section of the prescription form permits the instructional team to include additional pertinent information about the learner. This space can be used to note special adjustments in the learning environment or situation that can be seen as needed by the team after reviewing the learner profile.

Using the Information from the Learning Prescription

There are several potential uses for the learning prescription information given in later steps in the instructional development process. In Chapter 10, the prescription is used extensively in the process of instructional planning. The evaluation of instructional materials, identification of instructional methods, and determination of an appropriate sequence are all based to a large extent on the prescription.

The prescription is also frequently referred to in identifying school and community resources to be used in the instructional programs (Chapter 7). Another use can be found in Chapter 12, specifically the section on modifying and adjusting the learning environment.

Earlier, the need to evaluate a learner's needs and compile a new learner profile frequently was emphasized. This is also critical for learning prescriptions. As the learning and behavioral characteristics of the student change, the prescription will also have to be modified. It is recommended that the learner profile and learning prescription be jointly revised.

Lloyd's Prescription

The prescription developed for Lloyd, our learning disabled example, was presented in Figure 6–5. Because of his extremely low performance in reading, his teachers plan to emphasize the use audiovisual materials and observation of goal behavior. The goal behavior observation will involve Lloyd in closely watching demonstrations provided by the instructor and, in some instances, other students or workers in industry. Interviews, conferences, and discussions with people knowledgeable in welding will also be used. Along with the audiovisual media, his teachers plan to use some simplified reading materials to upgrade his reading skills.

Since it has been recognized that Lloyd tends to be hyperactive at times, the instructional team feels it is important that he work individually with a teacher or aide. Depending upon the situation, it should also be possible to have him work in small groups or with a partner on occasion. Finally, the team has added a special note that all activities and tasks should be of short duration in order to make the learning efficient. Larger tasks or activities will have to be broken down and completed in steps because of Lloyd's short attention span. It is expected, however, that gradually the time spent on each task can be increased as long as Lloyd's attention can be maintained.

SUMMARY

Identification and assessment of the educational needs of special needs students is an important, critical first step in formulating instruction. Accurate identification of special needs learners must be supported with and followed by a comprehensive assessment of the individual's verbal, social, numerical, cognitive, physical, perceptual, and language skills. Assessment of occupational interests and aptitudes is also vitally important in determining school program placement.

A variety of techniques to be used by the assessment/appraisal team (special and occupational educators plus psychologists, parents, administrators, and other ancillary personnel) are discussed. Compiling descriptive and instructionally useful information from classroom observations, assessment batteries, and other information sources is of primary importance. Once compiled, it is suggested that the information be displayed in a profile format to illustrate the learner's functional strengths and weaknesses. Strategies for using the profiled information in other activities, such as instructional planning and modifying the learning environment, are suggested.

Translating profiled assessment information into an individual prescription for the learner is essential for developing instructional units or modules. A concise learning prescription delineates *how* the student learns most effectively and efficiently. Such factors as appropriate learning modes—role playing or reading, for example—and appropriate interaction modes, such as independent, small group, and so on, are considered in preparing the prescription.

REFERENCES

Buffmire, J. A. *Information for inservice training development: A collection from field efforts of the RMRRC.* Salt Lake City: Rocky Mountain Regional Resource Center, 1975.

Dunn, R., and Dunn, K. *Educator's self-teaching guide to individualizing instructional programs.* West Nyack, N.Y.: Parker, 1975.

Education Amendments of 1976, Public Law 94–482. Washington, D.C.: Government Printing Office, 1976.

Egner, A. N., Burdett, C. S. and Fox, W. L. *Observing and measuring classroom behaviors.* Austin, Texas: Austin Writers Group, 1972.

Kay, E. R., Kemp, B. H., and Saunders, F. G. *Guidelines for identifying, classifying, and serving the disadvantaged and handicapped under the vocational education amendments of 1968.* Washington, D.C.: U.S. Department of Health, Education, and Welfare, Office of Education, 1973.

Lilly, M. S. Special education: A teapot in a tempest. *Exceptional Children,* 1970, 37, 43–49.

Lilly, M. S. Special education—A cooperative effort. *Theory Into Practice,* 1975, 14, 82–89.

Smith, R. *Clinical teaching.* New York: McGraw-Hill, 1974.

Vocational Education Amendments of 1968, Public Law 90-576. Washington, D.C.: Government Printing Office, 1968.

Wallace, G., and Kauffman, J. M. *Teaching children with learning problems.* Columbus, Ohio: Charles E. Merrill, 1973.

IDENTIFYING SCHOOL AND COMMUNITY RESOURCES

The development of a comprehensive instructional program for special needs learners involves several steps. One of these steps is the identification of resources that are available to assist and support both the instructional staff and the special needs learners. In order to effectively coordinate occupational and special education instruction, the participating members of the instructional team need to be aware of the resources and supportive services that are available within the school and in the community. For our purposes, resources are defined as those persons, services, or agencies that are available to students and instructional personnel for educational purposes. The two types can be identified as 1) those available within the school or

7

school district and 2) those available in the community (outside the school).

Resource utilization is a critical consideration when planning regular occupational programs as well as individual programs for special needs learners. In order to achieve the maximum educational output from a given instructional program, teachers and administrators need to be sure they have maximized their input of resources. In other words, the full attainment of goals will often depend upon full and efficient use of the available resources (inputs). This chapter, then, is designed to enable the reader to identify and inventory the resources available for the instructional program and coordinate the use of these resources.

WHY IS RESOURCE UTILIZATION IMPORTANT?

The task of designing and implementing educational programs for special needs learners is complex and challenging. As society has become increasingly concerned with the needs of persons with special problems, a multitude of educational programs and services have been generated by federal, state, and local governmental agencies, business and industry, labor, civic groups, and others. Because these programs and services were developed by different agencies and organizations, their objectives and approaches tended to be different, although they all, in some way, were focused on providing needed services to individuals with special needs. As a result, in any community there exist a number of resources which can be tapped by educators to facilitate programming for special needs learners. Many of these community resources (for example, vocational rehabilitation) provide services that are highly instrumental in educating the special needs learner and in insuring their successful transition to employment and independent adult living. Without the identification and systematic use of these resources, the educational process becomes increasingly complex and inefficient.

A similar problem exists with the coordination of resources available within the school or school district. In most medium and large districts there is a sizable number of instructional and supportiv staff responsible for providing special education, counseling, psychological services, remedial assistance, and other resources critical to programming for special needs learners. Here again, to use these resources effectively in instructional planning, they must be known to the regular class teachers who are to use them. Developing an awareness of the full range of resources and services that exist on a districtwide, as well as building level, is a critical step to utilizing these school resources systematically in educational programming.

SCHOOL RESOURCES

School resources are represented by the in-school instructional programs and services that are available to, or designed for, special needs learners. Five different types of school resources can be identified from the instructional staff that usually serves the special needs student at the secondary levels. These five major types are 1) career-related instruction, 2) special and supportive instruction, 3) special and supportive services 4) counseling, and 5) cooperative work experience instruction.

Career-Related Instruction

Occupational and practical arts teachers can be considered the resource personnel for providing career-related instruction. In addition to teachers, aides, paraprofessionals, student teachers or interns—all of whom have responsibility for providing *direct occupational instruction* at any level (junior high, high school, or area vocational center) can be included in this category. Vocational counselors and work coordinators are not included here but are discussed in later categories.

Special/Supportive Instruction

Special education teachers commonly provide the special or supportive instruction in basic academic skills in resource rooms and/or special classrooms. In certain situations teachers of basic math or English will also be providing supportive or special instruction. This resource category is designed to identify persons within the school whose primary responsibility is to provide direct special instruction, as opposed to special services (for instance, speech therapists or social workers).

Special/Supportive Services

Special or supportive services are typically provided by personnel who work with teachers or students on an itinerant consulting basis. Such services might include those provided by reading specialists, speech therapists, social workers, or numerous other trained consultants or specialists. Anyone who provides special or supportive services that are offered to the student in addition to direct instruction would be placed in this category.

Counseling

This fourth school resource category is self-explanatory. All personnel who serve in a counseling role, regardless of whether they are regular, vocational, or special education counselors, can be grouped in this category.

Cooperative Work Experience

All school personnel who are involved with placing and coordinating students on part-time jobs can be identified in this category. Coordinators from both the occupational program areas (e.g., WECEP or co-op coordinators) and special education (e.g., work study or prevocational coordinators) should be identified. This resource category should identify those staff members who are coordinators at least 50 percent of the time. Special work experience programs such as WECEP are explained in greater detail in Chapter 11.

Other School Resources

Depending upon the specific school situation, there are likely to be several resources that don't fit exactly into one or more of the above categories but are nonetheless critical to providing occupational programming for special needs learners. In some schools, program directors and the principal or assistant principals are considered resources because they facilitate much of the programming. Instructional media consultants and other personnel who coordinate instructional materials and resource centers represent another school resource.

Figure 7-1 illustrates by job title the variety of school resources that can be focused on serving the special needs learner. Most educators outside the field of special education fail to realize the vast number of supportive resources that exist within the school. As noted earlier, educators should be aware of the resources available within their school district.

You will note that in Figure 7-1 all of the identified school resources focused on meeting the needs of one or more special needs learners. For individual learners any one or a combination of the identified resources may be appropriate. You will also note that the major resource inputs come from both fields: occupational education and special education. In addition to the direct instructional staff (occupational, practical arts, basic academics, and special education teachers), supportive personnel function in a variety of roles and may be providing special assistance or instruction directly to the student or to the teachers involved in working with the student. The supportive personnel identified in Figure 7-1 are titles of supportive service positions commonly found in most, but not necessarily all, school programs.

COMMUNITY RESOURCES

With the introduction of career education, utilization of community resources has become an important aspect of all educational programs. Occupational educators have recognized for some time the importance of using community-based, specialized employer-employee knowledge in the

FIGURE 7-1. SCHOOL RESOURCES AND THE SPECIAL NEEDS STUDENT

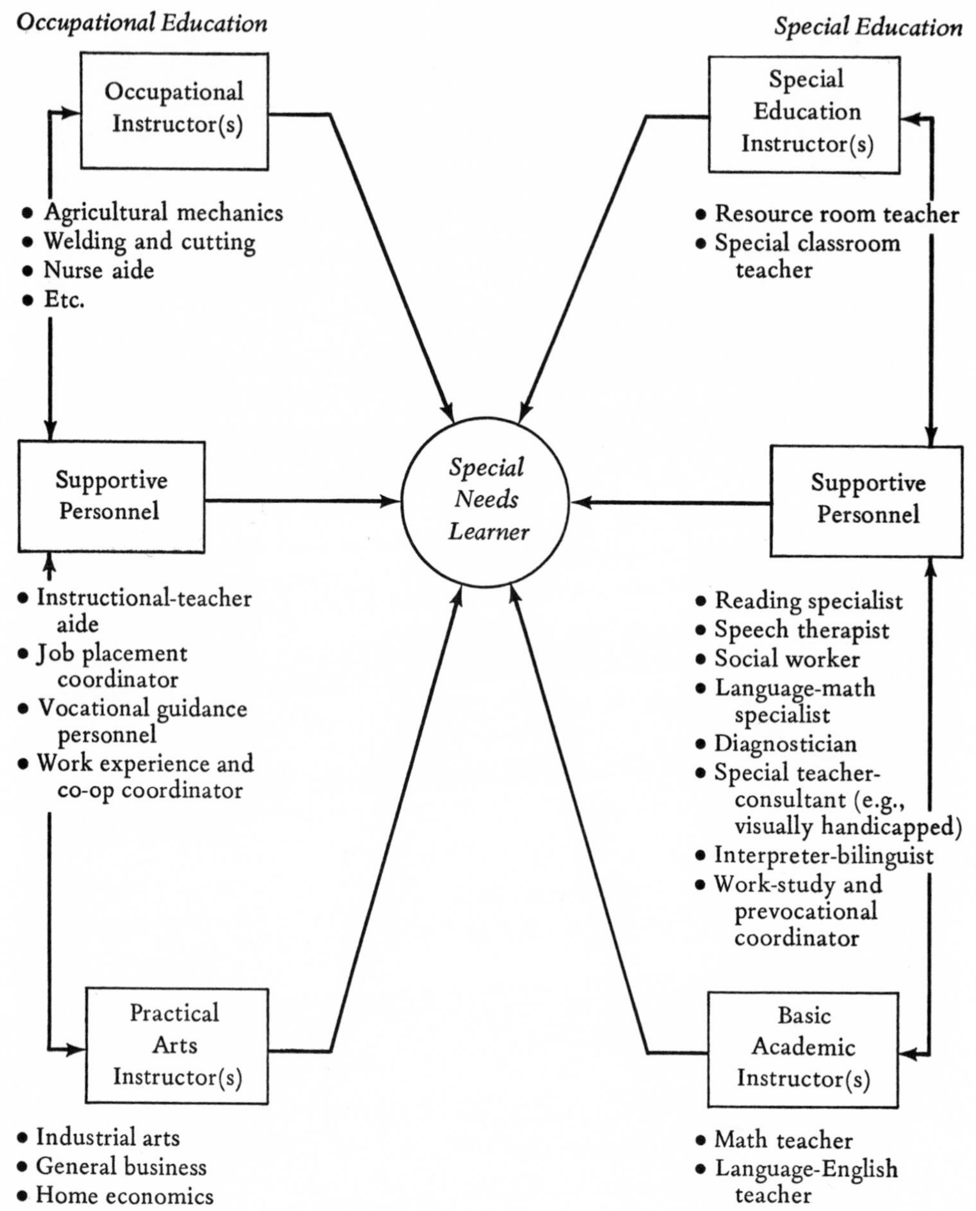

process of preparing students for active participation in the work force. Special educators have sought similar forms of special assistance and supportive services for the special needs student as well. As a result, a number of community-based agencies and organizations have been formed to provide ongoing services for handicapped and disadvantaged individuals. Several authors have noted that through utilization of community resources, the experience and knowledge of the citizenry can provide realistic instructional experiences for students.

Four distinct types of community resources can be identified (see Figure 7-2) on the basis of the agencies or organization through which the resources are available: 1) federal and state governmental agencies, 2) com-

FIGURE 7-2. COMMUNITY RESOURCES AND THE SPECIAL NEEDS LEARNER

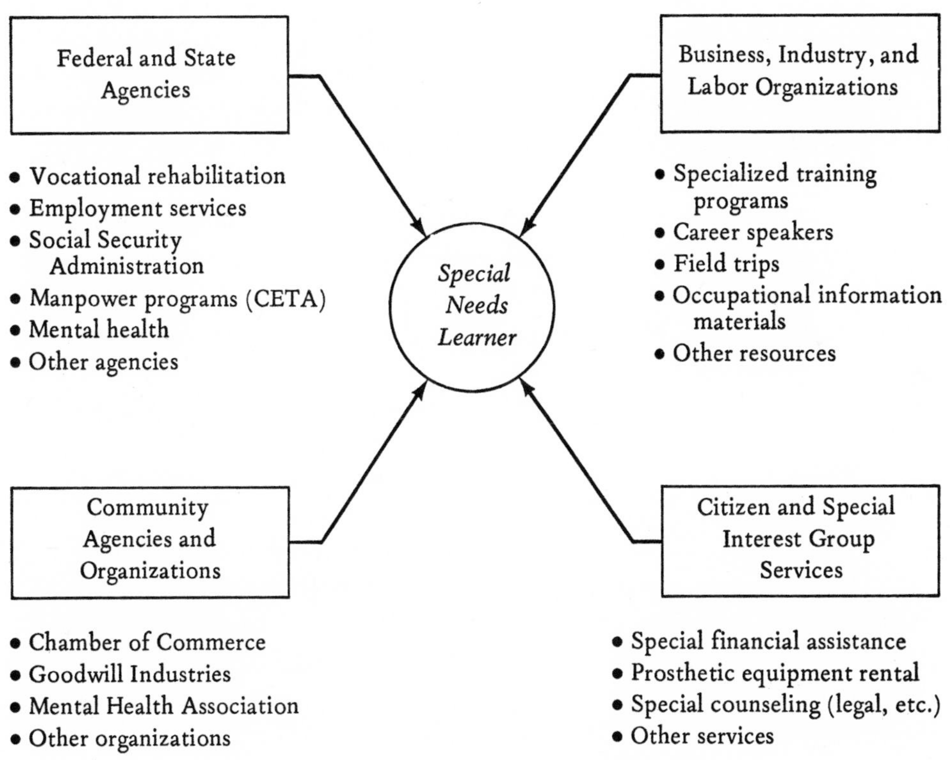

munity agencies and organizations, 3) business, industry, and labor associations or organizations, and 4) citizen or special interest groups.

A variety of different services are available through the four types of community resources, though the type and availability of resources in the form of supportive services will vary considerably from state to state and from community to community.

Federal and State Agencies

Federal and state agencies such as vocational rehabilitation and the employment service offer a number of special services and resources. Vocational rehabilitation provides services to persons near employment age who, because of substantial physical or mental disabilities, require additional services to become employable in competitive, sheltered, or home occupations. Some of the major services provided in this state-federal program include medical examinations, prosthetic devices (artificial limbs or wheelchairs and the like), vocational evaluation and guidance, transportation and basic living costs, on-the-job training expenses, and job placement services.

In addition to vocational rehabilitation there are a number of other agency resources that can and should be tapped by occupational and special educators working with special needs learners. Figure 7-2 identified the employment services, manpower programs (federally supported under the Comprehensive Employment and Training Act), Social Security Administration, and mental health as the principal agencies. Other resource agencies are identified later in this chapter.

Community Agencies and Organizations

This resource category includes agencies and organizations that generally tend to be nonprofit organizations. Although groups such as the Chamber of Commerce are not organized specifically to serve the handicapped and disadvantaged, they do provide a number of instructional materials, career speakers, and other resources that can be used in the occupational program. Other organizations such as Goodwill Industries or the local mental health association offer client evaluation services and other resources and forms of assistance.

Business, Industry, and Labor Organizations

Several of the national and local associations of manufacturers, businessmen, and labor personnel offer numerous types of resources, including specialized training programs, career speakers, field trips, and occupational information. While some of the programs, materials, and resources are not specifically directed at special needs learners, they do provide excellent opportunities and inputs for career preparation programs. There are, however, a substantial number of services and resources focused on different handicapped or disadvantaged groups.

Citizen or Special Interest Groups

This final community resource category identifies those civic groups that offer special assistance and services to persons with special needs. In most instances grants and other forms of individual assistance are provided to persons from groups such as Lions International or the Kiwanis.

A later section of this chapter will describe each of these resources in greater detail. These represent just a few of a vast number of community resources that can be tapped by the instructional team in developing and implementing instructional programs and support services for special needs learners.

INVENTORYING INSTRUCTIONAL RESOURCES

An efficient and effective way of identifying instructional resources is to develop an inventory of the resources existing both within the school program and in the community. An instructional resource inventory is similar in many respects to a directory and could logically be called a directory. Like the telephone directory, an accurate and complete instructional resource inventory will list 1) the names of persons and organizations providing the instructional resource(s), 2) the location and telephone number of individual(s) to be contacted in obtaining the resources, and 3) a brief description of the specific resource or service that is available.

Format for an Instructional Resource Inventory

A format for organizing an instructional resource inventory is shown in Figures 7-3 and 7-4. The format presented is designed to focus the development of the inventory on an occupational cluster such as health occupations or construction occupations. This organizes the inventory so that it will be useful to a number of teachers for identifying and describing the resources available to assist the learner in reaching a cluster-based career goal.

Sample information is included on the inventory forms in Figures 7-3 and 7-4 to illustrate their functionality. This format has been adapted from several other community resource identification forms developed by different schools and agencies. The form presented here has been field tested and refined by groups of teachers involved in inservice workshops.

Guidelines and Suggestions for Developing an Instructional Resource Inventory

The following guidelines and suggestions will be helpful in developing your own instructional resource inventory for a local instructional program. The suggestions that follow outline considerations procedures and techniques to be made or used when using the suggested inventory form.

1. The scope of the inventory will depend upon the type and size of the school district or program. In larger school districts an inventory may be developed on a per-building basis. In smaller school districts or programs, where the resources are decentralized, the inventory may include other cooperative school districts, multiple buildings, area vocational centers, and so on.
2. While developing the inventory it is important to keep in mind the information needs of the instructional staff who will be using it.

FIGURE 7-3. INSTRUCTIONAL RESOURCE INVENTORY FOR CONSTRUCTION OCCUPATIONS FOR SPECIAL NEEDS LEARNERS:

SCHOOL RESOURCES

District: Portage Public Schools

School(s): Lincoln High School; Jefferson Middle School; Lyle School

Developers: Karen Tinkman; John Lockman; Pete Benson

Date: September, 1978

RESOURCE CATEGORY	RESOURCE CONTACT PERSON	TITLE OR RESPONSIBILITY	LOCATION AND PHONE	DESCRIPTION OF SPECIFIC RESOURCE OR SERVICE
Career-related instruction	John Lockman	Teacher, building trades	Rm. 118, Lincoln H. S., ext. 27	Introductory carpentry; residential construction I & II
	Sam Smithson	Teacher, cabinetmaking	Rm. 126, Lincoln H. S., ext. 32	General construction concepts; exploration of const.
	Jan Tye	Teacher, construction	Rm. 213, Jefferson Middle School ext. 17	industry careers
Special supportive instruction	Karen Tinkman	Teacher, mentally hdcp.	Rm. 221, Lincoln H. S., ext. 12	Basic math and language arts instruction
	Bob Hammerman	Teacher, remedial math	Rm. 15, Lincoln H. S., ext. 15	Applied math and consumer math
Special & supportive services	Jan Jones	Reading consultant	Lyle School, 626-2572	Diagnosis & remediation of special reading problems
	Carolyn Bailey	Speech therapist	Central office, 628-2222	Diagnosis & remediation of speech & articulation problems
	Jenny Travis	Bilinguist	Lyle School, 626-3572	Assistance in communicating with students for which English is a second language
Counseling	Jere Chaffin	Counselor	Rm. 12, Lincoln H. S., ext. 3	Occupational interest and aptitude testing (GATB, SDS,
				OVIS); work adjustment counseling
Cooperative work experience	Pete Benson	Vocational co-op coordinator	Rm. 123 (a.m.) Lincoln H.S., ext. 19	Off-campus training stations
	Jack Samson	Work-study coordinator	Rm. 220 (a.m.) Lincoln H.S., ext. 11	On-campus training stations
Other school resources	Martha Hillier	Instructional materials	Library, Lincoln H. S., ext. 34	Development of special instructional materials for students with different handicaps

FIGURE 7–4. INSTRUCTIONAL RESOURCE INVENTORY FOR CONSTRUCTION OCCUPATIONS FOR SPECIAL NEEDS LEARNERS:

COMMUNITY RESOURCES

RESOURCE CATEGORY	RESOURCE CONTACT PERSON	TITLE OR RESPONSIBILITY	LOCATION AND PHONE	DESCRIPTION OF SPECIFIC RESOURCE OR SERVICE
Federal & State agency resources	John Jamas	VRS counselor	17 Wall St., Portage 627-3333	Postschool training support; funds to offset employer costs for extra supervision for on-the-job training; placement & follow-up services; funds for training materials
Community agencies & organizations	Larry Johns	Director, Portage Chamber of Commerce	185 Center St., Portage 628-3111	Career speakers for classroom presentations; advisory committee members; co-op training station
Business, industry, & labor organizations	Sam Cummins	President, United Construction Workers, Local #86	215 Court St., Portage 626-1315	Field trips to residential and commercial construction sites; student assistance fund
Citizen & special interest groups	Jack Gregory	President, Portage Lions Club	1515 W. Sherman, Portage 625-3646	Prosthetic aids (hearing aids, etc.); special financial assistance
Other resources				

Obviously, its principle users will be the individuals who are assisting in its development and who will collectively use it as a basis for planning and implementing programs for special needs learners. In addition, however, it may be a useful tool for counselors of various special students who may wish to solicit outside assistance in work adjustment or vocational counseling for individual students. Teachers not in occupational or special education may also find the inventory helpful in locating specific resources to assist with their instruction.

3. In some communities efforts either have been or regularly are undertaken to identify and tabulate community resources. *Initially, an attempt should be made to locate any existing resource listings or directories.* These listings may have already been prepared by organizations such as the local United Way or Chamber of Commerce and would represent the combined interests of a number of potential resources and special service providers.

   Before developing the school resource inventory, it is helpful to review the staff or personnel directory of the district. This will provide you with an overview of the position titles and responsibilities of everyone employed in the district. Several of the medium-sized and larger districts also publish detailed descriptions of the special education programs and services available. While these materials are generally distributed to parents, they can provide an excellent overview for occupational education personnel who may not be fully acquainted with the special programs in the district.

4. When individuals, agencies, or organizations are contacted in the process of developing the resource inventory, consideration should be given to their prospective involvement in an advisory capacity. It may be possible to invite selected individuals to serve as members of an advisory committee for the instructional program.

5. Existing citizens advisory committees are an excellent place to begin the search for community resources. Since one of the functions of such advisory committees is to coordinate community resources, they can frequently provide several excellent suggestions and leads for locating specific resource personnel and services.

6. When developing a resource inventory it is helpful to divide the resources to be surveyed into two broad categories—school resources and community resources.

7. Certain basic information is required in compiling and using a resource inventory for any educational program. Since most educational resources are identified by the individuals, agencies, or organizations who provide them, the basic information should be the name of the resource person or persons to be contacted. Additional essential information includes:

   a) Title or position of the resource contact person
   b) Short, concise description of the specific resource or supportive service available
   c) Location (address) of the resource contact person's office or business
   d) Phone number of resource contact person

8. Several different types of school resources should be considered (see Figure 7–1). Individuals representing the following areas should be included in the inventory:

   a) Specific career-related instructional programs (occupational and practical arts courses)
   b) Special services—reading specialists, diagnosticians, therapists, bilinguists, interpreters, and others
   c) Special education instructional programs, for example, special education class teachers or resource room teachers
   d) Basic education or remedial programs
   e) Vocational guidance personnel
   f) Job placement or work adjustment coordinators
   g) Work experience or work-study coordinators

9. In addition to school resources, a number of different community resources should be studied and included in the inventory (U.S. Department of Health, Education, and Welfare, 1972):

   a) Federal and state agencies. Among the several federal and state agencies with regional or local offices who provide various supportive services for special needs learners are the following:

      Federal Agencies

      Vocational Rehabilitation

      Employment Service

      Comprehensive Employment and Training Act (CETA) Administration

Social Security Administration
JOBS—National Alliance of Businessmen
Job Corps
National Youth Corps
Community Action Program
Veterans Administration
Bureau of Indian Affairs
Immigration and Naturalization Services
President's Committee on Employment of the Handicapped

State Agencies
State Employment Service
Mental health agency
State agency or school for the blind
State agency or school for the deaf
Public health agency
Family service agency
Department of welfare
Governor's Committee for Employment of the Handicapped

b) Community agencies or organizations. Numerous services and resources are available from such sources as:

Chamber of Commerce
Mental Health Association
Mental Retardation Association
Crippled Children's Society
Goodwill Industries
YMCA and YWCA
Opportunities Industrialization Centers (OIC)

c) Business, industry, and labor organizations. These organizations frequently provide or sponsor specialized training programs for individuals with special needs. They also provide such resources as field trips, career speakers or classroom presentations, and occupational and instructional information on various careers, career clusters, or industries.

d) Citizen and special interest groups. In addition to civic organizations such as Lions, Kiwanis, Rotary, and Elks, there are other organizations that frequently offer special services assistance. Certain special interest groups contribute in different ways to educational programs for the special student. These include:

National Association for the Advancement of Colored People
Congress of Racial Equality
Urban League
American Indian Education Association
Indian tribal councils
League of United Latin American Citizens

10. Once the resource inventory is compiled, administrators may wish to duplicate and distribute it to the appropriate staff.
11. Maintaining the currency and accuracy of the information in the resource inventory or directory is important. A system should be worked out for periodic review and updating of the data and distribution of revised versions to all users.

Guidelines for Using Resource Data Cards

Another system that teachers have found to be useful in identifying and inventorying instructional resources is an index card file. Figure 7–5 presents two cards (5x7 size) and how they can be used to catalog pertinent information on instructional resources and service resources. The index card format enables large amounts of resource information to be stored in a central file that can be made readily accessible to staff. The following are a series of suggestions for the process of developing a resource card index:

1. Discuss, as a group, the potential uses of the resource file and the information to be collected. This will enable you to carefully plan the format of the cards so that the appropriate information for each different type of resource is compiled. The two sample cards shown in Figure 7–5 suggest a need for two resource card files: one containing career-related instruction resources and the other listing resources offering special or supportive services.
2. Work in teams to organize the information collection process as well as to collect the resource information.

FIGURE 7-5. COMMUNITY RESOURCE DATA CARDS

Instructional Resources

CAREER-RELATED INSTRUCTION RESOURCE

Career cluster or occupation Janitor

Name of resource person Harold Graves

Title Janitorial Supervisor Address 411 Long Lake Blvd.

Phone 467-3322 Creston, Illinois

Appropriate for (students, grade level, etc.) Special needs students, grades 9-12

Type of resource (check all that are appropriate)

- ___ Field trip
- ✓ Classroom consultant
- ___ Instructional materials
- ✓ Instructional content resource
- ___ Speaker
- ___ Individual student tutor
- ___ Sponsor of short-term work experiences

Detailed description of resource Likes to work with students; has a full range of custodial services; excellent attitude toward the world of work

Service Resources

SUPPORTIVE SERVICE RESOURCE

Type of service

- ✓ Student assistance
- ___ Parent/family assistance
- ___ School/teacher assistance
- ___ Other (describe)___

Source of service (name of agency or organization) Neighborhood Youth Corps

Name of contact person Ron Barrett

Address 1400 W. Jasper Creston, Illinois

Phone 467-3228

Office hours 9-5

Record previous contacts or referrals below

Date	Student	Action
11/7/79	Harvey Devin	3 counseling sessions scheduled

3. After the information collection is complete, carefully sort and edit the information on the data cards to avoid duplications and misclassifications.
4. Develop a list or reference index of each of the resource titles that will enable the users of the card file to locate the pertinent resource data cards quickly and efficiently.
5. Conduct an inservice session to orient the staff to the use of the card index, and encourage them to add to and update the resource index on a regular basis.

INSTRUCTIONAL RESOURCES AND ADVISORY COMMITTEES

An effective means of identifying community resources is through the establishment and use of an advisory committee. In addition, advisory committees can play a functional and highly important role in overall program planning, development, and operation.

Historically, advisory committees composed of businessmen, employees, parents, and so on have been productive and beneficial in serving the needs of teachers, administrators, and students in occupational programs. Steering committees and citizens advisory committees have also been effectively used in other school programs, as well as governmental and community agencies serving individuals with special needs. Advisory committees, in and of themselves, have become widely recognized as a productive and functional instructional resource for school personnel.

Since the emergence of career education, the use of educational advisory committees has become increasingly critical. Several new roles and functions are being served by these committees as they attempt to initiate comprehensive community-based education. Advisory committees can be effectively used to support the instructional team in the following seven areas in their efforts to provide comprehensive career exploration and preparation programs for special needs learners (Cochran, Phelps, and Skupin 1974):

1. Identify and coordinate the use of various community resources for the instructional program.
2. Provide advice on the appropriateness and relevancy of instructional content.

3. Review and provide recommendations on instructional materials, facilities, and equipment.
4. Assist with student placement in cooperative work experience and full-time employment positions.
5. Develop and sponsor a comprehensive community public relations program.
6. Coordinate community need, manpower supply and demand, and follow-up surveys to collect relevant and supportive information for decision making.
7. Review and evaluate the total special needs program periodically.

Types of Advisory Committees

A number of different types of advisory committees can be used in program development and operation. Depending upon the local situation, it may be appropriate to consider:

1. Using existing career, occupational, or special education advisory committees or subcommittees of these committees.
2. Forming a joint advisory committee from existing career, occupational, or special education advisory committees.
3. Forming a new advisory committee representing the interests of the special needs instructional team, employers, agencies (governmental and community), students, parents, and representatives of the special needs community.
4. Expanding the role of child study teams (individual-student planning committees) to include the program advisement functions mentioned previously.

Guidelines and Suggestions for Advisory Committee Utilization

When establishing or utilizing existing advisory committees, several key considerations have to be made. To a large extent these considerations will depend upon the local district's policy regarding the use of advisory committees. However, there are some general guidelines that should be followed in most situations.

The suggestions and guidelines offered here are limited in scope and pertain only to the use of advisory committees for serving special needs occupational programs. More detailed information regarding the establishment and operation of advisory committees can be found in the references at the end of the chapter.

1. Determine the type of advisory committee needed in your local program situation. More specifically, what role, function, and purpose can an advisory committee provide in your situation, focused on developing and operating occupational programs for special needs learners?
2. Assess existing advisory committees to determine whether or not they can fulfill the role, function, and purpose previously identified.
3. Decide whether to initiate a new advisory committee, request a joint advisory committee using representatives from existing committees, or utilize existing advisory committees in the areas of occupational and/or special education.
4. Work with administrative personnel and other members of the instructional team to formulate a proposed school board endorsement for the new or joint advisory committee. Such an endorsement should clearly state the purpose of the committee and outline the specific commitment of the governing board regarding the committee.
5. Once administrative and school board endorsement has been obtained, several planning tasks need to be completed:
   a) Using some objective selection criteria, identify and select prospective advisory committee members to serve on the committee. The optimum size of the committee will depend upon the scope of the program. Effective committees usually range in size from four to eight nonschool personnel.
   b) Select a diverse and comprehensive advisory committee composed of representatives from the following groups:

      One or more teachers serving on the instructional team.
      Supportive service personnel (counselors, diagnosticians, social workers).
      Employers or prospective employers of special needs learners.
      Personnel from state agencies serving the special needs population.

Personnel from community agencies serving the special needs population.

Parents of special needs learners.

Past or present students.

c) Prepare and distribute a letter of invitation to serve on the advisory committee. The letter should be signed by the superintendent or chief school administrator and express the commitment of the district to occupational programming for special needs learners.

d) Once the committee membership is finalized, prepare and distribute an agenda for the initial organizational meeting. A list of possible introductory and discussion topics for the meeting is presented in the sample agenda shown in Figure 7-6. A roster of committee members should also be included with the mailing of the agenda.

FIGURE 7-6. INITIAL ADVISORY COMMITTEE MEETING AGENDA

AGENDA

Special Needs Advisory Committee Meeting

Date: September 6, 1978
Location: Millington High School
Time: 7:30 p.m.

Introductions of all members (administrator or teacher serves as temporary chairman)

Welcome and the special needs advisory committee charge (superintendent or chairman of the school board)

Overview of the program (temporary chairman)

Discussion of the advisory committee concept, operational guidelines, and development of the program of work

Annual program-of-work form distributed and discussion of tentative area of concern (see Figure 7-7)

Discuss agenda for next meeting

Set date, time, and location for next meeting

Adjournment

6. Planning for on-going advisory committee involvement is important. Experience with educational advisory committees has demonstrated that those committees which are the most productive have completed a certain amount of formalized long-range planning. An agenda item for an initial session of a special needs advisory committee meeting should be discussion of an Annual Program of Work for the committee. Planning documents of this type will vary considerably from district to district, depending upon the process used for planning. A simple, but functional program of work is illustrated in Figure 7-7.

Numerous other considerations beyond those listed here are obviously important. More detailed discussions of these considerations, along with example documents and case studies, can be found in the advisory committee references listed at the end of the chapter.

SUMMARY

Maximum utilization of community and school resources is important in providing a broad range of educational experiences and support services for special needs learners. This chapter discusses several types of human and material resources to be found in both the school and community. Suggestions and strategies for identifying and using such resources as in-school supportive personnel (reading specialists, aides, bilinguists-interpreters, therapists, and so forth) are provided. Advisory committees and preparation of resource inventories are effective techniques for identifying and using such community resources as vocational rehabilitation services, Goodwill Industries, local associations of retarded citizens, or career speakers among a host of others. A latter part of the chapter is devoted to guidelines for forming and operating special needs program advisory committees composed of local employers, employees, representatives of community agencies—such as social services, parents, and teachers—and support personnel (counselors, social workers, and others).

FIGURE 7-7. ANNUAL PROGRAM OF WORK, 1978–1979
SPECIAL NEEDS ADVISORY COMMITTEE, SANDMAN COMMUNITY SCHOOLS

AREA OF CONCERN	DATES FOR COMMITTEE REVIEW/DISCUSSION	COMMITTEE ACTIVITIES	RECOMMENDATIONS AND SUGGESTED SOLUTIONS
Employment opportunities for graduates	Fall meeting	Reviewed a recent regional manpower survey Interviewed local employment agency representative at meeting Discussed employment outlook with other area employers	Recommend opening the nurse aide program to more special needs students. Possibility of part-time work for some students at the sheltered workshop should be examined.
Status of dropouts	Winter meeting	Interviewed two recent dropouts at meeting Discussed problem with parents of dropouts Met with juvenile probation officer	Closer communication with parents of potential dropouts is recommended. Overall, however, the program does an excellent job of encouraging special needs students to stay in school.
Availability and coordination of community services	Early spring meeting	Discussed available services with VRS & employment service representative at meeting	Counselors and administrators should keep in closer touch with community service agencies by exchanging information such as memos, brochures, or placement information on a regular monthly basis.
Appropriateness of instructional objectives	Late spring meeting	Reviewed instructional goal statements for all programs before meeting Reviewed instructional objectives from state office of education	Specific recommendations made to individual instructors that certain goals should be deleted and others added. Also suggested a greater overall emphasis on developing basic skills in special needs students. Instructors need released time to modify and improve their instructional objectives.

REFERENCES

American Vocational Association. *The advisory committee and vocational education.* Washington, D.C.: American Vocational Association, 1969.

Burt, S. M. *Industry and vocational-technical education.* New York: McGraw-Hill, 1967.

Cochran, L. H., Phelps, L. A., and Skupin, J. F. *Guide for effective utilization of advisory committees.* Mt. Pleasant: Central Michigan University, 1974.

Hofstrand, R. K., and Phipps, L. J. *Advisory councils for education: A handbook.* Urbana: Rurban Educational Development Laboratory, University of Illinois, 1971.

Phipps, L. J., et al. *CRU system: A manual for community resource utilization.* Urbana: Department of Vocational and Technical Education, University of Illinois, 1974.

State of Illinois. *Advisory committee member* (Bulletin No. 29-672). Springfield: Division of Vocational and Technical Education, Illinois Office of Education, n.d.

State of Illinois. *Occupational education for disadvantaged and handicapped persons* (Bulletin No. 40-1273). Springfield: Division of Vocational and Technical Education, 1973.

U.S. Department of Health, Education, and Welfare. *Suggested utilization of resources and guide for expenditures.* Washington, D.C.: Government Printing Office, 1972.

CONDUCTING CAREER CLUSTER AND CONTENT ANALYSES

The instructional content provided in any education program is determined to a large extent by both the needs of society and the needs of individuals in that society. When educators become involved in curriculum development they are forced to interpret rather specifically the nature of these needs. Determining the needs of society, as represented by the need for a trained work force, will be the focus of this chapter. In the past, educators have used a variety of techniques and processes to make decisions about the need for new occupational programs or the need for improvements and changes in course content. Recently, the career education movement has suggested that clusters of occupations can be used to identify educational

programs and curricula and would have immediate relevancy for the world of work. Clusters of occupations used in this curriculum development approach usually reflect the major industries found within our society such as manufacturing, health, or public service.

Curriculum and instructional development in career-related instruction is focusing closely on the use of clusters because it reflects several contemporary and emerging educational needs. Some of these needs reflect:

1. The need to provide individuals with occupational versatility and mobility within and across different occupations
2. The need to consider diverse employability options for the increased geographic mobility that Americans possess
3. The need for individuals to adapt easily to the ongoing occupational, technological, social, cultural, psychological, and economic changes in the workplace and society
4. The need to provide greater flexibility in and a broader range of occupational choice patterns
5. The need to meet more adequately the needs of those youth who will not become college graduates

The cluster-based curriculum approach offers several positive alternatives for both the instructor and the student in occupational education. Five benefits to be derived by using this approach for developing instruction include the following:

1. The common elements of learning experiences that are provided in a cluster-based curriculum prepare the student for a cluster of related occupations, thus insuring some mobility among occupations within the cluster.
2. A curriculum based on the cluster concept has more relevance for those students interested in not just one but a variety of occupations. Occupational choice can be postponed until the time of entry into the world of work.
3. Later retraining, whether for advancement or for new occupations, is shortened due to the comprehensive nature of the initial curriculum design and instruction.
4. The elements of both academic and vocational instruction become more meaningful for the student when common job skills such as measuring are studied in their occupational application.

5. Curricula that are based on clusters of occupations provide a basis for examining the social, managerial, and other human relations and interactions aspects of work.

This chapter is designed to do essentially two things. First, it will introduce and describe a general process that local school personnel can use to determine curriculum content using an approach based on the identification of occupational clusters. Second, a suggested procedure for identifying curriculum or instructional content from occupational clusters will be presented. Thus, the two major sections of this chapter will focus on specifying career clusters and analyzing career clusters.

CLUSTERS FOR SPECIAL NEEDS LEARNERS

Many educators ask: How are clusters of occupations different for special needs learners? Or, can special needs learners really be expected to enter the same occupations as nonspecial learners? Two key points must be made before these questions can be answered:

1. As educators, we *cannot* assume that "generally" the employability potential of special needs learners is below that of nonspecial needs learners. The range or degree of variation in the basic functional abilities (reading, math, social skills, perceptual skills, physical abilities, and so on) of special needs learners is just as great, and some suggest perhaps greater than the range or degree of variation in functional abilities among nonspecial needs learners. While a specific special needs student may have limited or subaverage mental abilities, he may have excellent fine motor coordination, which would make him a highly employable in occupations such as circuit board assembler. Hundreds of physically handicapped persons have proved themselves to be highly competent as computer programmers, architects, lawyers, engineers, and in numerous other occupations to which they have been able to adjust successfully and compensate for their limited physical skills. Because of this wide range of variation in the basic functional abilities of special needs learners, it is impossible to make general statements that suggest they can only be employable at a certain level or in certain occupations.

2. It is important to realize that there is some research evidence that suggests special needs learners will tend to perform at the level of expectation held by those around them. Braun (1976) has prepared an excellent summary of the research on teacher expectations and their effects upon the learner's performance. In other words, if we, as educators, only expect learners with subnormal verbal skills to work in the warehouse or stockroom, and never be a receiving clerk or salesman; then it is likely that they will only express an interest in the former occupations. Some educators have referred to this as the "self-fulfilling prophecy of education."

Closely related to the idea of performance expectation levels is the concept of "instructional power." Marc Gold (undated) suggests that different teaching or training techniques have more power than others depending upon their effectiveness with the individual learner. His research with severely mentally handicapped persons suggests that the use of more powerful teaching techniques such as task analysis—where the instructional content is broken down to the learner's level of comprehension—can result in much higher levels of employability for the severely handicapped than ever before expected.

Based on this general framework, it appears that it is impossible to predict reliably the employment potential or capacity of special needs learners in general nor in broad disability areas such as the mentally retarded. Thus, it does not seem educationally feasible to establish separate occupational clusters and training programs that are designed to prepare special needs learners to explore and enter only those occupations for which we feel they can become competent. When designing cluster-based occupational programs that are exclusively for special needs learners, we must always ask ourselves to what extent can we establish a separate occupational cluster or program without limiting or restricting the basic right of all learners to find employment that is meaningful, satisfying, and rewarding.

CLUSTER ANALYSIS AND SPECIAL NEEDS LEARNERS

Over the years, occupational educators have developed a number of different techniques and processes for analyzing occupations. Several of these can be found in the references at the end of the chapter. The problem, however, has been that few of these techniques analyze or examine the basic functional abilities that workers must have to enter and maintain a given job. Because special needs learners are—by definition—limited in one or more of their basic functional abilities, this information is extremely critical if occupational and special educators are to counsel and prepare individuals to enter occupations. Consequently, when occupational and special education teachers attempt to analyze a job or series of tasks, they need to identify not only the specific occupational skills and knowledges required by the job holder, but also the basic skills and concepts which are implicitly required—math or measurement skills, perceptual skills, language and communication skills, social skills, and so on.

In order for the job or task analysis to generate useful information for teaching special needs learners, it often needs to be extensively detailed. To note only that being a machine operator, machinist, or auto mechanic involves reading a micrometer is not likely to provide sufficient information. Depending upon the specific nature and severity of the student's learning problem, it may be that the task of reading a micrometer would have to be further broken to identify the basic skills and concepts to be learned. An example is shown below:

TASK Reading a micrometer

a. Fine motor coordination
b. Recognition of three-digit numbers
c. Recognition of two-to-three-place decimals
d. Interpretation of unmarked graduations on a scale of 0–10

Although the basic procedure for conducting a job or task analysis for special needs learners is similar to those used by occupational educators, the analysis must also examine the basic skills and concepts involved, which, in turn, requires that the analysis go into greater depth and specificity in describing the job or task.

SPECIFYING CAREER CLUSTERS

The concept of clustering occupations into families or groups has been around for a good many years. Its popularity has increased considerably, however, with the advent of the career education movement in the public schools of our nation (Frantz 1973).

Career education has suggested the use of career clusters as a basic framework for curriculum development at the elementary, secondary and postsecondary levels. Clusters or families of closely related occupations (such as the clusters identified in Figure 8-1) serve as a basis for deriving curricula that are oriented toward providing career awareness, exploration, and

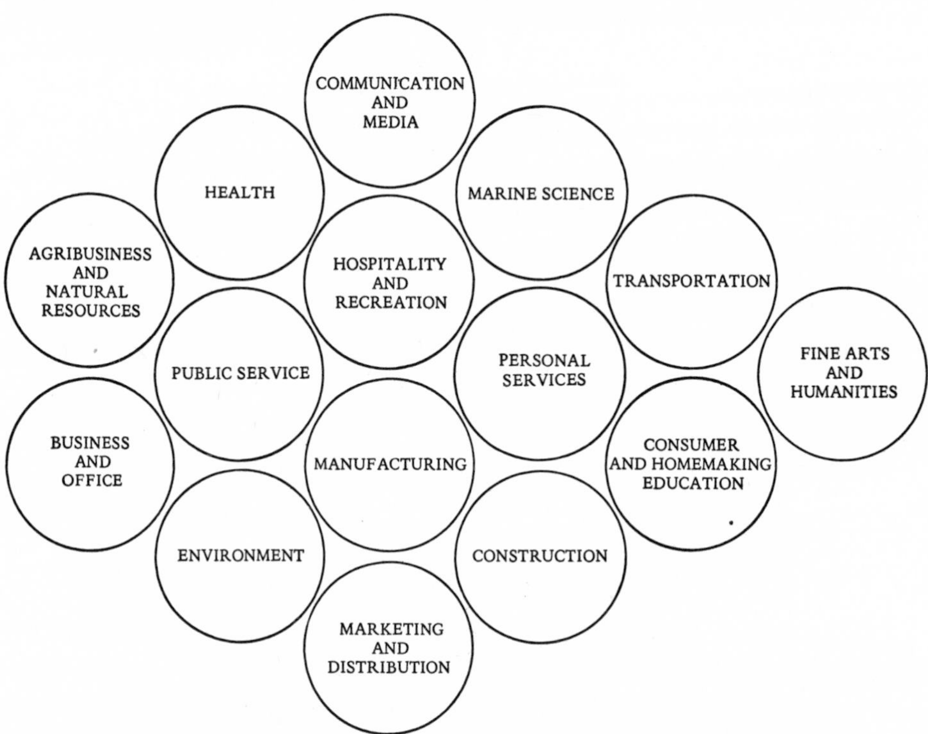

FIGURE 8-1. USOE CAREER CLUSTERS Source: U.S. Office of Education, *Career Education* (Washington, D.C.: Government Printing Office, 1971).

preparation. The normal progression of career development suggests that learning experiences focused on career awareness occur at the elementary level and that exploration and preparation experiences take place at the junior and senior high school levels. Career development is much more than a linear progression, however. It is a dynamic process in which supplemental awareness and exploration experiences continue to recur at the junior and senior high school levels and throughout life. The need to articulate and coordinate this process through career education at several levels has brought about a renewed interest in using the career cluster approach (Kenneke, Nystrom, and Stadt 1973).

A variety of different types of clusters have been developed and introduced in recent years. Some of these clustering schemes have been oriented toward serving a career counseling or guidance purpose. Most of the clustering schemes utilized for curriculum development have used the major industries as the criteria for clustering. Clusters such as construction, health, and manufacturing, which represent the different major industries in our economic system, are commonly identified. In recent years the most widely used clustering scheme has been the one proposed by the U.S. Office of Education (see Figure 8–1).

Specificity of Career Clusters

The specificity or breadth of an industry-based career cluster is an important consideration in curriculum development. Career clusters are broader in scope—include a greater variety of occupations—at the elementary school level than at the secondary level. Transportation is an appropriate cluster for serving the career awareness function at the elementary level. At the secondary level, however, where the focus is an exploration of several possible careers as well as preparation for a specific career, the broad cluster of transportation would be subdivided into a number of more specific clusters such as ground transportation occupations and air transportation occupations.

It is fairly easy to recognize that clusters become increasingly more specific (focusing on fewer occupations) as the curriculum objective moves away from career awareness and toward preparing students for career entry.

At the late secondary level (grades 11 and 12) most clusters are represented as vocational education programs such as auto mechanics, small engine repair, and auto body repair, all of which are part of the transportation cluster discussed earlier.

Cluster Specification Format

It is possible to use a number of different approaches in identifying and arranging occupations in one or more career clusters. The approach offered here will involve an occupational analysis and is similar to an approach developed in a cluster research project at Ohio State University (Taylor et al. 1972). The format for specifying clusters using this approach is presented in the form of a matrix and is shown in Figure 8–2.

This format can be used to identify clusters of occupations for either career exploration or career preparation programs. The major difference is that the number of occupational or job titles that are identified on the form is usually greater in a career exploration cluster, since the levels of occupations identified (from unskilled to highly skilled) are usually more diverse because the instructional goals are prevocational or exploratory in nature. Fewer occupations are identified for a career preparation cluster since the instructional objective here is to prepare the individual for job entry.

Also, it should be noted that the titles of career preparation clusters are more specific and narrower than titles of career exploration clusters. Figure 8–3 illustrates the specificity of several different career exploration and preparation cluster titles. Several subclusters focusing on career preparation can easily be identified in the broader career exploration clusters.

The Process of Career Cluster Specification

A general process for specifying the career clusters that can serve as a basis for instructional programs involves three steps. These are identified in Figure 8–4. These steps, which are discussed in detail later, are intended as a general framework for specifying clusters of occupations to serve as a curriculum development base. Modifications or extensions of the cluster specifi-

FIGURE 8-2. CLUSTER SPECIFICATION FORM

Check: ☑ Exploration Cluster
☐ Preparation Cluster

CLUSTER-RELATED INSTRUCTIONAL AREAS (Course titles and/or major instructional units)	CAREER CLUSTER: AGRIBUSINESS AND NATURAL RESOURCES OCCUPATIONS			
Landscaping	Groundskeeper		Landscape gardner Landscape designer	Landscape architect
Floriculture		Flower grower	Floral designer	Florist
Arboriculture	Tree-surgeon helper		Tree-trimming foreman Tree surgeon	Arborist
Turf management	Greensworker	Greenskeeper Irrigation controller	Superintendent, greens Sod grower Turf supplies salesman	Agronomist
Nursery	Laborer, nursery Moss handler Bagger-and-burlap man	Salesman	Salesperson	Garden center manager Nursery superintendent
Greenhouse	Greenhouse worker		Salesperson	Greenhouse operator or manager
Level:	Laborer Assistant Helper Worker Sorter or packer Loader Attendant Tender	Operator Driver Assembler Clerk Installer Aide	Craftsman Technician Complex operator Supervisor Inspector	Middle manager Foreman Official

FIGURE 8-3. A COMPARISON OF EXPLORATION AND PREPARATION CLUSTERS

CAREER EXPLORATION CLUSTERS	CAREER PREPARATION CLUSTERS
Transportation occupations	Automotive service occupations Auto body repair occupations Recreational vehicle service occupations Service station occupations • • •
Office and business occupations	Accounting occupations General office clerk occupations Mail and postal occupations Secretarial occupations Office machine occupations • • •
Health occupations	Dental occupations Environmental health occupations Nursing occupations • • •
Construction occupations	Residential construction occupations Building maintenance occupations • • •
Agribusiness and natural resources occupations	Agricultural mechanics occupations Ornamental horticulture occupations Forestry occupations • • •
Personal and public service occupations	Food production and service occupations Clothing production and service occupations • • •

cation form would have to be made if the clusters were to serve additional purposes, such as presenting career guidance information or being used as an instructional material by students.

The leadership in identifying and specifying career clusters should be provided by those members of the cooperative instructional team who represent occupational education. Special educators can provide assistance in identifying for inclusion possible occupations that may be uniquely appropriate for certain disadvantaged or handicapped students such as the blind or the deaf. For the most part, however, this activity, like the other instructional development activities, should involve occupational and special educators in a cooperative planning and development effort.

The suggested cluster specification form in Figure 8-2 is used to specify or identify one career cluster. If the cooperative instructional team is focusing on more than one area of occupational instruction, multiple forms will have to be used.

Identifying the Cluster. As suggested earlier, the specific title of an identified career cluster will depend upon the objectives of the instructional program. Broad cluster titles, such as transportation occupations or construction occupations, are appropriate for junior high exploratory programs, while more specific titles, such as auto service occupations or building maintenance occupations, are better suited to senior high career preparation programs.

The initially selected title should be considered a tentative selection. After the instructional areas are specified and the occupational titles identi-

FIGURE 8-4. SPECIFYING A CAREER CLUSTER

fied, the cluster title can be modified to accurately reflect the group of occupations for which career exploration or preparation instruction will be provided.

In some states such as Illinois, specific clustering schemes are used by the State Office of Education. Such schemes are frequently designed to reflect the manpower needs of the state. They are generally used to classify occupational education programs across the state for purposes of supervision and reimbursement. The clustering system used in Illinois is presented in Figure 8–5. Before beginning the task of specifying career clusters, you should be aware of any state or local curriculum clustering models that may already be in use. You may find that the existing schemes may or may not fit your specific instructional development needs. In either case, it is helpful to develop a brief written description of where and how the proposed cluster or arrangement of clusters fits into, or is an addition to, the existing clustering scheme.

Identifying Instructional Areas. The next task in the process involves identifying the career-related instructional areas. This step entails identifying the specific instructional programs, courses, or major units of instruction within a course, which the cluster will encompass. For instance, if an instructional team is attempting to specify a career cluster that would encompass several specific occupational programs or courses—auto mechanics and auto body repair, for example—these programs or courses should be listed in the left-hand column of the cluster specification form. If, however, the aim is to specify a narrower career preparation cluster, which encompasses only one specific occupational program, the instructional areas identified would be the major instructional units within the course or program. Figures 8–2 and 8–6 provide examples of different uses of the form to specify career exploration and career preparation clusters respectively.

Selecting Occupations. The final task is the identification and selection of occupations making up the cluster(s). Each of the boxes of the Cluster Specification Form provides a space for one or more occupational (job) titles to be listed. The most comprehensive and accessible source of job titles for this purpose is *Dictionary of Occupational Titles (DOT),* published by the U.S. Department of Labor. The two volumes of the third edition of

FIGURE 8-5. ILLINOIS CLUSTER MODEL

CLUSTER TITLES: Applied Biological and Agricultural Operations*; Business, Marketing, and Management Occupations; Health Occupations; Industrial Oriented Occupations; and Personal and Public Service Occupations.

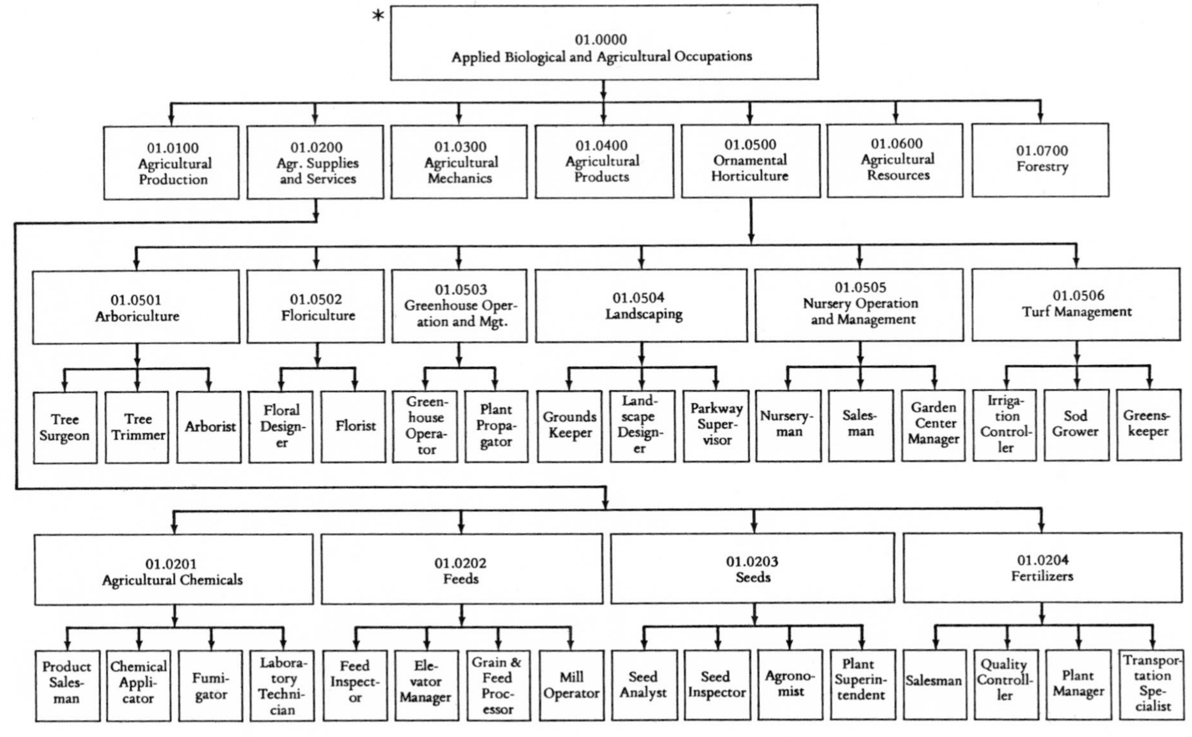

Source: Department of Adult, Vocational and Technical Education, *Suggested guidelines for the Planning of Sequential Programs at the Secondary Level* (Springfield, Ill.: Illinois Office of Education, 1975).

DOT provide a great deal of descriptive information for some 22,000 occupations. Occupations that *may* be particularly appropriate for special needs learners can be classified at four levels as shown on the form. General job title descriptors such as laborer, operator, and foreman are provided for each level along the bottom margin of the cluster specification form. These descriptors can be used as general guides in determining the level of each occupation included in the cluster.

Considerations in Selecting Occupational Titles

Traditionally, occupational education curriculum planners have used a number of criteria in selecting occupations for which instructional programs are to be developed. Many of these criteria are also appropriate for consideration here.

Employment Outlook. The present as well as anticipated future demand for workers trained in the cluster is a major consideration. Training people for jobs that do not exist has been a criticism of many occupational programs and does little to improve the outlook for persons with special needs who often have employment problems even with vocational training. Recent local or regional manpower surveys, advisory committees, state departments of labor, and federal publications such as *Occupational Outlook Handbook* (published every two years) can be helpful sources of employment outlook information. Also, data describing the current supply of trained workers obtaining or looking for employment in the cluster area should also be obtained from or by occupational curriculum planners of the local district.

It is unlikely that in most districts occupational and special education teachers will have the responsibility of collecting and organizing information on the employment outlook for career clusters in a local occupational program. They should, however, carefully review the available manpower information or request additional information, if necessary, before selecting occupations that are to be analyzed for the purpose of developing instruction.

FIGURE 8-6. CLUSTER SPECIFICATION FORM

Check: ☐ Exploration Cluster
☑ Preparation Cluster

CLUSTER-RELATED INSTRUCTIONAL AREAS (Course titles and/or major instructional units)	CAREER CLUSTER: AUTOMOTIVE AND POWER SERVICE OCCUPATIONS			
Auto mechanics	Automobile mechanic helper Used car renovator	Muffler installer Automobile accessories installer Tune-up man	Automobile mechanic Transmission mechanic Automobile service mechanic	
Small engine repair		Gasoline engine repairman Power saw mechanic Outboard motor mechanic Motorcycle repairman		
Auto body repair	Automobile body repairman Helper	Painter, automobile	Automobile body repairman	Shop estimator
Heating and air conditioning	Ventilation man Furnace installer & repairman helper Air cond. installer domestic		Furnaceman	
Service station	Automobile service station attendant			
Level:	Laborer Assistant Helper Worker Sorter or packer Loader Attendant Tender	Operator Driver Assembler Clerk Installer Aide	Craftsman Technician Complex operator Supervisor Inspector	Middle manager Foreman Official

Specialized Occupations. It is important to keep in mind that often the physically handicapped, as well as other individuals with special needs, are uniquely capable of entering selected specialized occupations. Specialized occupations, such as Volkswagen auto mechanics, are frequently overlooked or disregarded in manpower surveys because of the traditionally small demand for trained workers in such highly specialized occupations. Even though the demand for workers may be small, it may be sufficient to absorb a few well-trained and competent individuals with limited functional skills, such as blindness or deafness.

The Michigan School for the Blind in Lansing offers a vocational program for training Volkswagen mechanics. Because of the standardization of parts and design of the basic VW model over a number of years, blind individuals have the unique opportunity in this instance to develop and use a rather sophisticated mechanical skill. The two to five students who graduate from the program each year are placed in dealerships throughout the state. Such successful programs for the physically handicapped do much more than fill a need for trained manpower. They contribute significantly to raising the public's expectancy and attitudes for special needs individuals.

Student Career Interests. The specific career interests of the prospective students are sometimes overlooked in planning vocational curricula. Student career interests, as well as parent career aspirations for their children, have to be considered. It does little good to select occupations that do not reflect a high degree of student interest. Even though there may be a large demand for trained workers in an occupational field such as watch-making and repair, there is no guarantee that students will be interested in seeking training in that particular field. In selecting occupations for a cluster, and the cluster itself for that matter, be sure to select occupations that are appealing to the students, both for exploring different career options and preparing for entry employment.

Unique Considerations. One of the dangers in using the *DOT* or any standardized job descriptions for the purpose of specifying clusters of occupations is the lack of specific situational information. Similarly described jobs are often performed differently in different factories or businesses. It may be that one employer would be willing to re-engineer or modify a job for a physically handicapped person so that it would not involve the physical activities included in a standardized job description. While generally the mental, physical, and emotional characteristics of students should be considered in selecting occupations, it is equally important to be familiar with and consider the specific occupational placement possibilities for individual special needs students in the community.

Available Programs and Resources. Clusters and the occupations therein must reflect the basic content of existing educational programs. For purposes of immediate application of this instructional development process, the resulting instruction will likely have to take place in identifiable, existing programs. While cluster specification can serve to identify the need for new occupational programs, that is not the major purpose of the activity as it is described here. Thus, the clusters of occupations that are selected should reflect the curriculum content of those occupational or practical arts courses that are presently a part of the regular occupational program offering.

Career Preparation versus Career Exploration: A Final Note. If the intended focus of the instructional program is career preparation, certain of these previously mentioned considerations for selecting occupations are more important than others. Usually the primary consideration in formulating a career preparation cluster is the employment outlook. A cluster-based program that provides training and preparation for existing job opportunities represents a major objective of vocational education and career preparation programs at the secondary level.

If, however, the instructional focus is career exploration, the major consideration will probably be student interest. The interests of students in exploring the use and potential application of different tools, materials, or processes in different occupations becomes a major consideration in selecting occupations to be included in the cluster. Since exploration is the major goal, a much broader range of occupations (unskilled to highly skilled) can be included and less emphasis is placed on finding and including occupations particularly appropriate for certain special needs students. An underlying objective of the career exploration program should be that both the special needs students and the regular students find careers that are suited to their interests and potentials.

CONDUCTING A CAREER CLUSTER ANALYSIS

A career cluster analysis is a process of systematically determining instructional content. The relevant instructional content for the career exploration or preparation cluster(s) specified in the previous section of this chapter will form the content basis for developing instructional plans for special needs learners. The basic career cluster analysis process is graphically presented in Figure 8-7.

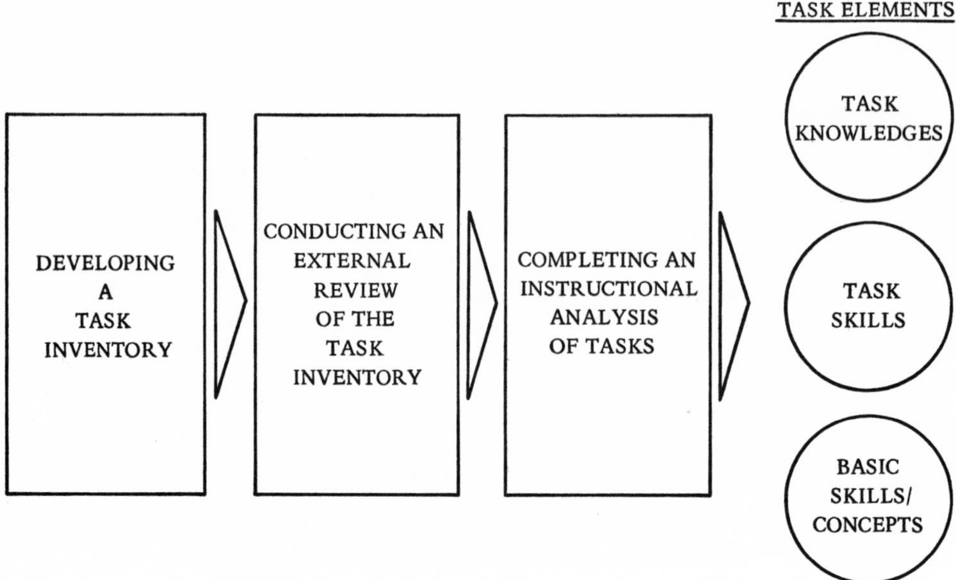

FIGURE 8-7. CAREER CLUSTER ANALYSIS PROCESS

Over the years a number of different systematic analysis procedures have been introduced for use in occupational and practical arts education programs. Trade, job, and task analyses have been commonly used in vocational education, while disciplinary content analyses have been developed by national curriculum projects in a limited number of practical arts areas, most notably industrial arts education (Cochran 1970). A career cluster analysis can be designed to draw upon the basic curriculum analysis procedures used by both fields.

Not unlike other occupational analysis techniques, the information gathered by career cluster analysis procedures can be used for a number of purposes:

1. To determine the task content of different occupations
2. To determine differences and relationships among occupations, useful for structuring occupations into career fields and career ladders
3. To determine training programs that can be reduced, or eliminated, or that need to be created

4. To determine the critical tasks (instructional content) that should be taught in a practical arts or an occupational education program
5. To determine the critical tasks to be included in occupational competency and certification tests
6. To provide career counseling information to assist students in obtaining realistic perceptions of occupations (Melching and Borcher 1973).

In this particular chapter, the career cluster analysis will focus on identifying and analyzing relevant instructional content in a specified cluster of occupations.

The three-step career cluster analysis process described below is useful in determing curriculum content for both special needs learners and non-special learners. Through program development experiences this cluster analysis approach was refined and adapted to specify the relevant curriculum content for *all* students who will be receiving individualized instruction. The steps in career cluster analysis process are as follows:

1. Developing a task inventory
2. Conducting an external review of the task inventory
3. Completing an instructional analysis of tasks

Establishing a Cluster Analysis Hierarchy

First, in order to analyze and define the instructional content for a career cluster, a set of commonly defined analysis levels is needed. This arrangement of different analysis levels can be referred to as a "hierarchy." Figure 8–8 presents a graphic illustration of an analysis hierarchy used in defining instructional content from a cluster of occupations. The hierarchy has three basic levels: cluster, task, and task elements.

The previously specified cluster of occupations can be broken down into a number of different tasks. The tasks can be further divided into the task elements of knowledges, skills, and basic skills/concepts.

As will be demonstrated in this analysis, the unique aspect of this analysis format is that the tasks specified as instructional content will be common to two or more occupations within the cluster. Once the tasks are

FIGURE 8-8. CLUSTER ANALYSIS HIERARCHY

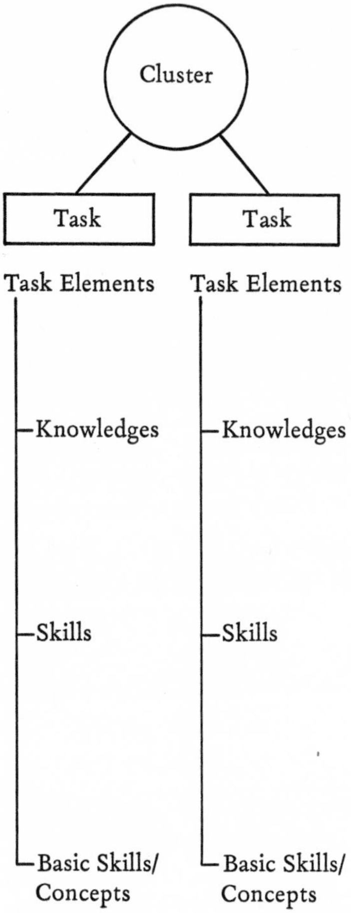

		DEFINITIONS	ILLUSTRATION: *Career Preparation Cluster*
Cluster		Cluster: A group of occupations, closely related by industry	*Auto Service Occupations*
Task	Task	Task: A unit of worker activity that can be divided into task elements for instruction	*Maintain and replace headlamps*
Task Elements	Task Elements	Task Elements: The three instructional components into which a task may be analyzed	
—Knowledges	—Knowledges	Knowledges: Basic cognitive concepts the individual must understand and comprehend to perform the task successfully	*Recognize headlamp identification numbers*
—Skills	—Skills	Skills: Basic psychomotor manipulations, movements, or complex operations the individual must demonstrate to perform the task successfully	*Install headlamps*
—Basic Skills/ Concepts	—Basic Skills/ Concepts	Basic Skills/Concepts: Specific capacities and abilities required of an individual in order to learn or adequately perform a task (U.S. Department of Labor 1965)	*Demonstrate fine motor coordination of eyes, hands, and fingers*

identified and listed in a task inventory (step 1), they can be validated by an external review source (step 2). Such external review sources as occupational advisory committees, employees or employers, or program graduates enrolled in advanced training programs can review and validate the inventory of identified tasks. Finally, the task elements of each task are analyzed. The task elements represent the most specific level of the cluster analysis hierarchy. Three specific task elements (knowledges, skills, and basic skills/concepts) are identified in the detailed instructional analysis that represents the third and final step in the career cluster analysis process.

Step 1. Developing a Task Inventory

Initiating a career cluster analysis involves developing a list or inventory of tasks. When developing a listing of the tasks performed in a career cluster, several considerations must be made, among them: What types of task statements can be developed, what existing sources of task statements can be used, and how are task statements to be written?

Types of Tasks. Several different types of task statements can be identified at this step in the process, and will depend largely upon the differing goals of the occupational or practical arts education program. Developers of career *exploration* programs will likely select task statements that are exploratory in nature and emphasize the recognition of 1) tools, materials, and equipment, 2) safe practices, 3) mathematical and scientific applications, and 4) general occupational information. Those individuals developing career *preparation* instruction, on the other hand, will emphasize the types of tasks directly required for successful job entry.

It is possible to develop task statements that will focus on nine different areas. Figure 8-9 lists the nine different types of task statements and provides an illustration of each type (Larson and Valentine 1974). As you will notice, a wide variety of different types of tasks may be developed and included in a task inventory. This diversity will accommodate a broad range of curriculum objectives in career exploration and preparation programs.

FIGURE 8-9. ILLUSTRATIVE TASK STATEMENTS

TYPE OF TASK STATEMENT	EXAMPLE OF TASK STATEMENT
Job operation or duty	Take pulse, respiration, and blood pressure
Safe practices	Recognize safety color designations
Equipment, tools, and materials	Identify different grades of plywood
Mathematical applications	Calculate revolutions per minute
Science applications	Recognize physical principles associated with torque
Specification interpretations	Interpret a lubrication service manual
Occupational terminology	Recognize medical abbreviations
Occupational information	Locate and use the want ads to find work
Work habits and attitudes	Dress appropriately for work

Sources of Task Statements. The most difficult and time-consuming part of this activity is developing the initial listing of tasks. To insure an adequate and comprehensive analysis, the inventory of task statements should be as complete as possible. Therefore, it is possible that a number of different sources can be used to locate task statements. Sources that may be most helpful include:

1. *Dictionary of Occupational Titles* (Vol. I)
2. Previously constructed job analyses or task listings
3. Curriculum or instructional guides
4. Procedure, service, or process manuals prepared by business and industry
5. *Occupational Outlook Handbook*

Here again, the goals or objectives of the career exploration or preparation program will likely determine which of these sources is most useful.

Writing Task Statements. Several important points should be kept in mind when writing task statements. They should be written at a consistent level of specificity so they can be readily converted into units or modules of instruction. As anyone who has developed curriculum using an analysis approach knows, this is much easier said than done. As you begin the process of writing task statements, you will note that some task statements you develop are too specific and will need to be combined with others. You will also probably write a number of statements that will need to be broken down into smaller tasks.

It is theoretically impractical to expect all task statements to be written at precisely the same level of specificity. However, a consistent and comfortable "range of specificity" should emerge as the task statements are developed. It is important to remember also that different teachers or curriculum developers will write at different levels of specificity. The important point is that each person developing task statements and conducting the career cluster analysis should refine and consistently use statements that are similar in their degree of specificity.

Some of the sources of task statements mentioned in the preceding section provide excellent examples of different specificity levels in task statements: "Disassembling an automobile engine" can be considered a much larger task in terms of complexity than "changing spark plugs." And, as is frequently the case, the smaller task in only one component of the larger task.

In developing task inventories for training programs for the Air Force. Fruchter, Morin, and Archer (1963) found that it was more effective if *what* and *how* phrases were not combined in a task statement. Below is an example of both "combined" and "separated" *what* and *how* statements.

COMBINED	SEPARATED
Conduct a credit card sales transaction using a presstype credit card imprinter	Conduct a credit card sales transaction (what) Operate a press-type credit card imprinter (how)

Even though more complete information may be provided by the combined statement, the number of meaningful combinations of "what" and "how" statements could lead to a list of tasks that is of unmanageable length.

Other general guidelines to keep in mind when writing task statements are:

- Be sure the task statements are grammatically consistent
- Eliminate unnecessary modifying phrases as much as possible. Example: "Use and interpret measuring rules accurately." "Accurately" need not be included in the statement; it can be assumed.
- Use multiple verbs like "remove and replace" only when it is anticipated that both operations will be covered in the same unit of instruction.
- Avoid using vague or ambiguous verbs such as coordinate, substantiate, operationalize, discuss, or verify.
- Make the task statements as short and concise as possible.

After the initial task inventory is developed, it may be helpful to identify each statement with an identification number. If task inventories for more than one cluster are being developed, it may also be helpful to use letter abbreviations to identify the different clusters. If data are to be collected and tabulated on each task statement, the use of code letters and numbers will make the process more efficient.

Figures 8-10 and 8-11 present two task inventories. One inventory was developed for a career preparation cluster in auto mechanics occupations and the other for a career exploration cluster entitled construction occupations.

Step 2. Conducting an External Review of the Task Inventory

Once a preliminary list of tasks has been identified for the clusters, it is important that they be reviewed and validated as essential instructional content. If the tasks represent a career exploration or preparation cluster, the relevant source of validation information feedback will be employers or employees who, to some extent, perform the tasks as part of their work.

When seeking curriculum validation information relative to an inventory of task statements, a variety of questions can be asked. The specific information requested from a particular validation source, such as an occupational advisory committee, will depend to some extent upon the ability of the source to answer the relevant questions and provide the information. For

FIGURE 8-10. TASK INVENTORY

Cluster: Auto Mechanics Occupations

Check one ☐ Career Exploration Cluster
☑ Career Preparation Cluster

ID. CODE	TASK
AM01	Service the components of the mechanical system
AM02	Service cooling systems
AM03	Service lubrication systems
AM04	Service fuel and carburation systems
AM05	Service ignition systems
AM06	Service exhaust systems
AM07	Service electrical systems
AM08	Service cranking motor systems
AM09	Service charging systems
AM10	Service standard transmissions
AM11	Service clutches
AM12	Service differentials
AM13	Service driveshafts
AM14	Service brake systems
AM15	Service suspension systems
AM16	Service hydraulic system components
AM17	Service air conditioning systems
AM18	Service emission control systems
AM19	Service front end alignment
AM20	Lubricate vehicle chassis and change engine oil and filter
AM21	Mount, balance, and rotate tires

instance, screw-machine operators are considered an expert validation source when attempting to determine the specific job skills needed by screw-machine operators. However, supervisors and employers of screw-machine operators may be better able to describe the basic skills and attitudes that make screw-machine operators "successful" at their jobs.

Validation Information. Depending upon the external validation source, a variety of different types of information can be obtained.

FIGURE 8-11. TASK INVENTORY

Cluster: Construction Occupations

Check one ☑ Career Exploration Cluster
☐ Career Preparation Cluster

ID. CODE	TASK
CON 01	Developing sketches for floor plans
CON 02	Reviewing sites and plot plans
CON 03	Selecting and purchasing property
CON 04	Surveying the lot
CON 05	Testing the soil
CON 06	Arranging finances
CON 07	Selecting and managing contractors
CON 08	Developing a set of working plans
CON 09	Building the substructure
	.
	.
	.

Employees performing the tasks listed in the inventory can best provide the following kinds of information about the task:

Whether or not the task is part of their present job
Frequency of task performance
Whether or not the task should be performed as part of their present job
The learning difficulty associated with the task
The prerequisite skills needed before the task can be performed effectively
The complexity of the task
The minimum level of acceptable task performance

Employers or supervisors can provide more specific feedback with regard to:

The basic skills, aptitudes, and attitudes required to perform the task

Importance of the task to the job as a whole
The commonality of task performance across more than one job

In a cluster-based instructional program two essential pieces of information are critical for instructional planners: 1) It must be known which tasks in the inventory are essential or desirable for entry employment in each of the occupations in the cluster, and 2) which tasks are common to more than one occupation within the cluster. The first piece of information dictates which tasks should be included in the instructional program, while the second can suggest a general sequence for the instruction, if one assumes that the most commonly performed tasks should be taught before specialized tasks are introduced.

Types of External Review. In occupational education and training programs a number of different sources have been used to review and validate curriculum content. Questionnaires, interview forms, and task analysis inventories have been used with advisory committees, employer organizations such as the Chamber of Commerce, employee organizations such as unions, employers, employees, and graduates currently enrolled in postsecondary training institutions.

The selection of the type of external review you decide to conduct will depend upon the size of the community and the availability of validation personnel or agencies. In smaller, rural communities the external review may involve only a small number of employers or employees or an advisory committee; it is unlikely that a large sample of employers or employees would be accessible.

Most occupational education programs have existing advisory committees which can be used for reviewing and validating a list of tasks performed by job incumbents. Suggestions and procedures for establishing and using an advisory committee for the special needs program were outlined in Chapter 7. However, because of the selective composition of advisory committees, they will probably be unable to validate tasks from a broad cluster of occupations. Oftentimes advisory committees can be used for the purpose of an initial pilot review of the task inventory. Based on their reactions, the format or content of the inventory can be expanded or modified and tasks added or deleted. Then, working through community contacts established by members of the advisory committee, the inventory can be administered to a larger, more representative sample of employers and/or employees. Several of the publications listed in the references contain detailed explanations and illustrations of different types of external review processes.

Instrumentation for an External Review. The specific format selected for presenting the task inventory for external review will depend upon the information of most importance in a cluster-based instructional program is 1) which of the identified tasks are essential, desirable, or unnecessary for entry employment in the identified occupations, and 2) which of the identified tasks are commonly performed in more than one occupation within the cluster.

The cluster analysis matrix format given in Figure 8–12 provides a sample form that will provide both kinds of information. Depending upon the size of the business, this form could be used with employers, supervisors, or employees as a data-gathering instrument in either an interview situation or a mailed survey questionnaire.

Step 3. Completing an Instructional Analysis

The final step in the career cluster analysis process is to conduct an instructional analysis of each of the tasks. Once the task inventory has been reviewed and evaluated by an advisory committee, employers, employees, or any of the other possible external validation sources, an appropriate decision can be made as to whether or not to include the task in the proposed curriculum.

In the process of carrying out the external review, a great deal of specific information about expected entry-level job performance is usually obtained that cannot be presented in the cluster analysis matrix. In order to utilize this information, it is important that a detailed analysis of each task be initiated. An instructional analysis develops specific instructional content for each task.

FIGURE 8-12. CLUSTER ANALYSIS MATRIX

Auto Body Maintenance Occupational Cluster

Directions: Listed below are a series of tasks performed in one or more of the selected entry occupations identified for this cluster. For each task that is "essential or critical" for successful entry performance in the identified occupation, place an "x" in the appropriate box. For each task that is a "desirable" competency in a worker entering the identified occupation, place an "o" in the appropriate box. Add any tasks that are essential (x) or desirable (o) to successful occupational performance which are not listed.

Name of Respondent: Al Hersche

Place of Employment: Al's Body Shop

Occupation: Estimation - Supervision

No. of Years in Occupation: 16

ID. CODE	TASK INVENTORY	SHOP ESTIMATOR	AUTOMOBILE BODY REPAIRMAN	PAINTER, AUTOMOBILE	AUTOMOBILE BODY REPAIRMAN HELPER
		CLUSTER OCCUPATIONS			
ABM 01	Remove, overhaul, and replace trim and hardware		X	O	X
ABM 02	Perform bumping operations	X	X	O	O
ABM 03	Remove and replace body components		X	X	X
ABM 04	Prepare surface for painting		O	X	X
ABM 05	Apply masking tape and paper			X	X
ABM 06	Operate spray paint equipment			X	O
ABM 07	Perform lacquer refinishing			X	O
ABM 08	Perform enamel refinishing			X	O
ABM 09	Remove and install glass		X	O	X
ABM 10	Prepare vehicle for delivery	O	O	O	X
ABM 11	Estimate damage repairs	X	X	O	
ABM 12	Select and use appropriate materials and supplies	X	X	X	X

Adapted from M. L. Reynolds, R. J. Lutz, C. B. Johnson, and L. A. Phelps, *Cluster Guide* (Series). Mt. Pleasant: Central Michigan University, 1973.

Occupational and special educators should be equally involved in this stage of the career cluster analysis process. The analysis essentially pulls together all of the data and information from employers, supervisors, employees, and graduates and forms a basis for instructional planning.

The instructional analysis should be completed by the teachers, coordinators, or consultants who were involved in the external review of the task inventory. Both formal and informal feedback from the reviewers should be carefully analyzed and considered during this phase. General teacher knowledge of student interests and aptitudes, as well as the occupational teacher's knowledge and experience regarding employment and work practices in the cluster, will also be important in developing the detailed instructional analysis.

The instructional analysis will focus on identifying the instructional elements of each task. Knowledges, skills, and basic skills/concepts were defined earlier (Figure 8-8) as the three components of a task that are critical to planning career-related instruction and providing meaningful career exploration or preparation experiences.

Instructional Analysis Format. A format and three examples of instructional analyses are provided in Figures 8-13 8-14, and 8-15. A one-page format is used to analyze each task separately. The form is designed in an open-ended format to permit the instructional personnel to identify and list a reasonable number of subelements in each of the three sections: task knowledges, task skills, and basic skills/concepts.

Task Knowledges. For each task it would be possible to list an infinite number of discrete knowledge elements. It is helpful, however, to consider identifying task knowledges at different levels. *Taxonomy of Educational Objectives for the Cognitive Domain* by Bloom and others (1956) is a helpful reference. Bloom's taxonomy identifies five basic levels of knowledge to be learned: knowledge (basic information), comprehension, application, synthesis, and evaluation. Each level represents an increasingly complex use of information and knowledge.

At the first level, information, such as understanding of specific facts, terminology, sequences, categories, or methods or procedures, is learned. An example of task knowledge statements at this level might be the following:

FIGURE 8-13. INSTRUCTIONAL ANALYSIS: EXAMPLE A

TASK: Complete a credit card sales transaction

Id. Code: RT08

TASK KNOWLEDGES	BASIC SKILLS/CONCEPTS
1. Identify and describe the information required on a credit card: a. Product description b. Quantity c. Customer number d. Customer signature e. Cost f. Tax	1. Recognize numbers as cost figures. Add to compute total cost. Compute tax by multiplication. Identify product names correctly.

TASK SKILLS	BASIC SKILLS/CONCEPTS
1. Follow a prescribed procedure for handling credit card transactions. a. Obtain card from customer b. Itemize purchases and tax on receipt form c. Set cost digits on machine d. Place card in roller machine e. Place receipt in machine f. Roll head over card g. Remove receipt and card for purchaser to sign h. Return card to purchaser i. Place store copy of receipt in predetermined location	1. Write legibly and spell accurately. Record information accurately. Hand-eye coordination.
2. Verify credit card information. a. Check signature on card b. Check expiration date on card c. Call telephone number to verify credit rating	2. Recognize dates (month and year) written as numbers (e.g., 5/76). Use the telephone to obtain specific information.

Identify the normal human pulse rate
Understand Ohm's law
Define the principle of torque
Identify sizes of type (printing)

The second level, comprehension, requires that one be able to interpret meaning from basic information. An example of task knowledge statements at this level might include:

Read a lubrication chart
Interpret medical abbreviations
Estimate area required for a floor display

FIGURE 8-14. INSTRUCTIONAL ANALYSIS: EXAMPLE B

TASK: Interpret recipes

Id. Code: FS 12

TASK KNOWLEDGES	BASIC SKILLS/CONCEPTS
1. Define specific nomenclature and vocabulary terms found in basic recipes: a. Weights b. Measures c. Directions d. Temperatures e. Ingredients	1. Measure weights of ingredients. Interpret temperature readings. Follow written directions. Identify ingredients by name. Dividing and multiplying recipe quantities.
2. Recognize the advantages of using standard food preparation recipes.	2. Quantity required per no. of persons to be served. Economy.

TASK SKILLS	BASIC SKILLS/CONCEPTS
1. Complete the necessary precooking procedures such as gathering ingredients and selecting pans.	1. Follow verbal directions. Follow written directions.

Application—the third level—focuses on skills such as organizing, generalizing, using, or otherwise relating learned information. Such task knowledge statements as the following represent the application level:

Determine outlet voltage using a voltmeter
Determine markup and margin for a product

The fourth and fifth levels, synthesis and evaluation, represent the most complex levels of information processing. Synthesis involves such tasks as

FIGURE 8-15. INSTRUCTIONAL ANALYSIS: EXAMPLE C

TASK: Complete a job application form

TASK KNOWLEDGES	BASIC SKILLS/CONCEPTS
1. Recognize and provide the following information on a standard application form: a. Name, address b. Telephone number c. Age, marital status, social security number d. Family information e. Educational background f. Employment background g. Personal and job references h. Military status i. Other pertinent information	1. Recognize and use numbers. Record information accurately. Follow written instructions.

TASK SKILLS	BASIC SKILLS/CONCEPTS
1. Read all of the directions. 2. Print clearly. 3. Spell accurately. 4. Provide all information requested.	(Note: Because this is a somewhat basic task involving different skills than those presented in Figures 8-13 and 8-14, there is probably no need to analyze the task further to derive more specifics.)

producing unique communications, outlining operational plans, and deriving abstract relationships. Evaluation involves determining the inherent worth of something based on judgment.

When staff are conducting an instructional analysis of a general task, it is important that the required task knowledges be carefully identified. By referring to the five levels of task information and knowledge during the instructional analysis they will then be able to detail the task extensively at the various levels. This detailed task information will be invaluable in 1) selecting tasks to be taught to individual special needs learners 2) specifying instructional objectives and subobjectives.

Task Skills. Task skills are the physical, manipulative components or operations of the task. For purposes of the instructional analysis, it is most appropriate to list the basic procedures, operations, or processes included in the task. This will define the composite skills in a procedural and developmental context that is generally more useful in instructional planning.

Simpson (1972) has developed a taxonomy for the psychomotor domain that is helpful in visualizing different types and levels of task skills. Seven major subdivisions are included in the taxonomy and are based on the degree of complexity of the task skill or psychomotor behavior. When attempting to specify the task skills involved in a given task, one can use the levels of this taxonomy as a reference check.

1.0 Perception	The process of becoming aware of objects, qualities, or relations by way of the sense organs. Perception may include sensory stimulation, cue selection, and translation.
2.0 Set	The preparatory adjustment or readiness for a specific experience or action. Set includes readiness to mentally perform an act, physically perform an act, and emotionally perform an act.
3.0 Guided response	The overt behavioral act performed under the guidance of an instructor (imitation) or in response to feedback gained from self-evaluation of performance (trial and error).
4.0 Mechanism	The learned response becomes a habit, and the

	learner has achieved a degree of confidence and proficiency in performance of the act.
5.0 Complex overt response	The attainment of complex motor skills or acts that include the resolution of uncertainty and automatic performance.
6.0 Adaptation	The altering of motor activities to meet the demands of new problem situations that require the individual to physically respond.
7.0 Origination	The creation of new motor acts or ways of manipulating materials out of understanding, abilities, and skills developed in the psychomotor area.

Basic Skills/Concepts. The instructional analysis format presented in the three examples (Figures 8–13, 8–14, and 8–15) provides for identification of the basic skills/concepts for both the task knowledges and task skills. This part of the analysis makes it especially appropriate for special needs learners. The key to doing an effective task analysis is to identify those basic competencies that the job requires. Identification of these basic skills and concepts provides information about the task and job which describes areas in which persons lacking these basic competencies may encounter difficulty. When matched against the learner's profile, developed and discussed in Chapter 6, it can not only be helpful in counseling students but also points out basic skills that will have to emphasized in the instructional program.

The basic skills/concepts provide another level of analysis that is more specific than the knowledges and skills involved in the task. They provide a deeper, more specific description of the functional abilities required in performance of the task. As a group, when teachers engage in this type of extensive analysis, it provides valuable insights into the complexity of tasks and, thus, how they can be taught in a variety of ways to students who exhibit different patterns of learning.

Figure 10–11 on page 251 provides a listing of basic skills and concepts used in instructional planning. There are eight general categories of basic skills/concepts which should be examined in each instructional analysis. When compiling an analysis, teachers should carefully determine whether or not there are certain basic skills or concepts in the following general areas which are part of the task knowledges or task skills:

Quantitative and numerical skills
Verbal skills
Cognitive skills
Perceptual skills
Language skills
Psychomotor and physical skills
Social skills
Occupational aptitudes

Tasks are seldom stated at a consistent level of specificity; that is, certain tasks as stated on the instructional analysis form are more complex and involved than others. For example, a task such as "completing a credit card sales transaction" (Figure 8-13) involves knowing several bits of information as well as the procedure involved. It is easy to see that a number of basic skills and concepts are prerequisite and important to the task knowledges and skills identified in Figure 8-13. This then is a fairly complex task when you actually get into the analysis of it.

"Completing a job application form" is a less complex task in several ways and requires a further explanation of the instructional analysis procedure. Because of the nature of the task, there appears to be more knowledge-based performance demanded. The only task skills or physical performance required is printing or writing legibly. With this type of task there really are no identifiable basic skills or concepts for the task skills. As the example in Figure 8-15 shows, this section of the instructional analysis form can be left blank. The extensiveness to which a task can be analyzed depends upon the nature of the task performance and the specificity of the task performance as it is stated initially.

SUMMARY

Relevancy of career exploration and preparation instruction to the world of work is vitally important. Job and task analysis has long been utilized by occupational and special educators as a basis for determining what specific skills, information, and attitudes are critical for employment. With the recent rapid changes in the workplace, it is suggested that a cluster of occupations be the basis for analysis. This approach suggests that if basic common tasks and information for a closely related group of occupations are learned, the individual will have a degree of mobility within the cluster. Providing increased mobility and expanded occupational options is as important for special needs learners as it is for all learners.

Techniques for identifying a cluster(s) of occupations are provided along with suggestions of clustering arrangements such as those that have been adopted by the U.S. Office of Education and state departments of education. Two types of clusters (career exploration and career preparation) are reviewed and discussed.

Once a cluster of occupations is identified, a process of instructional content analysis is initiated. The process involves 1) identifying the major common tasks associated with the occupations in the cluster, 2) obtaining validation information for the major tasks by conducting surveys or advisory committee reviews, and 3) completing an instructional analysis of the validated tasks. The instructional analysis is focused on determining the elements of each task: knowledges and information required, skills to be performed, and basic concepts to be learned.

REFERENCES

Bloom, B. S., et al. *A taxonomy of educational objectives: Cognitive domain.* New York: David McKay, 1956.

Braun, C. Teacher expectation: Sociopsychological dynamics. *Review of Educational Research,* 46, 1976.

Cochran, L. H. *Innovative programs in industrial education.* Bloomington, Ill.: McKnight, 1970.

Frantz, N. R. *Career cluster concepts.* Columbus: Center for Vocational Education, Ohio State University, 1973.

Fruchter, B., Morin, R. E., and Archer, W. B. Efficiency of the open-ended inventory in eliciting task statements from job incumbents. Lackland Air Force Base: Personnel Research Laboratory (AMD/AFSC), March, 1963.

Gold, M. W. An end to the concept of mental retardation: Oh, what a beautiful mourning. Champaign: Children's Research Center, University of Illinois, n.d. (Mimeograph)

Kenneke, L. J., Nystrom, D. C. and Stadt, R. W. *Planning and organizing career curricula: Articulated education.* New York: Howard W. Sams, 1973.

Larson, M. E., and Valentine, I. E. *Vocational education curriculum development handbook.* Fort Collins: Department of Vocational Education, Colorado State University, 1974.

Mager, R. F., and Beach, K. M. *Developing vocational instruction.* Belmont, California: Fearon, 1967.

Melching, W. H., and Borcher, S. D. *Procedures for constructing and using task inventories.* Columbus: Center for Vocational Education, Ohio State University, 1973.

Reynolds, M. L., Lutz, R. J., Johnson, C. B., and Phelps, L. A. *Program guide.* Mt. Pleasant: Central Michigan University, 1973.

Simpson, E. J. The classification of educational objectives in the psychomotor domain. *The psychomotor domain.* Washington, D.C.: Gryphon House, 1972.

Sjogren, Douglas. A functional approach to curriculum development. In J. W. Cunningham (Ed.), *The job-cluster concept and its curricular implications: A symposium.* Raleigh: Center for Occupational Education, North Carolina State University, 1969.

State of Illinois, Division of Vocational and Technical Education. *Vocational education.* Springfield: The Division, 1971.

Taylor, J. E., Montague, E. K., and Micheals, E. R. *An Occupational Clustering System and Curriculum Implications for the Comprehensive Career Education Model* (ED 061 427). Monterey, Calif.: Human Resources Research Organization, 1972.

U.S. Department of Labor. *Dictionary of occupational titles* (Vols. I and II, 3rd ed.). Washington, D.C.: Government Printing Office, 1966.

U.S. Office of Education and U.S. Department of Labor. *Vocational education and occupations.* Washington, D.C.: Government Printing Office, 1969.

U.S. Office of Education. *Career education.* Washington, D.C.: Government Printing Office, 1971.

U.S. Department of Labor. *Occupational outlook handbook.* Washington, D.C.: Government Printing Office, 1974.

DEVELOPING A COOPERATIVE INSTRUCTIONAL ARRANGEMENT

The importance and nature of cooperative teaching was discussed in Chapter 4. It has been widely recognized by educators and practitioners alike that instructional personnel from occupational and special education should work together closely in providing career exploration and preparation experiences for special needs students. An effective and efficient way of operationalizing these relationships is to develop a series of cooperative instructional arrangements for individual learners. ∾ The development of a formal cooperative relationship is the first major instructional planning activity presented in the System for Developing and Managing Instruction in

Chapter 5. Once the initial analyses discussed in preceding chapters (chapters 6, 7, and 8) are completed, the next step involves developing a planned arrangement to coordinate the specific instructional planning tasks. By formalizing a cooperative team arrangement at this point, occupational and special educators can utilize the information obtained to prepare specific instructional plans for special needs learners.

WHAT IS A COOPERATIVE INSTRUCTIONAL ARRANGEMENT?

A cooperative instructional arrangement is a vehicle for initiating the development of a formalized, cooperative plan for providing career-related instruction and supportive services for a special needs learner. Essentially, it is a plan for systematically coordinating available school and community resources for an individual learner. Since the instructional and support needs of each special needs student vary significantly, cooperative instructional arrangements must be made on an individual student basis. The cooperative instructional arrangement form (Figure 9–1) serves to indicate which teachers and other educational personnel currently are, or will be, working cooperatively to meet the special educational needs of the identified learner(s). When necessary, cooperative instructional arrangements can also include agencies outside of the school, such as Vocational Rehabilitation.

FUNCTION AND IMPORTANCE OF COOPERATION

Chapter 6 provided insight and suggestions for determining the unique, special needs of individual learners. In Chapter 7 we discussed and identified a variety of school and community resources that could be tapped to assist teachers of the special needs learner, as well as the learners directly. The occupational cluster(s), which special needs learners are exploring or preparing for, was carefully analyzed in Chapter 8 to determine essential content for the instructional program. We are now ready to begin incorporating this information into an individual plan for the learner.

The cooperative instructional arrangement form (Figure 9–1) can be used by occupational, practical arts, and special education personnel to

FIGURE 9-1. COOPERATIVE INSTRUCTIONAL ARRANGEMENT

Paul

CAREER-RELATED INSTRUCTION PROVISION	SPECIAL INSTRUCTION OR SERVICES PROVISION
Title of course in which student is enrolled Building Maintenance	Type of instruction/service provided for student special education (English, math, social studies)
Instructor(s) Theopolis Jackson	Instructor(s)/consultant(s)/specialist(s) Candy Jenkins
Location or building Cloverdale Area Occupational Center	Location or building Cloverdale H.S.
Planning period 10:00 – 10:30	Planning period 12:33 p. – 1:13 p.
Phone	Phone
COOPERATIVE WORK EXPERIENCE PROVISION	**SUPPORTIVE AGENCY PROVISION**
Job title	Agency name
Location of work station	
Work schedule	Contact person
a.m.	Telephone
p.m.	Description of specific service or instruction to be provided for the student
School coordinator	
Planning period –	
Job Supervisor(s)	
Phone	

ADMINISTRATIVE ENDORSEMENTS

School administrator(s)*	District Cloverdale Community Schools
(1) Wayne Logan	School(s) Cloverdale High School
(2) J. C. Jenkins	Cloverdale Area Center
Agency endorsement (if needed)	Date September, 1978

*e.g., Building principal, director of special education, and/or director of vocational education

determine other professionals who might also work with the identified learner. Completing the form can help the concerned teacher identify the nature of instruction or special services the student is receiving in his other classes. In many instances, the process of obtaining information for the cooperative instructional arrangement is the beginning of a mutual concern for the student and leads to other cooperative endeavors such as common lesson planning, supportive teaching, and so on.

COOPERATIVE ARRANGEMENT PROVISIONS

As suggested earlier, cooperative planning and teaching for special needs students may involve a number of different professionals. There are four basic provisions or options that can be identified in a cooperative instructional arrangement. Figure 9-1 illustrates a suggested form to be used and identifies the four options or provisions: 1) career-related instruction, 2) special instruction or services, 3) cooperative work experience instruction, and 4) supportive agency involvement.

Career-related Instruction Provision

This provision identifies the occupational or practical arts teacher. In addition to the identification of the course(s) for which the special needs student is enrolled, the location, telephone number, and planning period of the instructor is given to facilitate communication. Only individuals whose major responsibility is classroom or lab instruction should be identified in this section. Work or work experience coordinates should be given in the cooperative work experience section.

Special Instruction or Services Provision

Here the instructor or consultant/specialist who provides the special instruction or service is identified. This may be one person or more than one, depending on the different types of instruction or service the learner is receiving. A description of the types of special services or instruction should be provided along with the location, telephone number, and available planning time periods. It should also be noted that special education work/study or prevocational coordinators should not be listed here but, instead, identified under the cooperative work experience.

Cooperative Work Experience Provision

Since many special needs learners are educationally motivated by the opportunity to work, involving the work experience coordinator is essential in developing the cooperative instructional plan. The learner's job title, work station, and work schedule should be specified along with the name(s) of his or her job supervisor(s). The name and planning period of the school coordinator should also be included. The location of the work station may be either on-campus or off-campus and may be handled by a vocational coordinator or a special education work coordinator depending upon the local programming arrangement.

Supportive Agency Provision

In some instances, a key cooperator will be someone from a community or governmental agency such as vocational rehabilitation. When the special needs learner is receiving assistance from an external agency, it is helpful to list the name and telephone number of the contact person or case worker so they may be contacted directly.

Depending upon the student's educational program placement, the cooperative instructional arrangement planned for him or her may include any two of these component provisions. It is recommended that, when appropriate and necessary, more than two provisions be included in the cooperative arrangement. The example given in Figure 9–1 illustrates the optimal arrangement for coordinating two of the four possible provisions.

The instructional resource inventory discussed in Chapter 7 is an excellent place to locate the names of individuals who may be involved in the cooperative instructional arrangement. Figure 7–1 on page 138 is a helpful resource for identifying the broad range of potential school staff who could become involved in cooperative instructional arrangements.

ALTERNATE ARRANGEMENTS

In most cases, neither the learner's school placement nor his or her specific learning problems will require comprehensive involvement from all four of the cooperative provisions identified on the form. It is more reasonable to expect that secondary level students with mild learning or behavioral problems can be effectively served by a cooperating team of two or perhaps three professionals.

Several key factors, which will be discussed in the following section, will determine who the key cooperating professionals are for each student. However, it should be noted here that a total of six dual cooperative arrangements are functionally possible. These are listed below, along with an example (in parentheses) for each.

Career-related instruction (Welding instructor)	Special instruction and services (Resource room instructor)
Career-related instruction (Welding instructor)	Cooperative work experience (Industrial co-op coordinator)
Career-related instruction (Welding instructor)	Supportive agency (Vocational rehabilitation counselor)
Special instruction and services (Special education instructor)	Cooperative work experience (Prevocational coordinator)
Special instruction and services (Reading instructor)	Supportive agency (Employment service counselor)
Cooperative work experience (Work-study coordinator)	Supportive agency (Rehabilitation counselor)

Obviously, a number of different three-way cooperative arrangements are possible and feasible in certain situations.

ILLUSTRATIONS AND EXAMPLES

The following three case descriptions will offer some additional insights as to how the cooperative instructional arrangement is actually operationalized.

Paul

Paul (discussed in Chapter 1) is a multiply handicapped student who is enrolled in the building maintenance program at the local area occupational center. He attends the Cloverdale Area Occupational Center for half a day and works with Mr. Jackson who is the building maintenance instructor. At 12:30 each day Paul takes the bus back to Cloverdale High School for the afternoon, where he is in Ms. Wilkens's special education class for English, math, and social studies. Figure 9–1 gave the Cooperative Instructional Arrangement prepared for Paul by his teachers.

Although they have found it difficult to communicate regularly because they have different class schedules, Ms. Wilkens visited the center twice during the first two weeks of school in September to become familiar with what Paul would be learning. Both Mr. Jackson and Ms. Wilkens have made their principals aware of their plan to coordinate some of their instructional efforts to make Paul's experience in the building maintenance program as successful as possible. Both of the principals have heartily endorsed their plan and hope to be able to provide some released time for them to visit each other's program and communicate regularly.

Lloyd

Lloyd has some specific learning disabilities that are still causing him some difficulty in his junior year. Figure 9–2 illustrates the cooperative instructional arrangement developed for Lloyd by three of his teachers based on his class schedule for the fall semester. Lloyd has been assigned to

FIGURE 9-2. COOPERATIVE INSTRUCTIONAL ARRANGEMENT

Lloyd

CAREER-RELATED INSTRUCTIONAL PROVISION

Title of course in which student is enrolled Welding

Instructor(s) Matt Forbes

Location or building High School/Room 7

Planning period 8:45 – 9:30

Phone ______

SPECIAL INSTRUCTION OR SERVICES PROVISION

Type of instruction or service provided for student (1) Remedial English (2) Resource Room

Instructor(s)/consultant(s)/specialist(s) (1) Ms. Smith (2) Ms. Jenkins

Location or building High School/Room 22

Planning period 8:45 – 9:30

Phone ______

COOPERATIVE WORK EXPERIENCE PROVISION

Job title ______

Location of work station ______

Work schedule

a.m. ______

p.m. ______

School coordinator ______

Planning period ______ – ______

Job supervisor(s) ______

Phone ______

SUPPORTIVE AGENCY PROVISION

Agency name ______

Contact person ______

Telephone ______

Description of specific service or instruction to be provided for the student

______

ADMINISTRATIVE ENDORSEMENTS

School administrator(s)*

(1) Duncan Collier, Voc. Dir.

(2) ______

Agency endorsement (if needed) ______

District ______

School(s) Johnstown High School

Date October 18,

*e.g., Building principal, director of special education, and/or director of vocational education

Mr. Forbes for a two-hour block of vocational welding in the morning. Ms. Jenkins and Ms. Smith, English teacher, plan to emphasize some basic vocabulary, spelling, writing, measurement, and math skills that Lloyd will be using in the welding class. This particular cooperative instructional arrangement has worked extremely well because Mr. Forbes, Ms. Jenkins, and Ms. Smith all have first period as their planning period and this permits them to get together regularly to discuss Lloyd's progress and to plan for upcoming instructional units.

Coordinating instruction for Lloyd was also facilitated through reviewing and including his class schedule. The schedule (Figure 9-3) was included on the back of the cooperative instructional arrangement forms that were distributed to each person identified on the form.

FIGURE 9-3. LLOYD'S CLASS SCHEDULE

STUDENT CLASS SCHEDULE
Johnstown High School
Johnstown, Idaho

Student Lloyd Semester Fall Grade 11

PERIOD	CLASS	LOCATION	INSTRUCTOR
1 8:45-9:30	Intro. Chemistry		Jasper
2 9:35-10:20	Welding		Forbes
3 10:25-11:10	Welding		Forbes
4 11:15-12:00	Resource Room		Jenkins
5 12:00-1:00	Lunch		
6 1:00-1:45	English II		Smith
7 1:50-2:35	Amer. History		Turner

Phyllis

Four teachers have been involved in developing a cooperative instructional arrangement for Phyllis (see Figure 9-4). This arrangement is

FIGURE 9-4. COOPERATIVE INSTRUCTIONAL ARRANGEMENT

Phyllis

CAREER-RELATED INSTRUCTION PROVISION

Title of course in which student is enrolled: Clothing Construction

Instructor(s): Sue Loth

Location or building: 133/High School

Planning period: 1:00 p - 1:45 p.

Phone

SPECIAL INSTRUCTION OR SERVICES PROVISION

Type of instruction/service provided for student: Special education

Instructor(s)/consultant(s)/specialist(s): Candy Jenkins

Location or building: 26a/High School

Planning period: 1:00p - 1:45 p

Phone

COOPERATIVE WORK EXPERIENCE PROVISION

Job title: Seamstress

Location of work station: Courier Clothing

Work schedule

a.m.

p.m. 1:30 - 5:30

School coordinator: Lori Richards

Planning period: 1:00 - 1:45 p.

Job supervisor(s): Sam Pryor

Phone

SUPPORTIVE AGENCY PROVISION

Agency name: Dewitt County Health Facility

Contact person: Pat Porta

Telephone: 371-1880

Description of specific service or instruction to be provided for the student: Physical therapy

ADMINISTRATIVE ENDORSEMENTS

School administrator(s)*

(1)

(2) Ron Kinker, principal

Agency endorsement (if needed)

District: Community School District #61

School(s): Montclair High School

Date

*e.g., Building principal, director of special education, and/or director of vocational education

somewhat unusual because the placement coordinator, Ms. Richards, and a physical therapist from the local health care facility are involved, in addition to Ms. Loth and Ms. Jenkins—the clothing and special education teachers. Part of the morning Phyllis is enrolled in a clothing construction class, while in the afternoon she has a co-op work experience at a local clothing store. Ms. Jenkins regularly checks with Ms. Loth to see if Phyllis needs any supportive instruction and advises her on possible adjustments in the clothing class facility that may be needed to accommodate Phyllis's physical disability. Ms. Loth, Ms. Jenkins, and Ms. Richards meet frequently during their common planning period to discuss Phyllis's adjustment and progress in class and on the job. Every other week Phyllis visits the local health care facility to take physical therapy exercises with Mr. Porta.

DETERMINING FACTORS IN THE COOPERATIVE ARRANGEMENT

A number of different factors influence the establishment of a cooperative arrangement for developing and delivering instruction. The special learning problems or needs of the learner, student placement, availability of coordination time, program design, and location of cooperators are all influential in determining the optimum cooperative arrangement for a special needs learner.

Individual Learning Problems and Needs

If, for example, a seventh grade special needs student is having difficulty in his manufacturing class with some specific measurement concepts, the appropriate arrangement might necessitate cooperation between the manufacturing teacher and the resource room or basic math teacher. It is unlikely in this situation that cooperative work experience would be a viable option unless the individual is eligible for a special work program or needs the specific, on-the-job experience for a particular educational or economic reason. It is also doubtful that services from a supportive agency from outside the school would be important in remediating this particular learning problem.

Student Placement

Another determining factor is the total educational placement of the learner. If the cooperative arrangement is being established after the school year has started, the range of possible cooperators is limited, to some extent, to the professional educators with whom the student has daily or regular contact.

If, for example, a special education teacher is concerned about presenting a unit on "employment application forms" to a particular student, he or she might work with the student's vocational welding teacher or industrial co-op coordinator to determine the procedures and special considerations to be made in applying for employment as a welder at various businesses within the community.

In such situations, where students are placed in some or all regular school programs, the range of possible cooperators is largely limited to the teachers who comprise the learner's total educational placement.

Availability of Coordination Time

As the cooperative endeavor becomes more involved, this factor becomes most influential. Implementing a cooperative effort takes additional time of the teacher; there is no way to get around this. One may consider selecting cooperators who already have instructional coordination or consultation as part of their responsibilities. When the learning problem so dictates, attempts should be made to utilize the cooperative services of reading consultants, speech therapists, prevocational coordinators, and others whose job it is–(in part at least)–to work with teachers and students on an individual consulting basis.

It is also helpful to suggest to program directors and building principals the need for joint coordination meetings between occupational education personnel and special and basic education personnel. Joint staff meetings and concurrently scheduled planning periods can be extremely productive for implementing a cooperative venture.

Program Design

To a very large extent the cooperative arrangement is influenced by the existing program design or arrangement. For instance, in a large comprehensive high school a greater number and variety of career-related instructional programs, special services, and co-op or work-related programs are available. Thus, the potential for locating the appropriate cooperators is increased significantly over situations where the curriculum offering is limited or narrower in scope.

Location of Cooperators

The geographic location of important cooperating and supporting staff can cause problems also. Recently, many school districts across the nation have joined with other adjacent districts to construct area vocational centers. Coordination between area vocational center teachers and supportive teachers at the student's home school becomes extremely difficult and time consuming when the teachers are geographically separated.

A variety of strategies have been used in attempting to overcome this problem. Some area vocational centers have added special or basic education personnel to their staff, while others have employed liaison personnel to coordinate the instructional programs at the center with instruction at the home or sending school. Still other sending schools have found the problem to be critical enough to send selected members of their basic or special education staff to the area vocational center on a regular basis to meet with the occupational teachers.

COMMITMENT OF PERSONNEL

It is obvious that the important, critical consideration in initiating a cooperative arrangement is locating enthusiastic and committed teachers, consultants, or coordinators. Involvement of individuals who work with the student on a regular basis and who are committed to the idea of serving the students through a cooperative team approach is an absolute necessity. The willingness, commitment, and cooperative attitude of those professionals listed on the form are the only things that will make the arrangement work effectively for the learner.

ADMINISTRATIVE ENDORSEMENTS

In addition to commitment from the cooperating teachers, administrative endorsement for any plan of cooperation is also essential. Since the cooperative arrangement will be determined by optimum placement of the special needs learner, it is highly important that the appropriate administrative personnel be involved in formulating the arrangements for each student. It should be noted also that when instructional personnel take the initiative in planning to work cooperatively, such action provides a strong rationale that administrators can use to justify actions they take to expand and improve the services available to special needs students.

Administrators can lend their support for the cooperative instructional arrangement by permitting individual student scheduling options such as the following when necessary:

- Extensions of time for program completion by selected students
- Open entry and open exit scheduling that permits entrance or exit at different intervals as a student progresses
- Instruction on an individualized basis
- Flexible scheduling with modular-based instruction
- Laboratory-type hands-on courses for extended study or deficiency remediation.

In addition to providing scheduling flexibility, administrators can provide endorsement for 1) purchase of specially designed textbooks, instructional materials, and equipment, 2) modification of equipment or instructional materials, and 3) provision of necessary supplemental educational services for special needs learners in career-related programs.

Finally, as suggested by the examples provided earlier, a written administrative endorsement for the proposed cooperative instructional arrangement should be included on the form. This suggests that those administrators endorsing the plan are aware of the planned effort to coordinate instruction and services and are supportive of it.

A FINAL NOTE

A cooperative instructional arrangement is a formalized plan for coordinating career-related instruction and supportive services for individual special needs learners. The plan is based on the student's total educational placement, and it identifies both the instructional staff providing career-related instruction and special services offered the student on a regular basis.

The formalizing of an arrangement such as this represents a somewhat new departure in delivering programs and services for special students at the secondary level. Some occupational and special educators have worked together in cooperative efforts previously, but seldom has a planned, systematic approach to cooperation been suggested or widely implemented.

It should be readily recognizable, however, that planned cooperation between occupational and special educators will only be productive and fruitful for the student if the attitudes and commitments of those professionals who are involved demonstrate the true spirit of cooperation.

SUMMARY

Prior to developing individualized instructional programs for special needs learners, it is imperative that a cooperative instructional team be identified. Considerations and procedures for identifying and assembling a special needs learner's team are outlined in detail. The cooperative team usually involves two or more professionals representing: 1) classroom career-related instruction (vocational education or practical arts teacher), 2) special instruction or services (such as a resource room teacher), 3) a cooperative work experience coordinator (if appropriate), or 4) a supportive service agency representative (such as a vocational rehabilitation counselor if the student is eligible). A number of alternative and key considerations in formulating these cooperative arrangements, such as the involvement of administrators, are discussed.

REFERENCES

Antonellis, G. P., and James. G. B. *Cross discipline planning.* Salt Lake City: Olympus, 1973.

Gallagher, J. J. Vocational education, special education and vocational rehabilitation: A marriage of professionals needed for handicapped children. Address given at the National Conference on Vocational Education for Handicapped Persons, Pittsburgh, Pa., February 26, 1969.

Phelps, L. A., et al. The cooperative teaching concept. *Michigan Industrial Education Society Journal,* 33, 3, 6–7.

PLANNING INSTRUCTION

This chapter focuses on the critical and complex task of developing instructional plans for special needs learners. Instructional planning, which is the fifth component in the System for Developing and Managing Instruction, is similar in many respects to specific curriculum or lesson plan development. In the systematic instructional development process, planning follows the formalizing of cooperative instructional arrangements or teams. During instructional planning the learner's cooperative instructional team systematically incorporates data and information describing specific learner needs, available instructional resources, and the occupational competencies required in the world of work into a working instructional plan.

10

WHAT IS AN INSTRUCTIONAL PLAN?

Here, "instructional plan" is used in a somewhat limited context. It refers to 1) the specific modules or units of instruction to be taught and 2) any cooperative school-employer agreements or plans that may be initiated as part of the special needs student's program. A specific instructional plan developed by the cooperative team for a special needs learner could and should include a series of instructional modules and—when appropriate—a cooperative training agreement or plan for providing on-the-job, career exploration activities or work experience for the learner. Figure 10–1 illustrates these major components of instructional planning.

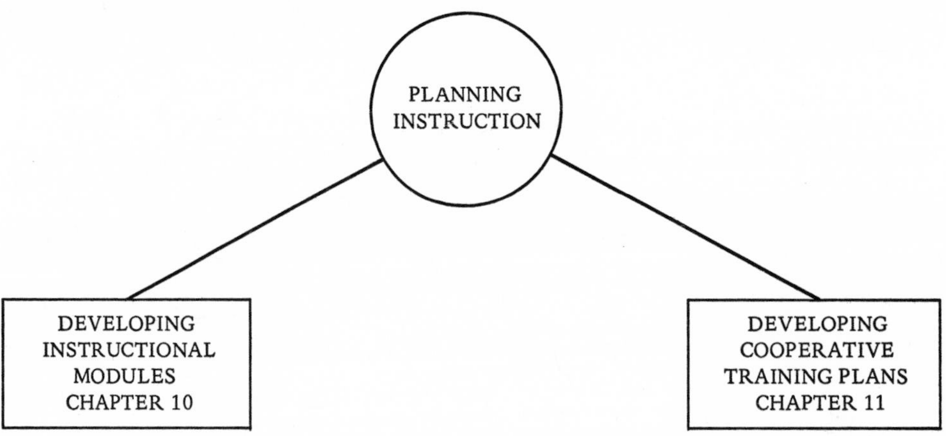

FIGURE 10-1. MAJOR INSTRUCTIONAL PLANNING ACTIVITIES

An "educational plan," which is frequently mentioned throughout this text, refers to *all* of the instructional development outcomes, including instructional planning, as they are focused on individual students. Ideally, the *total* educational plan for a special needs learner would include: a learner assessment profile, an inventory of available school and community resources, a career cluster analysis, a formalized cooperative instructional arrangement, a planned strategy for managing classroom instruction, and a system for monitoring and evaluating learner progress.

Certainly it is somewhat idealistic to think that we can conduct this type of formal, extensive educational planning for each special needs learner. While experience has shown that comprehensive individualized programs are effective and successful in meeting the needs of special students, it is not likely that all school districts and communities will be able to mount this type of effort in planning for individual students. We can, however, begin to approach the notion of individualized prescriptive educational planning for everyone by developing and using individual plans for our present special needs learners who clearly require individual attention because of the severity of their learning, emotional, or physical problems.

WHAT IS AN INSTRUCTIONAL MODULE?

A module is similar to what other instructional developers have traditionally called lesson plans or instructional units. The instructional module as discussed in this chapter will highlight a single concept, skill, attitude, or performance to be learned by the student. In some instances a module may convey or include a set of concepts, skills, attitudes, or performances to be learned.

In structuring and developing modules it is important that the topics of each module be related to the career cluster analysis activity discussed in Chapter 8. You will recall that a number of different types of broadly defined tasks can be derived from a career cluster analysis. Tasks such as "servicing brake systems," "filling out job application forms," or "computing board feet" are common examples. To make the logical extension of this career cluster analysis complete, in this chapter a task, which was defined earlier as "a unit of worker activity that can be divided into task elements," will form the basis for an instructional module. In other words, each "task" we previously identified will become a module.

WHAT IS INCLUDED IN A MODULE?

In order to develop a module, several specific instructional planning considerations have to be made. These will focus on such factors as the types of special needs learners receiving the instruction and the essential information needed by teachers to provide effective instruction. Because of these differences, teachers may not want or need to include the same instructional planning information suggested here. However, from research data and several years of experience in working with teachers of special needs learners on curriculum development, the authors have found that the following components of an instructional module appear to be critical:

1. *Performance objectives* that specify the occupational concepts, skills, and competencies to be learned.
2. *Basic skills/concepts* that specify the basic competencies to be developed by the learner *prior to or during* the instruction.
3. *Basic skill/concept content* identifies the specific content of the task, which can be taught by the special education or basic academic instructional staff.
4. *Instructional activities* that describe the specific experiences the teachers and learners will undertake in both occupational and basic or special instructional situations.
5. *Instructional resource materials* that will be used as a part of the instructional activities.
6. *A system for monitoring student attainment* of the performance objectives and basic concepts and skills in the module.

WHY ARE WRITTEN INSTRUCTIONAL PLANS IMPORTANT?

Well-developed, written instructional plans for special needs learners serve five critical purposes:

1. They provide a vehicle for communication and discussion between occupational and special educators, administrators, supportive and special services personnel, parents, and employers.
2. They enable teachers and coordinators to systematically develop reasonable, relevant, and meaningful instructional activities for individual special needs learners.
3. They aid teachers and other instructional staff in monitoring a student's progress throughout a course or instructional program.

4. Written plans can also be essential in the evaluation and improvement of instructional programs and supportive services.
5. Finally, written instructional plans, when coordinated by occupational and special educators, often provide for the maximum utilization of teaching effort, time, and materials.

A number of other secondary benefits point to the importance of written instructional plans. Written plans provide an overall sense of stability for the instructional process. As noted earlier, the development of plans provides a format for specifying and clarifying instructional objectives and teaching strategies to be used. Many teachers also feel that written plans, if well conceived, can increase their efficiency by providing them with an organization or structure for their activities in the classroom. In addition, written plans can provide a continuity of instructional content both throughout units of instruction as well as continuity throughout courses in junior and senior high school programs. Finally, formal plans are of great benefit to substitute teachers, and they can be very helpful to administrators in their efforts to document special services provided to special needs learners.

DEVELOPING INSTRUCTIONAL MODULES

The initial phase of instructional planning involves developing instructional modules. As mentioned earlier, an instructional module can also be thought of as a lesson plan or a unit plan for teaching. Typically, an instructional module will focus on *one* of the tasks listed in an inventory of tasks for a career cluster. Obviously then, a number of instructional modules will be included in a course or cluster-based instructional program.

A Format of Instructional Module Development

Numerous formats have been introduced in recent years for developing modules, lessons, and units of instruction. The specific format to be used in developing a module will depend upon the nature of the instructional planning inputs needed to deliver effectively the instruction to the learner.

Many of the planning inputs needed for instructing special needs learners are identical to the inputs required in developing effective instruction for students without special needs. However, since our primary target audience is special needs learners, and since special and occupational educators will be cooperatively delivering the instruction, some unique, supplemental planning inputs are required.

The inputs for instructional planning can be referred to as the components of the instructional module. Contained in an instructional module for a special needs learner are the following components:

1. Occupational performance objectives
2. Basic skills/concepts
3. Basic skill/concept content
4. Instructional activities
5. Instructional resource materials
6. System for documenting learner progress

The specific content of instructional modules is the primary consideration, rather than the arrangement of headings on the page. It is essential that an instructional module for most special needs students enrolled in occupational and special education programs include the six components identified above. A format, functional and easy to use, is important in making efficient use of the time that occupational and special educators devote to joint planning and instruction. Figures 10-2, 10-3, and 10-4 present an instructional module format that has been field tested and adopted by a sizable number of occupational and special educators. This is not to suggest that all of the teachers and coordinators who assisted in developing this form currently use the two-page form exactly as it is presented here. Some teachers have developed different column or section headings and rearranged some of the sections on the sheet. However, the consensus feeling among those who developed and use this form is that the format identifies the critical information needed to plan an educational experience for a special needs learner effectively and efficiently.

The following sections will introduce three students, discuss the development of the instructional modules by examining the purpose and intended use of the information, and list several guidelines to follow in writing each segment of the module.

FIGURE 10-2. SADIE'S INSTRUCTIONAL MODULE

CLUSTER PROGRAM: *Health Occupations: Nurse Aide*

task: *Take and record pulse*

Learner *Sadie*

I.D. No. *NA: 22*

Learner Progress	**Occupational Performance Objectives** Given the necessary materials, tools, equipment, and requisite knowledge, the learner will:	**Basic Skills/ Concepts**	**Basic Skill/ Concept Content**	Learner Progress
	1. List and describe different body areas from which pulses may be read.			
	2. Read a patient's pulse following a prescribed procedure:		Patient positions: sitting, lying	
	a. properly position patient	physical strength		
	b. locate pulse	touch discrimination	Rhythm (regular, irregular) tension (expansion, contraction, relaxed)	
	c. read the patient's pulse, noting rhythm, volume, and tension	touch discrimination		
		time measurement	Measure time in minutes and 30 and 15 second intervals	
		multiplication	Pulses counted times 2 (for 30 second interval) or 4 (for 15 second interval).	
	3. Chart the pertinent information regarding a patient's pulse rate	Reading comprehension	Read information and directions on a patient's chart	
		Recording information Form Completion Accuracy	Record written and numerical information on the patient's chart, including pulse rate, etc.	
		Numerical Concepts	Record pulse rates in number per minute	
		Technical vocabulary	Pulse, artery, radial (arm), patient chart	
Employable				Competent
Productive				Developing
Involved				Introduced
Introduced				

FIGURE 10-2. *(Continued)*

CLUSTER PROGRAM: Health Occupations : Nurse Aide

task: Take and record pulse

I.D. No. NA : 22

Occupational Instruction

Teacher Activities:

Provide individual or small groups demonstration on pulse taking and recording procedures.

After viewing the film, conduct a small group discussion on the basic concepts and techniques of pulse taking and reading.

Prepare simplified pulse charting forms and share with special education teacher.

Learner Activities:

Practice taking and recording classmates' pulses.

View film on pulse taking and recording.

Participate in small group discussions on bedside manner when taking vital signs.

Take their own and classmates' pulses on various conditions of physical activity.

Basic Skill / Concept Instruction

Teacher Activities:

Develop and use flash cards in teaching vocabulary related to pulse taking and recording.

Provide individual instruction on how to time 15 and 30 second intervals.

Learner Activities:

Practice counting the number of recurring events in 15 and 30 second intervals, i.e., number of drips from a slightly opened faucet.

Practice timing.

Instructional Resource Materials

Name / Title	Media	Source
"Temperature, Pulse and Respiration"	16 mm film	
Pulse intensity chart	wall chart	

Name / Title	Media	Source
Flash cards w/pulse-taking vocabulary		
Stop watch/watch w/second hand		

FIGURE 10-3. MARK'S INSTRUCTIONAL MODULE

CLUSTER PROGRAM:

task: All Clusters / Cooperative Work Experience
Apply for a social security card.

Learner: Mark

I.D. No.: 16

Learner Progress	Occupational Performance Objectives Given the necessary materials, tools, equipment, and requisite knowledge, the learner will:	Basic Skills/ Concepts	Basic Skill/ Concept Content	Learner Progress
Employable Productive Involved Introduced	1. Choose to apply for a social security card if he/she does not currently possess one.			Competent Developing Introduced
	2. Complete an application for a social security number by providing accurate and complete information.	Form Completion	Full name, name given at birth, place of birth (city, county, state), age on last birthday, Mother's full name at birth, father's full name, applied before?, sex, color or race, mailing address, date, signature	
		Accuracy	Verify and double check information provided	
		Technical Vocabulary	Social security number Railroad number Tax account number Treasury Department Internal Revenue Service	

FIGURE 10-3. *(Continued)*

CLUSTER PROGRAM:

task: All Clusters / Cooperative Work Experience
Apply for a social security card.

I.D. No. Mark

Occupational Instruction

Teacher Activities:

Discuss the purpose of social security, how the tax is deducted, etc, in small groups.

Organize and conduct a field trip to local offices of the Social Security Administration

Invite an employer to visit the class and discuss how social security deductions are computed and submitted to IRS.

Arrange for class to fill out application forms.

Learner Activities:

Students fill out application forms using personal information sheets

Students check each other's completed forms

Interview an employer regarding social security deductions

Basic Skill / Concept Instruction

Teacher Activities:

Obtain or prepare several copies of Application for Social Security Number forms.

Develop role-playing situations where students:
1. request and complete a replacement application form.
2. request and complete a request for change in social security records.

Have application form(s) brailled or translated to primary language if necessary.

Learner Activities:

Have students list on paper all information required on the application.

Practice stating information as briefly as possible (e.g., dates: 1/1/78)

Students take completed forms to the post office and submit

Practice printing required information clearly.

Students check each other's information sheets.

Instructional Resource Materials

Name / Title	Media	Source

Name / Title	Media	Source
Application for Social Security Number	form	post office

FIGURE 10-4. GARY'S INSTRUCTIONAL MODULE

CLUSTER PROGRAM:

task: *Construction*
Building a floor frame (model)

Learner *Gary*

I.D. No. CON-18

Learner Progress: Introduced	Involved	Productive	Employable	Occupational Performance Objectives Given the necessary materials, tools, equipment, and requisite knowledge, the learner will:	Basic Skills/ Concepts	Basic Skill/ Concept Content	Learner Progress: Introduced	Developing	Competent
				1. Measure, mark, and saw materials to length	Measure sizes	Sizes of framing members • Joists (need 4) 2"×6"×13⅞" • Header (need 1) 2"×6"×48" • Girder plate (need 1) 2"×4"×48" • Sill (need 1) 2"×4"×48"			
					Technical vocabulary	Floor joist			✓
						Header	9/15		✓
						Girder plate			
						Common nails-16d (d=penny)		✓	
						Box nails-8d		✓	
				2. Assemble the rough floor framing of a model structure a. nail joists to header b. toenail header and joists to girder plates and sill	Measure distance	16" between the 4 joists when measured from the center of one to the center of the next Actual distance between the joists 14⅜"			
					Hand-eye coordination	Driving nails straight-on and at an angle (toe-nailing)			

FIGURE 10-4. *(Continued)*

CLUSTER PROGRAM:

task: Construction
Building a floor frame (model)

I.D. No. CON-18

Occupational Instruction

Teacher Activities:

Assign students to groups in constructing floor frame models. Have special needs learners in different groups.
Demonstrate procedures for cutting stock and assembly to each group.
Prepare and use simple assembly drawings of floor frame with parts labeled.
Demonstrate toenailing with individual special needs learners.

Learner Activities:

Review assignments 84-85 in World of Construction Lab Manual
Practice toenailing framing members on scrap material.
Work in teams to construct the floor frame model.

Basic Skill / Concept Instruction

Teacher Activities:

Obtain and review floor frame assembly drawings. Review with individual students as needed.
Collect and label all tools. Use for identification test and vocabulary drill.
Have students practice measuring. Stress to overlearning in measuring the parts of the floor frame.
Obtain nail identification and size charts.

Learner Activities:

Measure and identify the correct size framing members (joist, header, sill) from several correctly and incorrectly cut samples.
Select 8d and 16d nails from a quantity of assorted sizes.
Practice marking 16" sections on the 2" × 6" header.

Instructional Resource Materials

Occupational Instruction:

Name / Title	Media	Source
World of Construction	Lab manual	McKnight Publishers

Basic Skill / Concept Instruction:

Name / Title	Media	Source
World of Construction	Lab manual	McKnight
nail identification and size chart	Chart	local hardware or Const. teacher
Sample framing members		
Quantity of assorted nails		

Three Illustrations: Sadie, Mark, and Gary

To guide us through this section of the chapter we will frequently refer to three of the special needs learners who were introduced in Chapter 1. As our high-school-level example, we will use Sadie, who is enrolled in a nurse aide vocational program and is also working part-time at the community hospital in a cooperative work experience program. "Taking and recording pulse" is the instructional module Ms. Healy and the other teachers are developing for Sadie (see Figure 10–2).

Mark is also a high school student, enrolled in an agricultural mechanics program. In addition, he also is working part-time as part of his special education work-study program. In the related instruction class, Mark's teacher will soon be introducing a unit on "applying for a social security card." Figure 10–3 illustrates the instructional module outlined for Mark for this particular unit.

Gary is a junior high school student (seventh grade) who is considered extremely bright, and he is highly interested in construction processes. Mr. Cary and several other teachers who work with Gary are planning a unit to introduce him to several mathematical and geometric concepts associated with residential construction. Figure 10–4 outlines the module they have developed dealing with "building a house model floor frame."

Cluster/Program

This heading at the top of the module (which can be printed on both sides of the sheet) identifies the cluster and/or instructional program in which this instructional module will be used. Chapter 8 focused on specifying occupational clusters and related instructional programs and should be used as a reference in completing this section of the module. The three examples used in the following discussion are taken from the health occupations, agricultural occupations, and construction occupations clusters.

As noted earlier, the example learners will highlight specific special needs students enrolled in each of these programs. Sadie will be our student in a health occupations cluster program at the high school level, Mark our student in an agricultural mechanics and special education work-study program, and Gary our student in a junior high construction cluster class focusing on career exploration and prevocational skill development in this area.

Learner Identification

So far, individualized instruction has been highly emphasized as an appropriate and effective instructional strategy for special needs learners. The instructional module we are about to develop is an individualized instructional plan. Thus, the name of the special needs learner for whom this plan is being developed should be placed in the blank in the upper left corner of the module planning sheet.

To aid the instructional team in developing this module, the learner analysis profile and learning prescription, which were discussed in Chapter 6, should be reviewed. It will be helpful to have these documents and other information on the student's learning needs available during the writing of instructional modules.

Task Statements

As with most curriculum plans, the component parts of the curriculum or course are broken down into units or lessons. As described in Chapter 8, the basis for occupational or career education curricula in *all* school programs can be viewed as a cluster of occupations. The specific competencies required for entry employment or exploration in one or more of the clustered occupations can be identified as "tasks." Tasks become the basic unit for curriculum development. Each instructional module is then focused on one particular task that either familiarizes the learner with, or prepares him or her for the occupations in which that task is performed.

Figure 10-5 is designed to clarify the relationship between the specificity levels of clusters and tasks in planning instructional modules. The example in Figure 10-5 illustrates that career exploration instruction generally has a broader base than preparation instruction. The exploration

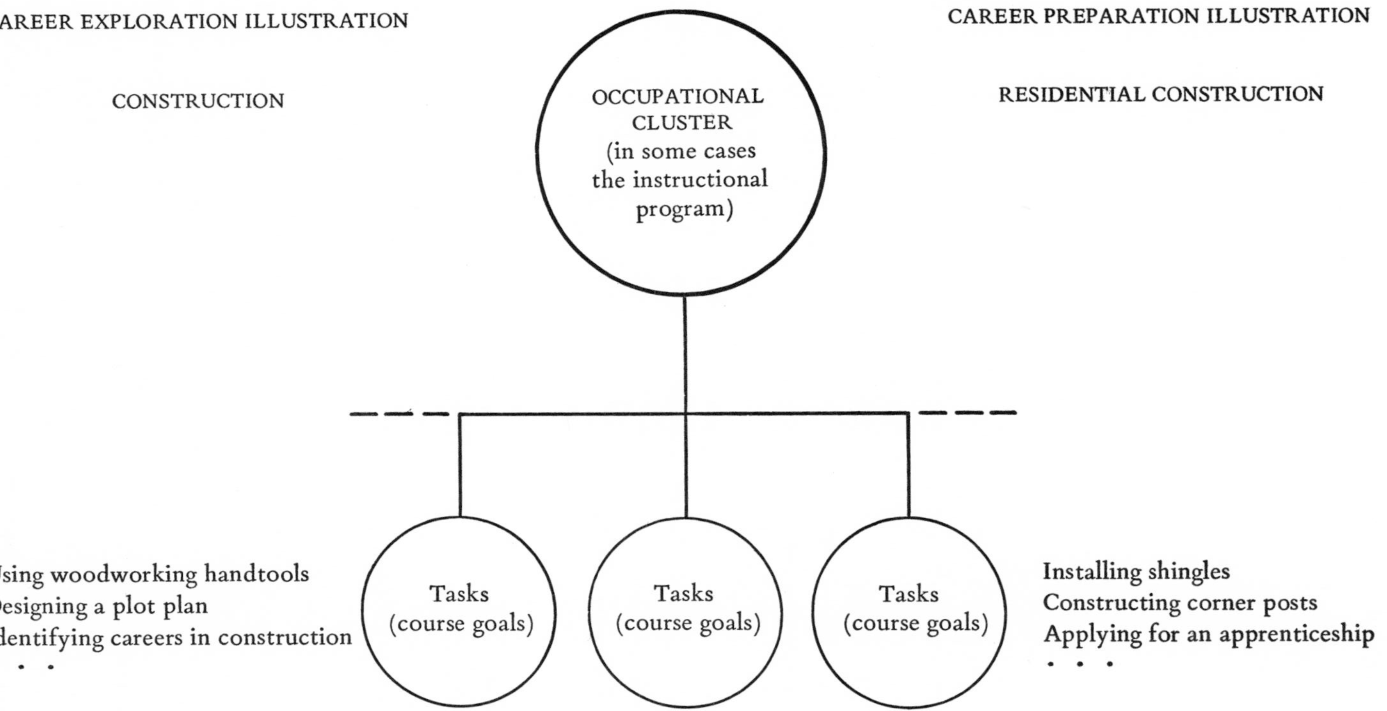

FIGURE 10-5. CLUSTERS AND TASKS

cluster title encompasses all of the construction occupations, while the preparation cluster focuses specifically on residential construction occupations. The tasks (or course goals) have a similar range of specificity.

At the top of the instructional module form (on both sides of the form) the cluster and task should be clearly identified. These headings are similar to such designations as "course" and "unit or lesson" commonly found in other instructional plans. If you refer to our earlier examples, you will note that Sadie will be learning to "take and record pulses," Mark to "apply for a social security card," and Gary to "build a floor frame model."

As you can infer from the examples, tasks should be general behavioral or performance statements that, in essence, describe the performance the learner will demonstrate when the instructional module has been completed.

Several specifics should be observed in writing task statements. First, attempt to write task statements at a consistent level of specificity. When instructional modules become disproportionate in complexity and depth, instruction can become sidetracked. Tasks should be simply stated, and the use of multiple or compound verbs in a task statement should be avoided (e.g., disassemble, overhaul, and service an engine). It is helpful if the task to be learned in the module can be completed within a week or shorter period of time by the special needs learner. Many special needs learners find it difficult to remain "on task" for a long period of time. (Several other suggestions for writing task statements and identifying different types of tasks can be found in Chapter 8 on page 178.)

Tasks can also be described in relationship to the courses in which they might be taught. Educators have traditionally identified the major purposes or goals of a course. One of the problems often encountered, however, has been that the goals of the course are too global; that is, they describe some far-distant future goal—being a contributing, independent member of society for instance. While many of these goals are valid and desirable, they provide little help in developing an individual's instructional plan.

Another problem has been that course goals seldom describe what the learner can do at the conclusion of the course. Goals are often translated into nondescriptive unit titles such as "family finances" that only identify the topic of the unit. It is more accurate to state the goal as "manage family finances efficiently." Course goals, when stated as tasks the learner will be able to perform upon completion of the module, are more useful.

Each of the six major components of the instructional module will be described in the following sections. After reading about each component, the reader is encouraged to review the example modules developed for Sadie, Mark, and Gary (Figures 10-2, 10-3, and 10-4).

Occupational Performance Objectives

A performance objective is an observable, behavioral description of what the learner will be able to do at the completion of the instruction. Performance objectives will specify the component behaviors or performances which, when collectively demonstrated, enable the learner to perform the task.

Performance objectives have become popular in educational circles in recent years for a number of reasons. The use of systems-oriented curriculum development models, the focus on greater accountability for the schools, and the recent interest in programmed instruction have all contributed to the popular use of performance objectives. There is considerable agreement in educational circles that clear and explicit statements of performance are important and necessary to curriculum, instruction, and evaluation. There is considerable debate, however, on how performance outcomes should be stated. Mager (1962), Gronlund (1970), Gagné and Briggs (1974) are among the numerous authors who have suggested different approaches to stating performance objectives.

This discussion of performance objectives and their use in instructional planning must be, at best, only superficial. Several excellent handbooks on specifying performance or behavioral objectives have been developed for the field by Gronlund, Mager, and others. These are listed in the references at the end of this chapter and should be consulted if an in-depth review is needed of procedures and techniques for writing and using performance objectives.

Why Specify Performance Objectives? A more direct and straightforward emphasis is being placed on learning in schools today. The appropriateness and effectiveness of teaching and instructional practices is being questioned more closely. Writing objectives that explicitly describe the anticipated learner performance do the following:

1. Enables teachers and students to distinguish between different types and levels of performance and subsequently aids them in determining which strategies for learning will be most helpful in individualizing learning.
2. Permits teachers to structure learning experiences specific to the needs of individual learners.
3. Insures that continuous re-evaluation of learner needs and achievement can occur and that the quality and effectiveness of the instruction can be determined.
4. Defines and delimits the purpose of the instruction and removes ambiguities of interpretation.

Objectives for the Special Needs Learner. Many regular class teachers in occupational education and other areas have raised a basic question regarding special needs learners: To what extent are the educational objectives different for the special needs learner? Actually, basic educational objectives are not, and should not be conceived of as being, different for special needs learners. Smith (1974) notes:

> *The general objectives of education for the intellectually normal as listed by the Educational Policies Commission (1946) are also appropriate for the mentally retarded. Civic responsibility, human relationship, self-realization, and economic efficiency are suitable broad objectives for all school children. They express the fundamental tenets of education in a democracy.*

It is fast becoming part of every educator's responsibility to assist the special needs learner to develop basic skills that in turn will lead to the development of adequate competencies for social, personal, and occupational situations and successful adjustment. All of this has the basic aim of preparing the individual for economic self-sufficiency.

Occupational educators maintain that certain sets of competencies and performance levels are essential for obtaining employment and, when transformed into minimum-level instructional objectives, must be essentially the same for all students if the graduates are expected to have a salable skill upon completion of the educational program. The majority of employers will only "hire the handicapped" if the handicapped individual can contribute to the economic viability of the business.

A Format for Writing Performance Objectives. The basic format to be used in writing performance objectives is illustrated in Figure 10-6. The performance objectives written for Sadie's module on "taking and recording pulse" identify the three performances she must be able to demonstrate at the completion of the instruction. The objectives were identified as either required task skills or task knowledges in the career cluster analysis that Sadie's teachers conducted using the procedures outlined in Chapter 8.

Within this format for developing performance objectives, there are three essential parts of the objective that will need to be stated.

FIGURE 10-6. OCCUPATIONAL PERFORMANCE OBJECTIVES

TASK: Take and record pulse

Given a watch, patient chart, and a classmate on whom to demonstrate, the learner will:

1. List and describe each of the different body areas from which pulses may be read.
2. Read a patient's pulse following a prescribed procedure:
   a. Properly position patient
   b. Locate pulse
   c. Read pulse, noting rhythm, volume, and tension
3. Chart the pertinent information regarding a patient's pulse rate

Optional Condition Statement:*

Given the necessary tools, materials, equipment, and requisite knowledge, the learner will:

*This condition statement was used in the development of cluster curriculum guides in the Vocational Education-Special Education Project, Central Michigan University, 1971–1974. From M. L. Reynolds, R. J. Lutz, C. B. Johnson, and L. A. Phelps, *Cluster Guide* (Series). (Mt. Pleasant: Central Michigan University, 1973. Copyright © 1973 by Central Michigan University. Used with permission.

Condition and situation statements describe the specific context under which the performance will be demonstrated. Since what the learner actually does is highly dependent upon the situation in which he or she is placed, descriptions of the performance situation and related conditions are important. For a given module or task you may choose to use a general condition or situation statement. For Sadie's module on "pulse taking," the following statement was developed:

> *Given a watch and patient chart, and a classmate on whom to demonstrate, . . .*

You will note that we have described the tools to be used and on whom the task is to be demonstrated. Several additional specifics—such as the position of the subject, and so on—could be included if they are considered appropriate by the instructor.

In some instructional situations teachers view condition or situation statements as less important and instead choose to emphasize the performance being demonstrated. In these instances, some teachers have found it helpful to use a general, standard condition or situation statement such as the optional statement given at the bottom of Figure 10-6.

Action and object of action words or phrases following the condition or situation statement is the second component of the occupational performance objective. The action or performance to be demonstrated is described in the verb tense. Selection of the action word or words for an objective is perhaps the most critical aspect of writing, because it defines the capability to be learned (Gagné and Briggs 1974) as well as the overt performance to be observed by the instructor. In the three performances listed in Sadie's module, she is required to:

1. List and describe . . . *different body areas*
2. Read . . . *a patient's pulse*
3. Chart . . . *pertinent information*

The objects of these action verbs are shown on the right and describe "what" the action is applied to.

As one can readily see, the selection of action words is the key to writing useful performance objectives. The action words must clearly describe what is to be observed as a result of the learning experience. Not only must action words be observable in order to measure successful performance, but they should also focus on a variety of capabilities to be learned. Many special needs students who are in mainstreamed programs *can* function at higher levels than their teachers expect. Thus, it is important that the objectives specified in instructional modules focus on the development of a *variety* of different capabilities to be learned.

Gagné and Briggs (1974) have identified five major types of human capabilities to be learned: intellectual skills, cognitive strategies, information, motor skills, and attitudes. When selecting action words in any of these human capability classifications, it is important to consider selecting verbs that represent a range of capabilities. For instance, "identify by name" is a commonly used action verb that represents a lower level intellectual skill than does "generating a solution to a problem." Selecting action verbs at varying levels of complexity enables teachers to determine the learner's level of performance capability and to select verbs representing progressively higher levels of performance in later lessons or units.

Criterion levels is the third component of a performance objective. Criterion levels describe the minimal qualitative or quantitative features of the performance. The basic purpose in specifying criterion levels is to identify when a student has successfully mastered the performance.

Criterion levels may be added to the action statements by including such phrases as "with 80 percent accuracy," "to comply with manufacturer's specifications," "as determined by the teacher," or "within thirty minutes." Each of these represents a qualitative or quantitative dimension of the performance in which the student will be engaged.

Another, and perhaps more functional approach to defining the performance criterion level is to use a series of standardized, performance level descriptors. The module format in Figures 10-2, 10-3, and 10-4 includes two columns labeled "Learner Progress" that can be used as criterion level indicators. As teachers use and develop consistent criteria for such levels as "productive" and "employable," this system for monitoring a student's progress in attaining each of the objectives becomes reliable and efficient. It is important to remember, however, that explicit and concise criteria for each of these levels should be developed by the occupational and special educators using them. An added benefit in specifying criterion levels in this manner is the opportunity it gives to make a graphic portrayal of progress made by students on a daily or regular basis. Chapter 13 will describe techniques for developing learner progress criteria and procedures for monitoring, reporting, and using learner progress information.

Basic Skills and Concepts

For any task one chooses to examine, there are a number of basic skills and knowledges required in order to perform the task successfully. For most nonspecial needs learners, these basic skills and knowledges are obtained as a result of their normal growth and development or through their early school experiences. Special needs learners, on the other hand, are usually designated as such because they fail to demonstrate these basic skills and understandings in daily behavior and performance patterns. Their lack of successful or normal performance and functioning in these areas has caused them to be identified as needing "special help" to aid in overcoming the learning, behavioral, or physical problems they have encountered in their growth and development.

Obviously then the identification and remediation of the basic skills the student is lacking is an important aspect of instructional planning. If we define "basic skills and concepts" relative to the task to be learned, it will be especially helpful in developing instructional modules. Basic skills and concepts are: *the competencies or abilities the learner will need in order to learn and/or perform the task successfully.* With this operational definition, we can identify the basic competencies in an instructional module designed for an individual student.

Identifying Basic Skills and Concepts. Each of the basic skills and concepts identified on the instructional module form are keyed to the occupational performance objectives. For instance, on Sadie's module (Figure 10–2) one of the objectives (2c) requires her to "read the patient's pulse." In order to do this successfully she must be able to "measure time" accurately, which is a basic skill.

In identifying the basic skills and concepts to be included in an instructional module, *two* important considerations must be made.

1. What are the basic skills and concepts required or demanded by this occupational performance objective or task? This determination can be made by referring back to the career cluster analysis presented in Chapter 8. Other job analysis data sources such as *Dictionary of Occupational Titles* can also be used to determine the basic skills and concepts people need in order to perform specific occupational tasks.
2. Is the learner already competent in the basic skills or concepts that are implied in the occupational performance objective or task? This determination can be made by reviewing the student's learner profile and other student needs assessment data, the collection of which is described in Chapter 6. When the cooperative team reviews the student information, if the individual has *not* demonstrated a deficiency in any of the basic skills demanded by task, then there is no reason to include the basic skill or concept in the instructional module.

Classifications of Basic Skills and Concepts. A number of curriculum research and development projects and federal agencies have attempted to develop classifications or lists of basic skills and abilities needed by individuals to function as independent adults as well as in specific occupational roles. The U.S. Department of Labor (1965) in *Dictionary of Occupational Titles* presents a number of different worker trait categories that specify the aptitudes (e.g., manual dexterity) required in various occupations. Researchers in psychology and special education such as Valett (1967) have developed classifications of basic learning abilities. Many of the basic skill classifications developed in this area have been based on human development theories.

More recently, two curriculum research projects focusing on occupational education for the handicapped have developed somewhat similar basic skill classifications. The Vocational Education-Special Education Project at Central Michigan University (1974) generated a list of task-related competencies and a list of employment-related competencies. The list of task-related competencies (e.g., recognizing numbers) was classified in four areas: knowledge, comprehension, numbers, and physical abilities. The employment-related competencies (e.g., opening a bank account) were identified in nine categories: self, awareness of job opportunities, job application, identifying information, social responsibilities, communication skills, transportation, business knowledges, and independence. The Illinois State University project (Hemenway et al. 1975), also focusing on special needs students at the secondary level, developed a Learner-Behavior-Task Demand Rating Scale that identified ninety-six different basic skills (e.g., planning ability). These basic skills—or behaviors, as they were defined in this project—were grouped into eleven different ability areas (e.g., cognitive, general health, psychomotor, and so on).

Both of these basic skill/concept classification arrangements were developed from a curriculum framework in which occupational and special education teachers were concerned with identifying and remediating basic basic skills special needs students lacked in developing their occupational competencies.

The Index of Basic Skills/Concepts. This Index, which is presented in Figure 10–8 is a consolidation of the competency and behavior lists developed in the Central Michigan and Illinois State projects. It presents and defines basic skills and concepts relevant to occupational education in eight major skill areas: quantitative and numerical, verbal, cognitive, social, perceptual, psychomotor and physical, language, and occupational aptitudes and interest. Definitions for each of these major skill areas are provided in Figure 10–7.

As you have seen in Chapters 6 and 8, this common list of basic skills and concepts can be effectively used for several purposes in the instructional development process:

1. To identify the areas in which a learner is strong or weak in certain basic skills or the understanding of basic concepts
2. To identify the basic skills and concepts required in a given occupation or cluster of occupations
3. To develop instructional content and strategies focused on remediation of basic skills needed in the student's area of occupational interest

4. To evaluate the learner's progress in attaining the needed basic skills

The Index of Basic Skills and Concepts is to be used as a reference by the cooperating instructional team to identify the basic skills and concepts to be included in modules for selected special needs students. This Index is intended *only* as a reference. It is not necessarily exhaustive or complete. Other lists, such as those mentioned earlier, may also be helpful aids. Teachers are encouraged to rearrange the basic skills by category, insert additional basic skills or concepts, or modify the Index in any way necessary for it to meet their instructional development needs.

FIGURE 10-7. MAJOR AREAS OF THE BASIC SKILL/CONCEPT INDEX

MAJOR AREA	DEFINITION
Quantitative and numerical skills	Involves the ability to count, record, perform basic arithmetic processes, measure, and otherwise use or manipulate numerical information
Verbal skills	Involves the ability to communicate in written and spoken forms
Cognitive skills	Involves the ability to follow instructions, remember, sequence information, plan, organize, and make decisions
Perceptual skills	Involves the ability to accurately perceive colors, forms, space, sounds, and odors
Language skills	Involves the ability to listen, understand, and express oneself using written and oral forms of language
Psychomotor and physical skills	Involves the ability to coordinate and perform physical movements
Social skills	Involves the ability to interact with others and act independently in an acceptable manner
Occupational interests and aptitudes	Involves the ability to determine one's occupational likes and dislikes and to adjust to changing work situations

FIGURE 10-8. BASIC SKILL AND CONCEPT INDEX

AREA: QUANTITATIVE AND NUMERICAL SKILLS		
01	Counting and recording	Reads, counts, and/or records numerical information accurately
02	Cardinal numbers	Reads, interprets, and writes cardinal numbers up to four digits
03	Ordinal numbers	Reads, interprets, and writes ordinal numbers up to four digits
04	Addition/subtraction	Performs simple addition and subtraction computations accurately
05	Multiplication/division	Performs simple multiplication and division computations accurately
06	Measurement	Performs or interprets the following measurements correctly and accurately a. distance-size b. weight-volume-balance c. liquids-solids d. time (measurement of) e. temperature-pressure-humidity f. torque g. electrical units h. vertical-horizontal i. degrees of a circle (angularity)
07	General numerical usage	Recognizes and affixes meaning to zip codes, social security numbers, street addresses, etc.
08	Fraction	Reads, interprets, and uses common fractions, e.g., ½, ¼, ⅓, etc.
09	Money	Recognizes common denominations of coins and bills and can make change accurately
10	Roman numerals	Reads, interprets, and writes common roman numerals
11	Approximations	Estimates and judges distances, height, weight, or size accurately

[1] Adapted from: Hemenway, R., et al., *Learner-Behavior-Task Rating Scale.* Normal: Illinois State University, January 1975; Reynolds, M. L., Lutz, R. J., Johnson, C. B., and Phelps, L. A., *Task-Related Competencies.* Mt. Pleasant: Central Michigan University, 1974; and U.S. Department of Labor. *Dictionary of Occupational Titles,* Third Edition. Washington D.C.: Government Printing Office, 1965.

FIGURE 10-8. *(Continued)*

	AREA: QUANTITATIVE AND NUMERICAL SKILLS	
12	Configuration	Discriminates differences in shape, form, texture, and size

	AREA: VERBAL SKILLS	
13	Reading	Reads with comprehension at the fifth grade level or above
14	Spelling	Spells common words accurately
15	Recording information	Maintains accurate records of performance on production
16	Verbal communication	Uses words effectively when asking or responding to questions
17	Written communication	Writes a series of sentences on a given subject
18	Match and differentiate	Discriminates accurately between items which are similar and dissimilar
19	Form completion	Provides complete information on common forms, e.g., social security card application
20	Telephone communication	Uses the telephone to obtain information
21	Accuracy	Checks, when necessary, to be sure that task was performed accurately

	AREA: COGNITIVE SKILLS	
22	Retention	Remembers critical information such as names, locations, procedures, etc.
23	Sequencing	Processes information accurately for determining an appropriate order or sequence for objects
24	Attentiveness	Concentrates on a task and is not easily distracted
25	Planning ability	Plans ahead for completion of a task
26	Organization	Approaches problems in a systematic manner
27	Decision making	Selects from among alternatives independently
28	Follows verbal instructions	Understands spoken instructions containing more than one idea

FIGURE 10-8. *(Continued)*

	AREA: COGNITIVE SKILLS	
29	Follows written instructions	Reads and follows written instructions as communicated by signs, safety labels, procedure manuals, etc.
30	Mechanical aptitude	Demonstrates a working knowledge of mechanical principles (e.g., levers, inertia, motion, etc.)
31	Perseverence	Sees the task through to completion
32	Transfer	Uses information gained from previously learned skills to a new task

	AREA: PERCEPTUAL SKILLS	
33	Auditory discrimination	Makes fine distinctions from sound cues and recognizes normal and abnormal sounds
34	Form perception	Sees details of objects, graphs, pictures and can compare difference in size and shape
35	Form discrimination	Recognizes differences between a variety of forms (two-dimensional), solid shapes, sizes, and textures
36	Space perception	Recognizes forms and objects in their spatial relationships accurately
37	Color discrimination	Recognizes primary colors, sees differences and similarities between shades
38	Touch discrimination	Determines size, shape, temperature, moisture content, or texture by means of touch
39	Perceptual information	Obtains information through sight, shape, size, distance, motion, color, and other unique characteristics
40	Olfactory discrimination	Differentiates a variety of smells

	AREA: LANGUAGE SKILLS	
41	Listening	Listens attentively and for the purpose of remembering when others are talking
42	Grammar	Uses appropriate grammatical expressions in sentence form

FIGURE 10-8. *(Continued)*

	AREA: LANGUAGE SKILLS	
43	Technical vocabulary	Recognizes and comprehends technical vocabulary words at a level sufficient for educational and social communication
44	Nonverbal expression	Reacts to voice tone, inflection, facial expression, choice of words, and gestures, and recognizes emotions and feelings
45	Generalizing	Draws conclusions, makes accurate assumptions from receptive language
46	Classification	Classifies meaningful language symbols, e.g., principal and bosses are authorities

	AREA: PSYCHOMOTOR AND PHYSICAL SKILLS	
47	Physical strength (check the appropriate level)	Uses physical strength to lift, carry, push, or pull objects in a variety of work situations: a. Sedentary work (mostly sitting and required to lift a maximum of ten pounds) b. Light work (considerable standing or walk or work movements while sitting and required to lift up to twenty pounds) c. Medium work (many work movements while sitting and required to lift up to fifty pounds) d. Heavy work (required to lift up to 100 pounds and/or carry up to eighty pounds) e. Very heavy work (required to lift over 100 pounds)
48	Hand-eye coordination	Coordinates movements of eyes and hands, and fingers rapidly and accurately
49	Eye-hand-foot coordination	Coordinates feet and hands in response to visual or auditory cues
50	Bi-manual coordination	Coordinates the use of both hands efficiently
51	Manual dexterity	Moves and coordinates hands with skill and ease in placing and turning motions; uses common hand tools

FIGURE 10-8. *(Continued)*

AREA: PSYCHOMOTOR AND PHYSICAL SKILLS		
52	Reaching, grasping	Reaches and grasps objects, adequately using upper extremeties
53	Finger dexterity	Manipulates small objects with fingers rapidly and accurately
54	Mobility	Walks or moves to appropriate locations with little or no problem
55	Equilibrium	Maintains body equilibrium to prevent falling or stumbling when walking, standing, running, or crouching
56	Kneeling, climbing, crawling	Demonstrates good use of lower extremities and body muscles in body movement

AREA: SOCIAL SKILLS		
57	Social acceptance	Likes and is sought out by peers
58	Sociability	Participates actively in group activities; seeks out friends
59	Sensitivity	Expresses feelings of warmth toward others; is sensitive to feelings and needs of others
60	Social invisibility	Blends in with groups and activities smoothly; exhibits behavior appropriate to the circumstances
61	Cooperativeness	Cooperates with peers and others for the accomplishment of a group task
62	Appropriate behavior	Does not exhibit inappropriate gestures, verbalizations, actions, mannerisms, etc.
63	Character	Considered dependable by peers and others
64	Punctuality	Is on time regularly for activities and events; accepts responsibility for tardiness
65	Self-initiation	Initiates work on task promptly and without being directed to
66	Responsibility	Assumes and carries out tasks in a responsible manner

FIGURE 10-8. *(Continued)*

AREA: SOCIAL SKILLS		
67	Attentiveness	Listens to directions; follows instructions; attends to task as required
68	Conformity	Accepts rules and regulations whether or not he/she agrees with them
69	Seeks help	Requests assistance from others and/or peers when encountering difficulty
70	Distractibility	Stays on task when others are nearby or after experiencing non-work-related problems
71	Loyalty	Never or rarely complains about peers, teachers, others, or tasks
72	Appearance	Dresses appropriate to the situation; well groomed
73	Absence of supervision	Works at a consistent rate when unsupervised; works well without direct, continuous supervision
74	Safety	Demonstrates a concern for and takes appropriate action to maintain safe conditions

AREA: OCCUPATIONAL INTERESTS AND APTITUDES		
75	Work adjustment capability	Adjusts to and performs tasks under the following conditions: a. Frequent changes in duties b. Assignment of specific tasks that seldom require independent action or judgment c. Working apart from others d. Stressful, unexpected, or risk-taking situations e. Making judgments and decisions on subjective criteria, e.g., feeling, common sense
76	Occupational interests	Prefers involvement in activities that: a. Involve things and objects b. Are routine and concrete

FIGURE 10-8. *(Continued)*

AREA: OCCUPATIONAL INTERESTS AND APTITUDES	
	c. Involve people and interpersonal communication
	d. Are scientific or technical
	e. Are abstract or creative in nature
	f. Involve processes and machines
	g. Result in tangible, productive satisfaction

A Key Question: Are the Basic Skills Prerequisites for Entering Occupational Education? In one sense the basic skills/concepts can be viewed as those skills that learners must have before they can undertake the learning of a task. This view suggests that certain developmental levels must be reached before students can be expected to undertake and complete successfully learning experiences that require higher levels of ability. Certainly this is reasonable and logical in situations where there are gross differences between the developmental levels in question. For example, it is obvious that a certain minimal level of hearing is a basic prerequisite if one expects to take or learn to take a patient's blood pressure (given the current medical technology for this procedure).

The major problem with this notion of prerequisite basic skills is that, in most instances, it is extremely difficult to determine which basic skills or concepts are essentially prerequisite to learning a given task. General patterns of motor development, socialization, and language development have been noted by child psychologists and others who have studied human development. Within any of these "general" patterns of development, however, certain sequential stages may not occur in the same sequence nor at the same age for all individuals. For example, some children learn to walk at ten months, others at sixteen or twenty months. Some learn to talk before they walk.

The point is essentially this: It is difficult to predict with precision exactly what level of basic skill one needs to attain in order to learn a given task successfully. Therefore, there is room to suggest that if the prospective special needs learner has attained certain minimal competencies that are important for task performance, that should be sufficient to permit the student to initiate the instructional module. In all likelihood, if the special needs student in question is recommended for placement in an occupational program, the specialists and professionals who are suggesting this placement can substantiate that she or he has attained at least minimum levels of competence in the areas critical to vocational achievement. If the basic skills and concepts are viewed by occupational educators as prerequisites and are used to screen students out of occupational programs, they have been seriously misused.

Basic Skill Enhancement or Refinement. The basic skills and concepts can also be viewed as abilities to be further developed and refined through career-related instructional experiences. Some occupational and special educators will view occupational instruction, such as "tuning up a two-cycle gas engine," also as an opportunity to increase the learner's basic skill in reading comprehension. It has been demonstrated that many special needs learners have poor reading comprehension primarily because they find traditional methods of reading instruction to be uninteresting. If, however, a student is enthusiastically involved in servicing a lawn mower engine, he is readily motivated to read when he realizes the information he needs to complete his project must be obtained by reading and accurately comprehending information in the engine service manual.

Successful remediation of certain basic skills can readily occur in career-related instructional programs. If occupational and special educators are successful in remediating and refining these skills the learner may, for all practical purposes, no longer have a special need. Once it is reasonably certain that he has obtained and demonstrated the necessary basic skills and occupational competencies to perform successfully on the job, the cooperative instructional team has successfully fulfilled its mission.

Basic Skill/Concept Content

The third major component of the module outlines the specific instructional content related to the basic skills and concepts previously specified. This section of the instructional module identifies specifically those things that the special or basic education instructor can directly emphasize in supportive instruction to assist in remediation of the identified basic skills and concepts.

For each basic skill and concept listed in the center column of the first page of the module, information detailing the specific content of the skill or concept is needed. Since special education and other supportive staff are likely to be unfamiliar with the vocational context of the task, it is extremely important that they be provided specific information enabling them to teach or remediate the basic skill or concept. Technical vocabulary, for instance, is a commonly listed basic skill/concept. To note that the student is deficient in technical vocabulary for his auto mechanics class is really of little help to the cooperating special needs or special education teacher. However, if the module being developed is focused on "performing a light tune-up," several technical terms pertinent to this module (e.g., "spark plugs, points, or dwell") can readily be identified. This information then is referred to as the basic skill/concept content for the remediation of language skills such as "increasing technical vocabulary."

This additional content information for each of the basic skills/concepts is provided so that the special education teacher or other cooperating instructional team members become familiar with the nature and scope of the task. Generating this information on the module leads to a clearer understanding of what the task actually involves and provides some meaningful, relatable content for each member of the cooperative team to teach.

Cooperating Teacher Involvements. An examination of the eight major areas of basic skills/concepts suggests that a number of different types of teachers could be involved in teaching the basic skill/concept content. A number of teachers and professionals in the school in addition to the special education staff could be involved. General or remedial math teachers could provide assistance for special students in the quantitative numerical skills area. Reading specialists and speech therapists could help in the verbal and language skills area. Physical and occupational therapists could provide various types of therapy and assistance in the area of psychomotor and physical skill development. Counselors or others may be helpful as cooperating team members in the social skills area.

These are just a few of the professionals who could become involved in the cooperative instructional arrangement in addition to the special education teacher. As noted in Chapter 9—Developing a Cooperative Instructional Arrangement—a number of situational factors such as the student's school placement or grade level are likely to be influential in determining who can provide the needed supportive services.

Monitoring the Development of Basic Skills

When the cooperative team is identifying the basic skills/concepts and the specific instructional content for each of these, they will undoubtedly be concerned with what level of skill or understanding students may already have in each area. For instance, under the technical vocabulary skill for Gary's task of "building a floor frame model," he may know—prior to instruction—some of the specific terms such as "floor joist" or "sill." As for "common nails" and "box nails," he may know what nails are but not be able to identify these two specific types. Other terms or concepts, such as "penny" (nail size), he may be totally unfamiliar with.

The second learner progress column on the right hand front side of the instructional module form is designed to help teachers keep track of progress students have attained in the basic skills and concepts. It is essentially an evaluation checklist, similar to the learner progress column on the opposite edge of the form, and can be used in an identical manner. As students attain the various levels of basic skill development—introduced, developing, competent—the special or basic education teacher puts a check or date notation in the appropriate column.

The example module describing Gary's task (Figure 10-4) shows that he is already competent in his understanding of the technical vocabulary terms "floor joist" and "header," and he has some understanding of "common nails" and "box nails" but needs to develop it further. Finally, the learner progress column notes that on September 15 he was introduced to the term "girder plate," a term with which the entrance test indicated he was not familiar.

Instructional Activities

There are two basic components to any instructional design: the content and the method. In other words, instructional plans must specify *what* is to be taught or learned, and also *how* it will be taught or learned. An instructional activity, as the term will be used here, represents the latter of these components. *Instructional activity* describes the teacher and learner activities to be used in conveying the instructional content outlined by the occupational performance objectives and the basic skill/concept content. The instructional activities are outlined on the back side of the single sheet instructional module format.

Several examples of instructional activities designed for individual special needs learners in different career exploration and preparation programs are presented in Figures 10–2b, 10–3b, and 10–4b. It will be helpful to review the instructional activities designed for Sadie, Mark, and Gary, since they will be referred to throughout this section.

Methods of Instruction. The instructional activity can generally be regarded as a description of the instructional methods to be used. It will, however, involve more than simply stating the method such as lecture or demonstration. In order for the methods of instruction and their purpose to be fully understood by the occupational and special education team, the specific activities to be engaged in by the teachers and the learners during the module need to be described.

Involvement in Planning. Here again, it is important that occupational and special education personnel be collectively involved in selecting and planning the instructional activities for each module. Tips and suggestions provided by special educators will help occupational educators adapt their teaching methods to suit the learning style of the special learners they have in class. Conversely, occupational educators can provide instructional materials and general descriptions of certain occupational tasks—reading a micrometer, for example—which will be helpful to special educators in teaching job-related skills such as measuring.

Designing Instructional Activities. There are basically six steps that the team should follow in designing the instructional activities for a module.

1. *Select the general method or instructional approach.* We have noted in earlier chapters that special needs learners, as a group, vary significantly in the ways by which they learn. One of the basic principles, therefore, in selecting methods is to consider first a wide variety of methods, then attempt to select a general instructional approach that can effectively convey the content and that is also appropriate for the learner's style.

   Johnson and Johnson (1970) have identified twenty-five general instructional methods or approaches. Figure 10-9 provides a brief description of each of the twenty-five methods. This list should be reviewed carefully as the first step in designing an instructional activity.

FIGURE 10-9. GENERAL INSTRUCTIONAL METHODS

Comparative analysis. A thought process, structured by the teacher, employing the description, classification, and analysis of more than one system, group, or the like so as to ascertain and evaluate similarities and differences.

Conference. A one-to-one interaction between teacher and learner where the individual's needs and problems can be dealt with. Diagnosis, evaluation, and prescription may all be involved.

Demonstration. An activity in which the teacher or another person uses examples, experiments, and/or other actual performance to illustrate a principle or show others how to do something.

Diagnosis. The continuous determination of the nature of learning difficulties and deficiencies, used in teaching as a basis for the selection—day by day or moment by moment—of appropriate content and methods of instruction.

Directed observation. Guided observation provided for the purpose of improving the study, understanding, and evaluation of that which is observed.

Discussion. An activity in which pupils, under teacher and/or pupil direction, exchange points of view concerning a topic, question, or problem to arrive at a decision or conclusion.

Drill. An orderly, repetitive learning activity intended to help develop or fix a specific skill or aspect of knowledge.

Experimentation. An activity involving a planned procedure accompanied by control

From Johnson, S. R., and Johnson, R. B. *Developing Individualized Instructional Material.* New York: Westinghouse Learning Corporation, 1970. Used with permission.

FIGURE 10-9. *(Continued)*

of conditions and/or controlled variation of conditions together with observation of results for the purpose of discovering relationships and evaluating the reasonableness of a specific hypothesis.

Field experience. Educational work experience, sometimes fully paid, acquired by pupils in a practical service situation.

Field Trip. An educational trip to places where pupils can study the content of instruction directly in its functional setting, e.g., factory, newspaper office, or fire department.

Group work. A process in which members of the class, working cooperatively rather than individually, formulate and work toward common objectives under the guidance of one or more leaders.

Laboratory experience. Learning activities carried on by pupils in a laboratory designed for individual or group study of a particular subject matter area, involving the practical application of theory through observation, experimentation, and research, or, in the case of foreign language instruction, involving learning through demonstration, drill, and practice. This applies also to the study of art and music, although such activity in this instance may be referred to as a studio experience.

Lecture. An activity in which the teacher gives an oral presentation of facts or principles, the class frequently being responsible for notetaking. This activity usually involves little or no pupil participation by questioning or discussion.

Manipulative and tactile activity. Activity by which pupils utilize the movement of various muscles and the sense of touch to develop manipulative and/or perceptual skills.

Modeling and imitation. An activity frequently used for instruction in speech, in which the pupils listen to and observe a model as a basis upon which to practice and improve their performance.

Problem-solving. A thought process structured by the teacher and employed by the pupils for clearly defining a problem, forming hypothetical solutions, and possibly testing the hypothesis.

Programmed instruction. Instruction utilizing a workbook or mechanical and/or electronic device which has been "programmed" to help pupils attain a specified level of performance by 1) providing instruction in small steps, 2) asking one or more questions about each step in the instruction and providing instant knowledge of whether each answer is right or wrong, and 3) enabling pupils to progress at their own pace.

Project. A significant, practical unit of activity having educational value, aimed at one or more definite goals of understanding and involving the investigation and solution of problems.

Reading. Gathering information from books, periodicals, encyclopedias, and other printed sources of information, including oral reading and silent reading by individuals.

Recitation. Activities devoted to reporting to a class or other group about information acquired through individual study or group work.

Role-play. An activity in which students

FIGURE 10-9. *(Continued)*

and/or teacher take on the behavior of a hypothetical or real personality in order to solve a problem and gain insight into a situation.

Seminar. An activity in which a group of pupils, engaged in research or advanced study, meets under the general direction of one or more staff members for a discussion of problems of mutual interest.

Sensitivity training. An activity in which a group and a trainer meet to self-consciously examine their immediate feelings and perceptions about themselves and each other in order to gain skill in authentic communication, leadership, behavioral flexibility, or social sensitivity.

Shopwork. An activity emphasizing skill development through experience in woodwork, metal work, or other industrial processes and procedures.

Skill practice session. All activity in which pupils have opportunity to put into practice those skills and understandings previously learned through other instructional activities.

2. *Identifying Teacher Activities.* Once the general instructional method or methods is selected, the team must begin to consider the specific activities they will have to carry out. Teacher activities for both the occupational instructional and basic skill/concept instruction should be listed. In starting, teachers should not attempt to develop an instructional procedure but should instead identify several *different* alternative activities that could be used to teach the content. Because special needs learners tend to vary so greatly in their learning needs, and because the motivation of individual students may change during the course of instruction, a variety of teacher activities should be planned. When one activity or technique doesn't work, the instructional team can immediately refer to the module and then begin trying another activity.

   The teacher and learner activities should be written as short descriptive statements describing the interaction of teacher-student-instructional materials or media.

3. *Identifying Learner Activities.* Learner activities will describe what the learner will be doing in both the occupational education and basic or special education classes. The learner activities will, of course, be directly related to the teacher activities. Here again, it is best to describe a number of *different* types of activities rather than a sequence of learning activities that all special needs learners will be involved in.

4. *Incorporating Special Teaching Techniques.* The real key to a successful and effective special needs program rests on the ability of the instructional team to adapt and use special teaching techniques that effectively reach the special needs student. It has been noted by Gold (1972) and others that we have a severe lack of instructional technology for teaching the handicapped. The ability to devise effective techniques that are different from what we do with "regular" or nonspecial needs students is at the heart of the instructional development process.

   Even though educators lack the technology needed to reach every special needs learner, a number of special techniques, procedures, or teaching tricks (if you care to call them that) have emerged from the fields of rehabilitation, special education, psychology, and learning theory. Probably the most comprehensive list of these is presented in Robert Smith's book, *Clinical Teaching* (1974). Figure 10–10 provides a summary list of special teaching techniques that are most appropriate for mildly or moderately handicapped learners.

FIGURE 10–10. SPECIAL TEACHING TECHNIQUES AND PRINCIPLES

Reinforcement of desired behavior. Providing immediate and appropriate reinforcement following a behavior that is to be increased or strengthened.

Use a token system, punch card, or green-stamp system to provide an ongoing reward/reinforcement system.

When teaching new skills, reinforce the learner's correct response on every occasion.

Reinforce reasonable degrees of progress toward the final goal.

To eliminate undesirable behaviors, competing or incompatible behaviors must be found and introduced. As these contending behaviors occur, the positive one(s) should be heavily reinforced.

Certain behaviors can be changed simply by removing certain negative conditions or inhibitors. It is important to be aware of these factors and remove the ones necessary to expand and strengthen desired behaviors.

After a behavior has become established, changing the reinforcement from a regular to variable-ratio schedule will assure its stability.

Exercise. Opportunities to repeat and practice experiences in a variety of ways.

Adapted from R. M. Smith, *Clinical Teaching: Methods of Instruction for the Retarded,* 2nd ed. (New York: McGraw-Hill, 1974.) Used with permission.

FIGURE 10-10. *(Continued)*

Distributed practice. Practice in learning concepts and most other material should be spread out, or varied according to the characteristics of each student as well as the nature of the material.

Active participation. Action involvement in a task readily facilitates learning and has several advantages:

It focuses the learner's attention on the task at hand.

It fosters greater efficiency in learning.

It provides a dynamic source of feedback.

It gives more opportunities for meaningful reinforcements for desired behavior.

Overlearning. Practicing a task beyond the point of initial mastery. Improvement in learning, retention, transfer, and relearning will be facilitated by overlearning.

Stressing accuracy. Stressing accuracy instead of speed will reduce the chance of learner's practicing errors. This is especially important in the learning of new material and basic concept formation.

Minimal change. Shifts in concepts and instructional content focus should be as minimal as possible. Retention and continuity of generalization can be maintained if the progressive steps are small and blended together well.

Utilizing the learner's strengths. It is important to utilize the learner's strengths (e.g., nanipulative skills) to enhance development of weaker areas (e.g., quantitative reasoning).

5. *Using Prescriptive Teaching Techniques.* Prescriptive teaching techniques are those techniques that can be matched to certain learning problems or characteristics. As suggested throughout this chapter, the instructional team must attempt to plan and implement instructional content and teaching techniques that are specifically focused on remediating the learner's special needs. Carter (1975) has identified and indexed a number of common learning problems exhibited by special needs learners and suggested prescriptive teaching techniques for each learning problem. Prior to examining the learning characteristics and prescriptive techniques offered by Carter (Figure 10-11), another word of caution regarding the generalizability of these techniques should be provided. The techniques provided for each learning problem area are only *suggested* techniques. It is not accurate to assume that all special needs learners exhibiting these

individual learning characteristics will benefit from each or all of the prescribed techniques.

The instructional team can readily incorporate these prescriptive techniques in a module by crosschecking the basic skills/concepts identified on the module with the problem characteristic categories identified by Carter. For instance, the first problem characteristic category, "reads slowly," matches the basic skill/concept of reading in the Verbal Skills area.

FIGURE 10-11. LEARNING CHARACTERISTICS AND SUGGESTED TEACHING TECHNIQUES FOR SPECIAL NEEDS LEARNERS

CHARACTERISTICS	SUGGESTED TECHNIQUES
Reads slowly	Supply information in forms other than the written text.
	Allow student to practice reading very brief selections in class.
	Build motivation by showing place of reading in life and employability.
	Use yourself and others as models of people who like to read.
	If possible, arrange for a tutor.
Is slow to grasp generalizations	Move from the simple to the complex.
	Try to always relate sub-concepts to major concepts.
	Present ideas or concepts in various ways.
	Summarize every lesson.
Has difficulty with abstract ideas	Present actual sample of each object studied, and give concrete example of each concept introduced.
	Relate abstractions to reality in terms of the student's perception.
	Build instruction on student's experience.
Fails to broaden perspective	Plan short, local field trips.
	Teach local transportation means.
Solves problems slowly, can't make decisions	Provide information on the problem-solving and decision-making processes.

From R. M. Carter, "Teacher Behavior and Classroom Casualties," *American Vocational Journal,* 1975, 50, 6. Used with permission.

FIGURE 10-11. *(Continued)*

CHARACTERISTICS	SUGGESTED TECHNIQUES
	Analyze case situations for ways to identify and solve problems. Give student practice in solving practical problems as identified by the class. Use cooperative planning to solve organizational problems in the classroom.
Perceives time differently	Teach time concepts. Reorient your own emphasis on time. Relate punctuality to employability.
Has poor visual perceptions or perceives shapes differently	Make use of audio means of learning. Use large, clearly defined visuals; employ high intensity contrast. Allow student to handle objects. Refer to physical and psychological therapists.
Lies or stretches the truth	Use group feedback techniques. Role-play reversal situations. Relate behavior to dependability. Teach honesty as it applies to employability.
Is prejudiced or biased	Emphasize that all people possess the same human qualities. Stress the richness of cultural diversity. Organize a "learn about people" fair. Provide a model of an unprejudiced behavior.
Is overconcerned with surface appearance	Serve as a model who values people for what they are, not for their outward appearance. Use value clarification techniques. Use encounter devices.
Is insecure	Be consistent and fair. Make ground rules understandable and enforceable. Use devices to build self-confidence. Move the student toward responsibility for self and learning.
Feels trapped by fate	Permit student input into decision making. Give instruction in decision making in society.

FIGURE 10-11. *(Continued)*

CHARACTERISTICS	SUGGESTED TECHNIQUES
	Through school activities, show how individuals affect events. Show community action projects run by local people.
Feels isolated and ignored	Use participation gimmicks in class. Develop friendship skills and attitudes. Use group feedback and analysis techniques. Involve student in planning committees for school activities.
Is uneasy in social situations	Provide instruction in social behavior. Practice social behavior in class. Involve students in extracurricular activities.
Is sensitive to own differences	Teach human variability concepts. Build tolerance of self and others. Use positive group feedback techniques. Discuss problem frankly.
Demands structured environment	Develop cooperative ground rules for classroom activities. Teach concepts related to self-confidence. Build from dependence to independence.
Verbalizes excessively	Record and analyze conversations. Teach interaction principles. Use transactional analysis. Plan nonverbal activities, including manipulative activities.
Is physically aggressive	If possible, provide energy outlets. Relate aggression to its consequences. Refer to counselor.
Is argumentative	Analyze transactions in class. Record class verbalizations. Show how contentiousness can affect employability.
Uses sarcasm directed at people	Portray probable effect on human relationships. Use group feedback techniques. Role-play reversal situations.

FIGURE 10-11. *(Continued)*

CHARACTERISTICS	SUGGESTED TECHNIQUES
Expresses hostility toward people and ideas	Use transactional analysis. Use encounter group activities. Teach human relations concepts, showing results of hostility in terms of human relationships. Use counselors as resource persons. Plan step-by-step improvement.
Lives in a deteriorating environment	Teach community action concepts. Build toward leadership behavior. Teach managerial skills. Work on practical housing ideas. Teach consumer protection.
Has grooming problems	Teach grooming skills. Relate grooming to employability.
Appears apathetic, lazy, or bored	Build motivational devices into classwork. Relate content to reality. Check for malnourishment. Investigate sleep patterns.
Displays atypical behavior	Record actions for purposes of analysis. Teach socially acceptable behavior. Show results of behavior in terms of employability.

6. *Checking the Appropriateness of an Instructional Activity.* Once the instructional team has completed the development of an instructional activity it is helpful to evaluate its appropriateness. This self-check evaluation can be helpful in improving any part of the activity before it is implemented. In assessing the appropriateness of the planned activity, the following questions should be addressed:

    a) Are several techniques or possible approaches to teaching the module listed?

    b) Are the learner activities too formal, perhaps too dry, and potentially boring or are they adventuresome and appealing?

c) Are the methods, techniques, and materials focused on overcoming a learning problem or are they busywork?

d) Do teachers and students have a choice of possible teaching-learning activities?

e) Does the instructional activity lock the teacher in or is it adaptable to different situations and creative or vicarious learning experiences?

f) Is one or more of the teacher or learner activities overused within this module or in several successive modules?

g) Have new or different instructional activities been substituted for ones that really work or that the learner really enjoys only for the purpose of change?

Instructional Resource Materials

It is extremely difficult, and impossible for all practical purposes, to consider the selection and use of instructional materials separate from the instructional activities. At times the availability of certain materials will dictate their use of a particular activity. More often, however, the selection of a particular activity. More often, however, the selection of a particular activity will imply the use of certain instructional materials.

This section will discuss identifying or selecting special instructional resource materials as part of developing or planning of modules. The analysis and evaluation of existing course materials, in light of their appropriateness for special needs learners, will be discussed in Chapter 12.

The instructional resource materials section of the module form is designed to identify those materials that will be needed to implement the suggested instructional activities. The module format presented earlier suggests that three items of information are required in identifying the instructional resource materials: title or name of the material, the media (i.e., film loop, transparency, etc.), and the source or reference notation describing where the material can be obtained.

What Kinds of Instructional Materials Are Appropriate? Instructional materials, like the instructional activities, must be selected to meet the needs of individual special needs learners. Thus, there is no one type of material that is more appropriate than another.

The interests of the learner are probably the most important consideration in determining the appropriateness of materials. Special needs learners with low level reading skills, perceptual problems, and short attention spans seldom attempt to read anything that is not of major interest or importance to them. Many special educators have found that publications like hot rod and motorcycle magazines are excellent motivators for getting students interested in reading. Before one can attempt to enhance reading or other similar basic skills, capturing the learner's interest in the occupational task is of crucial importance. In occupational and special education classes, selecting and using materials highly related to the learner's avocational or vocational interest is critical.

In many cases, instructional materials may have to be modified to make them appropriate for special needs learners. Regular texts or other printed information may have to be brailled, tape recorded, or purchased in large print versions for the visually handicapped student. Simplified and nonverbal materials containing symbols, charts, and graphic illustrations are important modifications for special learners with general reading difficulties. Numerous other suggested modifications can be made based on the learner's specific disability. Most of these, however, such as translating materials for Spanish-speaking students, are logical and straightforward.

Using Multimedia Materials. It is likely that different types of instructional materials or media will be required in implementing a set of instructional activities. A number of the principles and suggested special teaching techniques mentioned in the previous section are incorporated in the use of multimedia, multisensory instructional materials. Materials that involve the use of more than one sense (visual, auditory, tactile, olfactory, and salvatory) reflect the notion of using whatever sensory input channels are available to overcome difficulties being encountered with other channels. If, for instance, a learner is blind, his ability to hear and feel will serve as the primary channels through which he can process information. When special needs individuals lack the use of one or more sensory input channels, they tend to refine and maximize the use of their available senses and can pick up significant amounts of information as a result.

Figure 10-12 lists nineteen different types of media and indicates which are multisensory in nature. Obviously, those media that utilize multisensory involvement tend to be used more frequently with special needs learners than those which have limited sensory involvement.

Selecting and Sharing Instructional Materials. Undoubtedly, most of the instructional resource materials that are identified will be used with the students. In some instructional situation it is likely that the materials will

FIGURE 10-12. TYPES OF INSTRUCTIONAL MEDIA

	SENSORY INVOLVEMENT				
	VIS.	AUD.	TAC.	OLF.	SALV.
Demonstration with real objects or materials	X	X	X	X	X
3-D models—mockups	X	X	X	X	X
Games—simulators	X	X	X	X	X
Sound/slide programs	X	X			
Filmstrip—cassette/record	X	X			
TV—broadcast, closed circuit	X	X			
Video and/or audio recorder	X	X			
Film, 16mm—BW/color, sound	X	X			
Film loop, 8mm	X				
Filmstrip	X				
Slides	X				
Overhead transparencies	X				
Books, magazines, texts, booklets	X				
Pamphlets, brochures, manuals, workbooks	X				
Newspapers, cartoons	X				
2-D displays, charts, graphs, posters	X				
Drawings, photographs, schematics, maps	X				
Opaque projectuals	X				
Telephone, intercom		X			

Adapted from M. L. Reynolds, R. J. Lutz, C. B. Johnson, and L. A. Phelps, *Cluster Guides* (Series). (Mt. Pleasant: Central Michigan University, 1973.)

focus on occupational concepts. It is important that all of the materials to be used in both the occupational and special instructional activities be closely reviewed and jointly selected by the team. Considerations such as reading level, the learner's specific interests, and so on must be made.

As occupational and special teachers collectively plan the instructional strategies and materials to be used, an interesting interaction takes place. As the planning discussions continue, the special-basic education teacher or remediation specialist begins to learn more about the nature of the task the student is or will be learning. This happens as a natural outgrowth of the occupational teacher's explanation and description of how he or she teaches the task and the materials generally used. As this interaction continues, the special-basic education teacher can begin to identify and further refine the basic skills/concepts needed to perform the task. Through reviewing the occupational instructional materials and planning discussions, the special-basic education teacher begins to feel more comfortable in understanding the specifics of the task. Once the team gets into the instructional activities and materials to be used, a mutual feeling of confidence usually begins to emerge.

A great deal of useful instructional material can be identified by simply sharing materials with other teachers. Occupational teachers, by sharing with each other, can keep abreast of new commercially produced materials as well as teacher-prepared materials within their department. When occupational and special educators share and review instructional materials, not only can they become better acquainted with each other's instructional program but they can frequently offer suggestions regarding improving instructional materials. Special educators can help in substituting complex words and concepts with simpler ones. Occupational teachers can suggest job-related examples or applications for math problems.

Sources of Instructional Materials. A number of recent audiovisual and media catalogs list instructional materials that are appropriate for special needs learners. A very useful index describing over 500 vocational instructional materials for special needs students was published by the Northwest Regional Educational Laboratory in 1972 (Towne and Wallace 1972). This document and others listing instructional materials are contained in the references at the end of the chapter. The instructional media or resource center of a college or school library is also an excellent place to locate instructional materials directories that are comprehensive, descriptive, and current.

Checklist Progress Evaluation System

In addition to serving as a form for instructional planning, the module can also be used to monitor the special needs learner's progress. By closely monitoring a student's progress, a team can make adjustments and improvements in the plan as it is being implemented. Earlier sections of this chapter briefly mentioned the learner progress columns used to monitor attainment of the occupational performance objectives and the basic skills/concepts.

In earlier chapters heavy emphasis was placed on the need for continuous re-evaluation of the learner's achievement as well as various aspects of his or her general educational development. Emphasis was also placed upon developing performance objectives that would describe in observable, measurable terms what the learner was actually able to do. Both of these concerns are included in the instructional module format in the form of the learner progress column.

Learner Progress. Figures 10–2, 10–3, and 10–4, which were presented earlier, illustrate a four-column progress checklist that is placed next to the performance objectives section to the left on the module form. Within this four-column format teachers can record dates or checkmarks indicating the levels of attainment this particular learner has achieved regarding each of the performance objectives.

It should be noted that there is no technical reason or specific rationale for using four levels. Teachers can use any number of appropriate descriptors to depict the learner's progress. It may even be that the instructor chooses to place a checkmark or date in a single column next to the objectives when the learner has demonstrated successful performance of the objective. A four-step progress record, which includes the performance levels of introduced, involved, productive, and employable, has been found to be highly usable by the large group of occupational and special education teachers who have field tested and adopted this module format.

Another progress assessment column is located on the front, right-hand side of the module format and serves a function and purpose identical to that of the learner progress column on the left. The only differences are that three levels of progress are suggested (introduced, developing, and competent) and assessment is focused on the learner's attainment of the basic skill/concept content.

Using the Progress Checklists. During instruction, the team will frequently be together for at least two purposes: 1) to discuss how things are going and 2) to plan future modules. The progress checklists are designed to facilitate the first purpose.

It is recommended that the team develop some operational criteria or definitions for each of the progress levels identified in the two columns. If criterion levels are identified during the planning of the module, it facilitates planning and modifications during the early periods of instruction. You will remember that Gary (Figure 10–4) was already competent in some of the basic skill areas. With each of the levels defined, accurate and appropriate instructional content can be identified for individual learners who already have exhibited mastery of some or several of the performance objectives and basic skills/concepts.

Specifying Criterion Levels. Developing functional definitions for each level in the progress-monitoring columns is not an easy task; yet the degree to which the instructional team is able to identify and agree on what constitutes "employable" or "competent" performance is the key to successful monitoring of learner progress. Failure to specify the level of performance to be attained can result in misunderstandings of the target performance and inconsistency in communicating the performance and level of performance to parents or the learner during instruction.

Quantitative or qualitative criteria should be defined for each performance objective and basic skill. Criteria such as the following are generally appropriate for identifying terminal performance levels:

Correctly apply the three principles
Complete the task within fifteen minutes
Correctly identify eight out of ten

Provide the information requested on the form with 100 percent accuracy
In accordance with manufacturer's specifications

Descriptors for the interim or formative levels of performance—introduced, involved and productive—are also useful. Figure 10-13 provides some general example definitions for each of the formative levels for the occupational performance objectives.

Summarizing Learner Progress Information. Chapter 13 will address the problem of evaluating learner progress and reporting evaluative information. In this chapter the monitoring system used on the module form will

FIGURE 10-13. CRITERION LEVEL DESCRIPTORS FOR MONITORING LEARNER PROGRESS

OCCUPATIONAL PERFORMANCE OBJECTIVES

Introduced. The learner has become acquainted with the general task, as well as its function and/or purpose through previous experiences or instruction. However, the learner has not yet begun to develop or demonstrate any significant, recognizable competency in performing the task.

Involved. The learner has begun to develop and/or demonstrate minimal competence in performing a few selected parts (subskills) of the task.

Productive. The learner has developed and/or demonstrates a minimal level of competence in performing several parts (subskills) of the task. The learner would be employable in specialized, entry-level occupations requiring only minimal skills.

Employable. The learner has developed and/or demonstrates a level of competency that would make him or her employable in a normal, competitive work setting.

BASIC SKILLS/CONCEPTS CONTENT

Introduced. The learner has become acquainted with the basic skill or concept through previous experience and/or instruction.

Developing. The learner has demonstrated some capacity to perform the basic skill, and/or interpret and apply the basic concept.

Competent. The learner is capable of accurately and repeatedly performing the basic skill, or interpreting and applying the basic concept.

be incorporated into a total system for summarizing and reporting learner progress information using a learner performance record. Progress or achievement profiles are extremely useful in reporting progress information to prospective employers, parents, future teachers and others.

SUMMARY

Planning of instruction must include planning for both in-school and out-of-school instruction. This chapter focuses on the first of these while Chapter 11 will address the latter. Specific modules or units of instruction should logically be developed from an occupational cluster analysis process and be based on the major tasks identified.

Six components are essential in outlining an instructional unit or module for a special needs learner: 1) performance objectives that specify the occupational concepts and skills to be learned, 2) basic skills/concepts that specify the basic competencies to be developed by the learner prior to or during the instructional module, 3) basic skill/concept content that identifies those parts of the task that can be taught by special education or basic academic instructional staff, 4) instructional activities that describe the specific experiences the teachers and learner will undertake in both the occupational and special instruction situations, 5) instructional resource materials to be used as an integral part of the instructional activities, and 6) a system for monitoring learner attainment of the performance objectives and basic concepts/skills in the module. A module format along with examples, procedures, and suggestions for developing modules or units with these components is provided.

REFERENCES

Bailey, L. J., and Stadt, R. *Career education: New approaches to human development.* Bloomington, Ill.: McKnight, 1973.

Briggs, L. J., *Handbook of procedures for the design of instruction.* Pittsburgh, Pa.: American Institutes for Research, 1970.

Carter, R. M. Teacher behavior and classroom casualties. *American Vocational Journal*, 1975, 50, 55–57.

Clark, D. C. *Using instructional objectives in teaching.* Glenview, Ill.: Scott, Foresman, 1972.

Gagné, R. M., and Briggs, L. J. *Principles of instructional design.* New York: Holt, Rinehart, & Winston, 1974.

Gold, Marc W. Research on the vocational habilitation of the retarded: The present, the future. In N. R. Ellis (Ed.), *International review of research in mental retardation* (Vol. 6). New York: Academic, 1972.

Gronlund, N. E. *Stating behavioral objectives for classroom instruction.* New York: Macmillan, 1970.

Hemenway, R., et al. Illinois State University Informal Vocational Learner-Behavior-Task Rating Scale. Normal: Illinois State University, January 1975.

Johnson, S. R., and Johnson, R. B. *Developing individualized instructional material.* Palo Alto, Calif.: Westinghouse Learning Press, 1970.

Mager, R. F. *Preparing instructional objectives.* Palo Alto, Calif.: Fearon, 1962.

Mager, R. F., and Beach, K. M. *Developing vocational instruction.* Palo Alto, Calif.: Fearon, 1967.

Popham, W. J., and Baker, E. L. *Planning an instructional sequence.* Englewood Cliffs, N.J.: Prentice-Hall, 1970.

Reynolds, M. L., Lutz, R. J., Johnson, C. B., and Phelps, L. A. *Cluster guide* (Series). Mt. Pleasant: Central Michigan University, 1974.

Reynolds, M. L., Lutz, R. J., Johnson, C. B., and Phelps, L. A. *Program guide.* Mt. Pleasant: Central Michigan University, 1974.

Reynolds, M. L., et al. A project to train vocational education teachers and special education teachers to work cooperatively in occupational preparation of handicapped persons. Mt. Pleasant: Central Michigan University, 1974.

Smith, R. *Clinical teaching: methods of instruction for the mentally retarded.* New York: McGraw-Hill, 1974.

Towne, D. C., and Wallace, S. *Vocational instructional materials for students with special needs.* Portland, Oreg.: Northwest Regional Educational Laboratory, 1972.

U.S. Department of Labor. *Dictionary of Occupational Titles* (Vol. 3). Washington, D.C.: Government Printing Office, 1965.

Valett, R. E. *The remediation of learning disabilities.* Palo Alto, Calif.: Fearon, 1967.

DEVELOPING COOPERATIVE TRAINING PLANS

Much has been written about the importance and use of cooperative occupational education, work-study, and work experience as an essential vocational programming component for special needs learners. Programs of this type, in which the learner actually gains on-the-job experience, are crucial to a successful transition from school to work. The purpose of this section is to provide an overview of several different cooperative work experience programs or approaches that can be used in a special needs learner's instructional plan. The three basic types of work experience programs will be discussed and the role of the teacher-coordinator described. Also discussed will be the three key functions performed by the special

11

needs teacher-coordinator—developing training agreements, analyzing work stations, and evaluating the learner's work performance. Finally, the importance of and strategies for sequential programming will be presented.

This abbreviated discussion of work experience programs will focus only on the special considerations related to placing special needs learners in on-the-job situations. Several excellent comprehensive texts on planning, managing, and evaluating cooperative school-work programs are listed in the references at the end of the chapter for readers desiring more information.

It is important to note that the term "cooperative" is used here in a different context than it was in Chapter 9 and previous chapters where we described the cooperative instructional arrangement and the cooperating team of occupational and special educators. Cooperative work experience programs have traditionally been viewed as cooperative activities between the schools and the local business community. In essence, the business community cooperates in the occupational education of the learner. In this chapter we have expanded our initial concept of cooperation among in-school personnel to now include cooperation between the cooperative team of school personnel and employers in the community.

Before considering the process of developing cooperative training plans and its role in instructional planning, it will be beneficial to examine three different types of programs that utilize the work environment for learning. Special needs learners, depending upon their specific educational needs, can be served in any of the three basic types of cooperative work experience programs.

TYPES OF COOPERATIVE WORK EXPERIENCE PROGRAMS

Specifying the different types of cooperative work experience programs is not an easy task. Over the years occupational and special educators and rehabilitation personnel have used a multitude of different program titles and arrangements to implement programs providing learning experiences within sheltered and competitive work settings.

The three types to be presented here—cooperative occupational education, work-study, and work experience—differ primarily in the educational goals they are designed to achieve. Cooperative occupational education generally provides a capstone educational experience in which the competencies obtained in an occupational course can be further refined by on-the-job experience. The primary objective is to provide the learner with a job skill. Work-study programs, as they have been defined and developed in secondary special education programs, focus on providing learners with general, prevocational competencies through in-school and out-of-school work experiences. Work experience programs as well are designed to provide the student with general, prevocational competencies, but they also build in an emphasis on exploration and experimentation in different careers.

Cooperative Occupational Education

This program combines the learning experiences gained through regularly scheduled supervised employment in the community and occupationally oriented in-school instruction. The employing community serves as a laboratory where students have an opportunity to apply the principles and practices they have learned in school (State of Illinois 1972).

Generally, in cooperative occupational education plans the student has an established career objective, classroom instruction related to the career objective is provided, and there is an established work station and close supervision is provided by the school (Mason and Haines 1972).

Work-Study

Occupational education and special education personnel have implemented work-study programs for a number of years with different intents. Kolstoe and Frey (1965) and Smith (1974) have described special education work-study programs as involving work experiences within the school or in the community that are closely supervised by secondary level, special education personnel. Conversely, vocational educators have defined work-study as a program to provide financial assistance, through part-time employment, to students who have been accepted for full-time enrollment in vocational training (State of Illinois 1972). The primary purpose of vocational education work-study is usually to provide earning power and financial assistance for the student who is, frequently, enrolled in higher education. This definition of work-study has been generated from several pieces of legislation that authorize federal expenditures for vocational education.

The work-study program described by special educators is similar in several respects to the cooperative occupational education program. It differs in two respects, however. Special education work-study frequently involves using work or training stations (placements) within the school, whereas cooperative occupational education stations are usually community based. The second difference is that cooperative occupational education students are required to have taken or enroll concurrently in an occupational education course that provides them with a basic entry-level job skill. If, for instance, students are working part-time in an insurance office, they might also be enrolled in a second-year typing course or a bookkeeping course. This usually results in the cooperative occupational education student being placed in a higher level position.

Work Experience

Programs of this type are designed to provide students with exploratory and maturing experiences through employment or observation in the work place. In most instances when part-time work is involved, it need not be related to the occupational goals of the student. In fact, one of the objectives of most work experience programs is to assist learners in identifying and refining their career goals. A number of different programs of this type have been designed specifically to serve disadvantaged youth and adults who are early school leavers or potential dropouts, and who need both the social, emotional and maturational benefits and the career exploration opportunities essential for a successful transition or adaption to the world of work.

While some of these programs are highly similar to cooperative occupational education or special education work-study, they can be considered a separate type because a major purpose is career exploration *and* experimentation.

Probably the most prominent work experience program for special needs learners is the Work Experience and Career Exploration Program (WECEP), sponsored by the U.S. Department of Labor. WECEP is a school-supervised and school-administered program that includes part-time work as an integral part of the educational program aimed at motivating youth toward education and preparing them for the world of work. The program is designed to serve fourteen- and fifteen-year-old youth who are dropout-prone or who otherwise suffer educational disabilities.

WECEP was initiated as an experimental program to focus on those students who developed feelings of frustration or failure in academic achievements and who were waiting for their sixteenth birthday to drop out of school. However, providing employment and exploratory opportunities to this group required changes in the child labor laws, which are regulated by Employment Standards Division of the U.S. Department of Labor. The U.S. Office of Education also indicated that changes in the child labor regulations were necessary for the full intent of Congress to be served in providing vocational education for special needs populations under the 1968 Amendments of the Vocational Education Act.

During the early 1970s the Employment Standards Division waived the age restrictions to allow fourteen- and fifteen-year-old youth in approved programs in selected states to work up to twenty-eight hours a week when school was in session and up to four hours on a school day, any portion of which may be during school hours. As a result of the experimental programs these time periods were changed to maximums of twenty-three hours per week and three hours per day.

Each school district must meet the standards for approval as established by the state office of education. Applications for program approval must meet the following criteria (U.S. Department of Labor, 1975):

1. Any student aged fourteen or fifteen whom authoritative school personnel determine can benefit from the program can participate.
2. School credit toward graduation is received for both in-school related instruction and on-the-job experience.
3. Regularly scheduled classroom instruction devoted to *both* job-related and to employability skill instruction should be provided.
4. Appropriate instructional time in those classes required for graduation shall be allotted.
5. Assignment of twelve to twenty-five students to one teacher-coordinator.

6. A designated teacher-coordinator shall supervise and coordinate the work and education aspects of the program and make regularly scheduled visits to the work stations.
7. A written training agreement signed by the teacher-coordinator, the employer, and student (and approved by a parent or guardian) shall be prepared prior to the student's participation in the program.
8. Student learners can be assigned to work in any occupation except the following:
   a) Manufacturing and mining
   b) Occupations declared to be hazardous for the employment of minors between sixteen and eighteen years of age
   c) Occupations where the student learner would, in effect, displace a worker employed in the establishment of the employer.

THE COOPERATIVE WORK EXPERIENCE TEACHER-COORDINATOR

The teacher-coordinator is the central figure in establishing work experience programs for special needs learners and has numerous responsibilities. You will recall that Chapter 9 discussed and emphasized the role of the cooperative instructional team. In situations where the student is ready to be placed in an in-school or community-based work station, the teacher-coordinator assumes a major role in the cooperative instructional arrangement (see Figure 9-1).

To maximize the in-school resources fully, the teacher-coordinator should operate within the cooperative instructional arrangement format suggested in Chapter 9 where several examples of cooperative instructional arrangements involving teacher-coordinators are given. Arrangements of this type will greatly facilitate or maintain communication between the teacher-coordinator and occupational and special educators, counselors, school administrators, and job supervisors regarding individual learners.

Generally, placement occurs after the occupational and special education members of the team have provided the learner with the appropriate entry-level occupational and general social competencies necessary for him or her to function at a minimum level on the job. This may not always be the case, however, especially with the present expanding need to provide earlier opportunities for work to students who are potential dropouts.

A teacher-coordinator fills multiple roles when working with special needs learners. He or she is not only a coordinator of instructional activities within the school but between the school and the employer as well, coordinating the experiences encountered in the work setting with the instructional modules being implemented by himself or herself and other members of the cooperative instructional team. To fill this role adequately, the teacher-coordinator (Floyd et al. 1973) has the following responsibilities:

Secure jobs for students
Teach job-related class
Prepare training plans
Work with job-training supervisors
Visit students on the job
Prepare reports
Request or issue work permits and waivers
Keep student records
Evaluate student performance
Select or assist in selecting students to participate
Secure services of resource people
Hold individual student conferences
Promote program
Visit parents of students and prospective students
Organize an advisory committee
Develop instructional materials

A successful coordinator spends a great deal of time working and communicating with the community. His or her primary purpose is to coordinate in-school experiences with the supportive services and resources available in the community to assist the student encountering difficulties.

MAJOR COORDINATION FUNCTIONS

Teacher-coordinators perform several functions and use a multitude of forms in planning, coordinating, and evaluating work experience programs. The forms are a necessity primarily because of state and federal legal constraints—authorizing work permits, for instance—and the need to correlate the efforts and activities of unique in-school instruction and on-the-job experience for several students. Coordinators use forms or instruments for such functions as conducting community and student surveys, interviewing students, compiling application information and student data, rating employers and their supervisory personnel, and other operational functions of the program. Multiple examples of different forms, instruments, training plans, and so on can be found in the references at the end of the chapter.

Three of the functions commonly performed by teacher-coordinators (and use of associated forms) require some special consideration when special needs learners are involved. Many of the occupational or job analysis forms, training plans, and learner evaluation forms typically used are not appropriate or functional for outlining instructional activities and plans for special needs learners. In addition, many of these forms don't facilitate in-school coordination between the teacher-coordinator and special education and/or occupational education teachers.

Occupational or Training Station Analysis

Chapter 8 focused on the identification and analysis of occupational clusters. The purpose there was to systematically identify the competencies and relevant content for career exploration or preparation instruction in an occupational cluster or set of clusters. The procedures outlined focused on identifying the knowledges, skills, and basic skills/concepts required to successfully work in the occupational cluster area. It was noted that most occupational or job analysis criteria fail to consider the basic skills, concepts, and aptitudes, which special needs learners may lack, that are required in a job. Thus, it is critical that a part of the initial job analysis focus on these factors so that potential work experience trainees with special needs can be carefully matched to work stations where their limited functioning capacities are not required in their job performance.

Figure 11-1 shows a form that can be used to examine the essential personal characteristics or aptitudes required in an occupation being considered as a training station. The form was adapted from criteria used by Peterson and Jones (1964) in their efforts to develop personal characteristics

FIGURE 11-1. OCCUPATIONAL TRAINING STATION ANALYSIS FORM FOR USE WITH SPECIAL NEEDS LEARNERS

	Job Title: Auto Mechanic Helper		
ESSENTIAL PERSONAL CHARACTERISTICS	Low	Average	High
SOCIAL SKILLS			
1. *Self-expression.* Communicate, ask for assistance, question		✓	
2. *Sociability.* Interact with other employees or public		✓	
3. *Work independence.* Work without supervision or guidance	✓		
4. *Appearance.* Cleanliness, good mannerisms, neatness in appearance	✓		
5. *Teamwork.* Perform in close coordination with other jobs		✓	
TIME FACTORS			
1. *Pace.* Perform at a consistent rate of speed		✓	
2. *Attendance.* Be reliable in attendance and punctuality		✓	
3. *Simultaneity.* Perform several activities at nearly same time			✓
4. *Timing.* Perform timed, scheduled activities; be aware of time		✓	
PERFORMANCE SKILLS			
1. *Accuracy.* Perform within well-defined tolerances			✓
2. *Dexterity.* Make fine manipulations, coordinated movement			✓
3. *Choices.* Select among alternatives, make decisions.	✓		

Adapted from R. O. Peterson and E. M. Jones, *Guide to Jobs for the Mentally Retarded* (Washington, D.C.: American Institutes for Research, 1964.) Used with permission.

FIGURE 11-1 *(Continued)*

ESSENTIAL PERSONAL CHARACTERISTICS	Job Title: Auto Mechanic Helper		
	Low	Average	High
PERFORMANCE SKILLS *(continued)*			
4. *Direction.* Follow procedures, instructions, or directions		✓	
5. *Memory.* Remember locations, procedures, nomenclatures, etc.		✓	
6. *Caution.* Use care in activities that pose personal hazard			✓
TOLERANCE			
1. *Repetitiveness.* Have tolerance for monotony or repetition		✓	
2. *Perseverance.* Perform continuously, over normal periods		✓	
3. *Stamina.* Have physical stamina, strength, resist fatigue			✓

requirement profiles on jobs that would be appropriate for employable retardates.

When the data from this form is combined with a description of the actual job activities performed, for example, changing tires or servicing batteries, sufficient occupation analysis information is available to consider special needs learners for placement. However, before decisions can be made on whether or not a specific special needs learner can function effectively in the training station, the essential personal characteristics data should be compared with the learner profile data. When contrasted with the learner's profile of basic skills and occupational interests developed in Chapter 6, and when other pertinent information from parents, student records, and so on is considered, the teacher-coordinator is ready to make an initial decision with the help of the cooperative instructional team, on placement of a special needs student in the training station.

Formulating Training Agreements and Plans

The essential form used most frequently by teacher-coordinators is the training agreement or training plan. Once the training station and the job-related activities have been reviewed and analyzed by the teacher-coordinator and employer, the next step is formulating an agreement between the employer and school to authorize the work experience. Figure 11–2 illustrates an example form for the training agreement and plan.

This particular form has been modified from a conventional form for use with special needs learners and the instructional module planning process discussed earlier. For the employer's benefit, the form includes descriptive information about the learner. The in-school cooperative instructional team (the primary supporting teachers) is identified. The identification of related occupational and special education or supportive service personnel indicates to the employer that a concerted in-school effort will support the on-the-job learning experiences of the special needs learner.

Information describing the training site and job activities is crucial for the cooperative instructional team. If the job supervisor and teacher-coordinator can identify the specific activities the learner will be or is involved in at the training station, the appropriate instructional modules can be developed or selected for in-school instruction. If instructional modules or units similar to the ones described earlier are developed and used, an articulated instructional effort involving the occupational teacher, special or basic education teacher, and teacher-coordinator can be generated.

In certain school situations you may find that the special needs students' schedules cannot be structured to involve occupational education, special education, and cooperative work experience program placement simultaneously. Frequently, it is difficult to schedule students into these three programs concurrently because they must enroll in certain academic courses to fulfill graduation requirements. Also, all school districts may not be able to offer comprehensive programs in all three areas at the secondary

FIGURE 11-2. TRAINING AGREEMENT AND PLAN

Montclair High School Work Experience and Career Exploration Program
Jenkinsville, Iowa

Learner Phyllis Address 711 Kenyon, Jenkinsville Zip 68312
Phone 360-1212 Age 11 Birth date 3-12-61 S.S. No. 222-13-7661
High school Montclair Grade Junior Sex F
Date employment begins 1-15 Expected completion date 6-15
Starting rate of pay $3.12/hr. Daily schedule 1:30-5:30 p.m.
Total hours per day 4 Maximum hours per week 20

LEARNER'S COOPERATIVE INSTRUCTIONAL TEAM (IN-SCHOOL)

Occupational instructor Sue Loth Course Clothing Construction
Special services instructor Candy Jenkins Course or service Special ed.
Teacher-coordinator Lori Richards Related course Employment Orientation

COOPERATIVE TRAINING SITE

Employer Courier Clothing Address 1450 Abbas Avenue Phone 361-2161
City Jenkinsville Zip 68312 Supervisor Sam Pryor
Job title: Alteration Tailor

JOB ACTIVITIES	RELATED INSTRUCTIONAL MODULES	ID. NO.
Resew seams	Handstitching machine sewing	CTS-03 CTS-10
Remove stitching	Handstitching	CTS-03
Shorten pants	Alterations	CTS-08

FIGURE 11-2. *(Continued)*

JOB ACTIVITIES	RELATED INSTRUCTIONAL MODULES	ID. NO.
Alter suit/sports coat	Alterations Garment construction	CTS-08 CTS-06
Perform waist alterations	Alterations Garment construction	CTS-08 CTS-06

RESPONSIBILITIES OF PARTICIPATING PARTIES

A. Trainee will abide by the regulations and policies of his or her employer and the school.

B. The employer assumes the responsibility of providing the trainee with the broadest experience in keeping with the job activities.

C. The coordinator will arrange for in-school related instruction, consultation, and advisory service to parties concerned with this training program.

D. The employment of the trainee shall conform to all federal, state, local laws and regulations, including nondiscrimination against any applicant or employee because of race, color, or national origin.

E. This training program shall NOT be interrupted without prior consultation among the trainee, employer, and coordinator.

SIGNATURE OF PERSONS APPROVING THIS PROGRAM

Learner Phyllis Jobe *(signature)*

Employer Sam Pryor *(signature)*

Parent Mrs. Larry Jobe *(signature)*

Coordinator or school official Lori Richards *(signature)*

Date January 30

level. As a result, the teacher-coordinator may frequently also serve in the role of the occupational instructor or supportive services instructor.

Assessing Learner Performance

Another activity involved in coordinating cooperative experience programs is evaluating the learner's on-the-job performance. For special needs learners job performance evaluation, when conducted by the job supervisor, can be most helpful if it is focused on the basic skills, aptitudes, and attitudes that the learner demonstrates. Direct feedback to the instructional team during the work experience, as well as at the conclusion of on-the-job training, can be helpful in determining future placements or continuation of current placement, the need for additional supportive services, or the need to modify the in-school instructional program.

Figure 11–3 provides an example evaluation form for job supervisors to use in assessing such basic skill areas as social adjustment, personal adjustments, occupational skills, and personal habits. After completing a learner evaluation, the teacher-coordinator and supervisor should review and discuss the results and, if necessary, develop some specific action recommendations.

Work Experience Forms for Special Needs Learners

In addition to the forms mentioned previously, placing a special needs learner on a part-time job typically requires that certain additional state and federal forms be completed and submitted. The principal ones, which are required by federal child labor regulations, are applications for work permits, proof of age certificates, approval of certain occupations that are usually prohibited for minors, obtaining a handicapped worker certificate, and employing a student learner. Copies of these forms can be obtained from state or federal offices of the Department of Labor. Teacher-coordinators should also be familiar with any additional state forms required to place any underage or special needs learners in cooperative work experience stations.

FIGURE 11-3. COMPREHENSIVE WORK EXPERIENCE
STUDENT EVALUATION FORM

Trainee Phyllis Training station Courier Clothing
School Montclair H.S. Period of training from 1-15 to 2-15
Days absent 1 Job description Alteration Tailor

Please check (x) the level of functioning.

	ADEQUATE	SHOWS PROGRESS	UNSATIS-FACTORY	
				I. OCCUPATIONAL SKILLS
1.		X		Assumes responsibility
2.		X		Works without constant supervision
3.		X		Follows instructions
4.	X			Shows respect for tools and equipment
5.		X		Completes assigned work
6.	X			Works safely and carefully
7.		X		Pursues extra tasks
8.		X		Reports to work on time
9.		X		Effective use of time and materials
10.	X			Willingness to do same job repeatedly
11.	X			Knows terminology of job
12.				Accepts corrections and criticism
13.		X		Able to do job in time allotted
14.	X			Is accurate in job duties
15.		X		Is physically capable of doing job
16.	X			Attendance
				II. SOCIAL ADJUSTMENT
17.	X			Gets along with other workers and supervisor
18.	X			Demonstrates good manners
19.	X			Communicates well with people
20.		X		Exhibits mature attitudes
21.	X			Displays honesty
22.	X			Is loyal to employer

FIGURE 11–3 *(Continued)*

	ADEQUATE	SHOWS PROGRESS	UNSATIS-FACTORY	
				III. PERSONAL ADJUSTMENTS
23.	X			Makes friends with other employees
24.	X			Seeks ways to self-improvement
25.	X			Avoids improper mannerisms
26.	X			Demonstrates self-confidence
				IV. PERSONAL HABITS
27.	X			Proper dress for job
28.	X			Personal hygiene and grooming
29.		X		Keeps work area neat and clean

30. What can the student do to help herself improve? Depend less upon others for assistance

31. What can the school do to help the student improve? Encourage to rely less upon her co-workers for assistance because of her physical problem

32. What occupational skills did you as employer develop in the student? Very few – she has an excellent background in clothing construction and alteration

Date 2-15 Signature Sam Pryor
Employer or supervisor

Adapted from J. E. Wiggins et al., *Guidelines for the Establishment of Work Experience-and-Study Programs for Handicapped Children in Colorado* (Denver: Colorado Department of Education and Department of Social Services, 1971).

AN ARTICULATED PROGRAM FOR SPECIAL NEEDS LEARNERS

On-the-job work experience is one critical and essential component of instructional plans for special needs learners, but it is still only a component part of the plan. Although many occupational and special educators at the secondary level consider work experience to be the key component, it still must be articulated with prevocational, in-school experiences and full-time job placement and follow-up. This articulation is of crucial importance and must be managed carefully and prudently for there to be a successful transition from school to work and independent adult living by the special needs learner.

Smith (1974), Kolstoe and Frey (1965), and others have generally described a series of six sequential phases that provide a comprehensive perspective on an articulated program for special needs learners at the secondary level.

In-class activities on an exclusive basis. Prior to any type of work placement, students should receive a heavy concentration of prevocational information. The emphasis should be placed on procedures and techniques for interviewing, completing application forms, recognizing the social demands of work, and other similar considerations. Whenever possible, these concepts should be taught in situations that replicate the work environment, as nearly as possible, in the special classroom.

In-class activities with short-term, on-campus work experience. This arrangement provides an opportunity for the learner to relate his classroom instruction to solving practical, job-related problems. He has an opportunity to try out some of his skills in a closely controlled environment. Possible in-school training stations could include:

Elementary teacher aide
Lunchroom assistant
Library aide
Maintenance assistant
School bus maintenance
Clerical assistant
Warehouse material handler
Messenger-guide
Audio-visual media assistant

The adults supervising this kind of placement should be familiar with the program objectives. The work performed should not be artificially contrived, but should be useful. Financial remuneration should be provided. The purpose of the placement is to enable the learner to evaluate his own performance, therefore the emphasis should be on accuracy as opposed to speed.

In-class activities in combination with heavy on-campus work experience and some off-campus, community-based work experience. This type of placement provides for the introduction of new work environments and situations for the learner. A stabilizing environment is still considered critical to adjustment in this type of program, however. The in-class experiences are used to strengthen the student's deficiencies in selected areas and to help him maintain the basic skills he previously developed. Emphasis in the on-campus work experience should be placed on application of academic skills.

In-class with half days of off-campus work experience. Here again a move toward greater independence and responsibility is evident. The learner should be closely supervised and shifted from one training station to another to acquaint him with a variety of occupational experiences. At this stage it becomes critical that the responsibilities of the supervisor and coordinator become clearly delineated. Training plans and agreements such as the one given in Figure 11–2 should be developed. Records of performance and evaluation should also be maintained by both the coordinator and employer.

Total off-campus work experience. By the time the learner has progressed to this stage (usually eighteen or nineteen years of age) he or she has systematically worked out and overcome any major weaknesses that might impede success in occupational, social, personal or self-sufficiency functioning. It is the coordinator's responsibility to see that the learner is placed in a permanent position when this level is reached. Vocational rehabilitation can provide assistance in the placement process, also.

Follow-up. When a learner is placed in a permanent position, it should be noted that a considerable investment has been made by the public school and the supportive service agency. To insure that this investment is not lost, regular and systematic follow-ups should be made for at least three years. These assessments should examine the job performance of the individual, his or her development of independent living skills, and level of social integration. If the responses of either the individual or the employer indicate a problem or potential problems, efforts must be initiated to provide whatever remedial or rehabilitative services are necessary.

SUMMARY

Three basic types of work experience programs are described and discussed: cooperative education, work-study, and work experience. Each serves an important role in providing special needs learners with opportunities to explore first hand and to prepare for entry into the world of work. The recently developed WECEP (Work Experience and Career Exploration Program) model designed to serve fourteen- and fifteen-year-old dropout-prone youth is discussed in detail. The roles and tasks of the work experience teacher-coordinator who works with special needs learners is also examined. Finally, procedures for conducting training station analyses, developing training plans and agreements, and evaluating the special needs learner's on-the-job performance are reviewed.

REFERENCES

Baxter, J. *Labor laws and their application to special education-vocational rehabilitation work study program.* Lansing: Michigan Department of Education, 1971.

Floyd, G. L. Work experience and career exploration guide book. Joliet, Ill.: Joliet Public Schools, 1973.

Kimbrell, G., and Vineyard, B. S. *Strategies for implementing work experience programs.* Bloomington, Ill.: McKnight, 1972.

Kolstoe, O. P., and Frey, R. M. *A high school work-study program for mentally subnormal students.* Carbondale: Southern Illinois University Press, 1965.

Mason, R. E., and Haines, P. G. *Cooperative occupational education.* Danville, Ill.: Interstate Printers, 1972.

Peterson, R. O., and Jones, E. M. *Guide to jobs for the mentally retarded.* Washington, D.C.: American Institute for Research, 1964.

Smith, R. M. *Clinical teaching: methods of instruction for the mentally retarded.* New York: McGraw-Hill, 1974.

State of Illinois. *An articulated guide for cooperative occupational education.* Springfield: Board of Vocational Education and Rehabilitation, Division of Vocational and Technical Education, 1972.

State of Illinois. *WECEP: Work experience and career exploration programs.* Springfield: Division of Vocational and Technical Education, 1972.

U.S. Department of Labor. Part 570–Child labor regulations, orders, and statements of interpretation. *Federal Register,* 40, No. 172, September 4, 1975.

Wiggins, J. E. et al., *Guidelines for the establishment of work experience-and-study programs for handicapped children in Colorado.* Denver: Colorado Department of Education and Department of Social Services, 1971.

IMPLEMENTING INSTRUCTION

When implementing the instructional program for special needs learners, occupational and special educators consider that the following are critical: sequencing of instructional modules and concepts, appropriateness of instructional materials, usability and safety of facilities and equipment, and providing appropriate feedback in the form of reinforcement for special needs learners. ∾ Joint planning and cooperation between occupational and special educators has been heavily emphasized in preceding chapters. However, once the learner enters the class, there is an understandable tendency for the instructor to rely solely upon his or her capacities as a teacher as the individualized plan is implemented. Once the instructional plans have been formulated, precautions must be taken to insure that the cooperative effort and spirit is carried forward into the implementing phase. ∾ Several types of cooperative activities may be appropriate when the implementation phase begins:

12

1. Resource or remedial teachers can visit the occupational lab or work site to provide specific instructional services to each special needs learner.
2. Teacher aides, teacher cadets, or advanced students can be used to provide individualized attention in the occupational, laboratory, resource room, or special class.
3. Instructional team meetings can be held during preparation periods to discuss specifics for implementing certain modules or learning experiences.
4. Essential information can be exchanged at regular faculty or staff meetings regarding individual learners.
5. The instructional team can jointly:
    a. Analyze the instructional materials being used by the learner and modify them as needed.
    b. Discuss and provide certain reinforcements for positive behaviors they are trying to instill in the learner.
    c. Inspect the tools, equipment, and materials the learner is or will be using and modify, replace, or add to each as needed.

SEQUENCING INSTRUCTION

Learning occurs over time. The sequence of events through which learning occurs is "planned" in most educational programs. In some instances, however, the instructional planner may not always consider or analyze alternative sequences for providing instruction. Often the sequence of instruction is established from the teacher's previous experience in teaching the course or a particular unit. These previous experiences may or may not reflect several critical principles of sequencing instruction for special needs learners, and they are not likely to reflect a "variety of different sequences" which are often essential in instructing special needs learners.

Sequencing instruction can be defined at two levels. Initially, teachers have to determine a general sequence of tasks or instructional modules that is appropriate for the special needs learner receiving the instruction. Once this is resolved, the question of how shall the component skills of each module be presented must be addressed. This discussion will focus primarily on the first problem, that of sequencing modules or units of instruction. Many of the principles of instructional sequencing, however, will also apply to the sequencing of subordinate or component skills within the module.

Sequencing Principles

A number of general principles for sequencing career-related instruction are presented by Mager and Beach (1967) and serve as an excellent framework for considering sequencing problems. Depending upon the specific learning styles of selected special needs learners, certain of these principles may be more important than others. Clues as to which of these sequencing principles may be most appropriate for a given student can be obtained by reviewing the learner profiles and learning prescriptions developed in Chapter 6.

Interest Sequencing. Motivation for learning is a fundamental problem for many disadvantaged and some handicapped learners. Thus, one of the basic sequencing principles when beginning instruction involves selecting instructional modules or tasks in which the learner exhibits a high degree of interest. The most efficient, and often the most effective, means of determining a student's interests prior to instruction is to hold a series of short, informal discussions with the student and the parents. Sequencing of instruction based specifically on student interests is essential until the student begins to realize the "spin-off" tasks, concepts, and skills that are related in some manner to his major occupational interest. Once a learner's awareness of and interest in broader, related areas of the course is generated, it is appropriate to consider other criteria for sequencing instruction.

Illustration: Jamie approached his welding teacher on the first day of class expressing his urgent need to repair the kickstand on his motorcycle. That afternoon during his planning period the welding teacher and Jamie met in the lab. In twenty minutes, the instructor used the cracked kickstand bracket to introduce Jamie to the basic principles of arc welding, certain safety precautions, and several other concepts by repairing the bracket with Jamie's close supervision. By capitalizing on

Jamie's immediate and intense interest, the instructor was later able to introduce Jamie readily to a variety of skills related to arc welding, many of which also encouraged him to improve his reading and writing skills.

Logical Sequencing. In certain instances the nature of the subject matter will dictate that one instructional module be taught before another, for example, one must be able to read a thermometer before being able to accurately record and chart a patient's temperature. However, the decision as to which tasks or concepts are absolutely prerequisite to others is seldom that simple. Generally, there is not nearly as much reason for logical sequencing as most teachers would like to believe. It should be realized that an individual does not necessarily have to understand the thermo-physical principles of arc welding before he or she can repair a motorcycle kickstand bracket, nor does one have to be able to add three-column numbers manually before he can compute a billing if a calculator is used.

Illustration: Tasks that involve trouble shooting or identification and diagnosis of service problems are usually taught by logical sequencing. Jan, a physically handicapped student, was attempting to follow the basic trouble-shooting procedure outlined in a programmed instructional text for her introductory electronics course. The suggested procedure was based on inductive logic. That is, she was attempting to locate problems in the branches of individual circuits before testing each of the major circuits. Her instructor recommended that she use the alternative trouble-shooting procedure based on deductive logic, which was more appropriate to the task of locating a bad component in a complex circuit board. This procedure enabled her to "narrow down" the location of the bad component by testing the major circuits first.

Skill Sequencing. Sequencing instructional units in a skill development pattern is more appropriate for vocational education programs than practical arts programs. Skill sequencing has been utilized extensively in programs where singular career ladders have been viewed as the primary structure for instruction. It is especially important in short-term training programs that the person be trained for entry level employment (auto mechanic helper, for instance) before providing additional instruction or training enabling him or her to be employable as an auto mechanic.

Frequency Sequencing. Frequency sequencing is a principle that is highly consistent with the concept of career cluster analysis discussed in Chapter 8. The cluster analysis approach suggests that those tasks common to the greatest number of occupations in the cluster should be the initial focus of instruction. Similarly, the frequency sequencing principle suggests that those skills that are performed most frequently on the job should be taught first. The remaining modules or tasks are then sequenced in order of decreasing frequency of performance. Here again, if the training period is short, the student will at least have the skills he or she will use most frequently on the job. For example, in most instances pumping gas is more important for a service station attendant than being able to repair three-speed transmissions.

Graduated Sequencing. There are a number of simple considerations related to graduated sequencing that have been noted by developers of programmed instructional materials. Johnson and Johnson (1970) have identified seven commonly used graduated sequences:

1. Simple to complex
2. Facts to generalizations
3. Concrete to abstract
4. Practical to theoretical
5. Meaningful to unknown
6. Past to present
7. Present to future

While all of these graduated sequences have not been empirically tested to determine their effectiveness with all types of special needs learners, there is substantial research evidence to suggest that most of them are appropriate for educable mentally handicapped students.

Illustration: Sara was about to open a checking account because she had just received her first check from the school district for working as an aide in an afternoon kindergarten class. Ms. Jenkins, her learning resource room teacher, saw this as an opportunity to reinforce and perhaps further improve Sara's math skills. Once she had learned the practical aspects and importance of balancing her checkbook and keeping accurate records, the next step was to introduce units on "banking service charges" and "interest," since it was necessary that she be able to interpret these on her bank statement each month. The next concept presented in the sequence was "borrowing money." In this unit an in-class discussion and field trip to the bank were used to facilitate her understanding of how much the bank paid her in interest for keeping her money versus how much she would be charged for borrowing money. By this time the sequence, which had begun with the very practical, concrete, and meaningful task of "maintaining a checking account," had progressed to the more theoretical concept of comparing interest rates for lending and saving.

Total Job Practice. One of the potential hazards in using the modular or unit approach in developing instructional plans is that students may never have an opportunity to practice the entire job. As the component skills of a task are learned and practiced, it is important that they be integrated; that is, the skills are practiced in conjunction with the previous tasks that have been learned. As more tasks are learned and integrated, the resulting performance more closely replicates the complex nature of total job performance. Mager and Beach (1967) conservatively recommend that at least 5 percent of the total instructional time for vocational instruction should be devoted to total job practice. With most special needs learners, it is likely that more than 5 percent will be needed for total job practice.

Formulating Instructional Sequences

Frequently, teachers utilize the sequencing principles described in the previous section with little forethought or planning. Decisions on how to sequence a particular set of tasks or modules are frequently based on either the teacher's approach to the subject matter content or his or her teaching style. Generally, they either view the instructional content as being teachable in only a limited number of ways because of the nature of the content, or they have strong personal preferences for certain sequences. The preferences may be based on previous success in teaching to the student's interests or teaching the tasks by the sequence in which they are performed in business or industry.

Both the inherent nature of the instructional content and the teacher's teaching style are major considerations in instructional planning and need to be carefully addressed when occupational and special educators are determining an appropriate instructional sequence for a special needs learner. The forms shown in Figures 12-1 and 12-2 can be helpful in formulating instructional sequences considering the nature of the instructional content and a teacher's style of teaching.

Instructional Sequencing Worksheet

The instructional sequencing worksheet (Figure 12-1) assists educators in examining different possibilities for sequencing a set of instructional modules or tasks. Occupational and special educators commonly use the worksheet to analyze what type of sequence may be most appropriate for a special needs learner. Completing this worksheet enables the teachers to visualize different possible sequences and to recognize approximately when students will begin new modules.

Instructional Sequencing Master Schedule

When several special needs learners are involved in different instructional modules concurrently, it can become difficult for teachers to remember on a daily basis the various sequences for individual students. To effectively monitor and manage individualized programs that are to be coordinated with other teachers' efforts, teachers can use a tool like the instructional sequencing master schedule (Figure 12-2).

The master schedule is a composite of the instructional sequencing worksheets on each special needs learner. For a set of tasks or instructional modules, the sequence for presentation of the modules is identified for each student.

Several different factors and situations can be monitored with the master schedule. As shown in the example, some students will have similar, or perhaps even identical sequences planned for them (Patti, Jim, Harry).

FIGURE 12-1. INSTRUCTIONAL SEQUENCING WORKSHEET

Directions: In section 1 list the tasks or instructional modules the student is to be taught in the coming weeks. You can list as many as ten if you care to. Once the tasks or modules are listed, develop some alternative sequences for presenting these to the student, using the three sequencing criteria provided. This can be done readily by writing the identification numbers for each task/module in the appropriate boxes.

Learner Greg Course Construction Grade 8

I. Tasks or Modules to be Taught

ID. NO.	MODULE TITLE OR TASK STATEMENT	ID. NO.	MODULE TITLE OR TASK STATEMENT
1	Using woodworking hand tools	6	Planning a project
2	Constructing joint samples	7	Reading blueprints
3	Selecting wood fasteners	8	Using measuring tools
4	Operating power hand tools	9	Sharpening hand tools
5	Selecting construction materials	10	Selecting finishes

II. Alternative Instructional Sequences

	Initial Task or Module									Final Task or Module
1. Student Interest Sequence	6	5	4	1	8	3	10	2	7	9

Name of Student Greg

Interest sequencing rationale Greg is extremely interested in building a doghouse for his father's new hunting dog.

2. Graduated Sequence										

Type (not appropriate)

3. Other types of relevant sequences (i.e., logical, skill, frequency, or total job practice):	1	2	7	8	6	5	4	3	10	9

Skill development

FIGURE 12-2. INSTRUCTIONAL SEQUENCING MASTER SCHEDULE

Course Construction School Lincoln Junior High

Instructor Mike Cary Marking Period 1st

Directions: List below the tasks or instructional modules to be focused on during this marking period. For each learner, identify the: 1) date she or he will start working on this set of modules or tasks (entry date), 2) the planned sequence in which each will be introduced, and 3) the type of sequence (i.e., student interest, graduated, frequency, etc.). As the learner completes each task or instructional module it can be checked off.

Tasks/Modules To Be Taught

ID. NO.	MODULE TITLE OR TASK STATEMENT	ID. NO.	MODULE TITLE OR TASK STATEMENT
1	Using woodworking hand tools	6	Planning a project
2	Constructing joint samples	7	Reading blueprints
3	Selecting wood fasteners	8	Using measuring tools
4	Operating power hand tools	9	Sharpening hand tools
5	Selecting construction materials	10	Selecting finishes

Proposed Instructional Sequence

LEARNERS	ENTERING DATE	INITIAL									TERMINAL	SEQUENCE
Greg	9/3	6	5	4	1	8	3	10	2	7	9	stud. interest
Patti	9/3	1	2	7	8	6	5	4	3	10	9	skill develop.
Jim	9/3	1	2	7	8	6	5	4	3	10	9	skill develop.
Harry	9/3	1	2	7	8	6	5	4	3	10	9	skill develop.
Herm	11/1	4	6	10								stud. interest

Some students will enter at different dates and have different sequences planned for them as a result (Herm). In instances where students have already demonstrated a satisfactory level of competence in one or more of the tasks or modules, their list of modules to be accomplished on this form may be shorter (also Herm).

As suggested earlier, a major benefit is that the teacher using a master sequencing schedule can note the types of sequencing patterns he or she is using. If all students are given the instructional modules in the same sequence, it may be an indication that sufficient individualizing is not taking place.

Sequencing of Instruction: A Final Note

Techniques and procedures for sequencing instruction have received only limited attention in research on learning, and education has few suggestions to teachers on how to sequence concepts—or any instructional content for that matter—for special needs learners.

It should also be noted that throughout this section we have assumed that instructional modules should be presented in a linear sequence. For some special needs students and teachers this may not be the case. If sustaining a student's interest in a specific task is difficult (as it often is with learners with emotional problems), it may be necessary to shift back and forth between different modules on a daily or more frequent basis. Thus, the student may be working on more than one module at a time. Since it is often difficult to "plan" for these types of sequences, the format of the sequencing worksheet does not take this into consideration. Also, some teachers actually prefer to have some students (usually those with average or above average capabilities) involved in more than one instructional module or task at a time. This is a characteristic of teaching style in many instances.

The underlying purpose in using the instructional sequencing worksheet and master schedule is to help the instructional team "visualize" the types of instructional sequences they are using with different students. Frequently, before teachers can make decisions about the appropriateness of their sequencing, they must be able to visualize it.

ANALYZING AND MODIFYING INSTRUCTIONAL MATERIALS

As suggested in Chapter 10, utilizing a variety of different types of instructional materials is often critical to successful remediation of learning problems in mildly handicapped students. However, it must go far beyond the simple selection of a variety of media. Instructional personnel need to analyze carefully each instructional material they intend to use. Once analyzed, the characteristics of the material (such as the reading level) need to be compared with the learning characteristics of the specific special needs learners who will use them. If necessary, as is often the case, appropriate modifications can then be made to the instructional materials.

Analyzing Instructional Materials

There are two basic types of analyses that can be completed to determine the appropriateness of a specific instructional material for a special needs learner. First, a readability analysis can be conducted on print materials. This analysis is particularly useful in evaluating materials to be used with students having different types of reading and comprehension difficulties. The second type, a format and content analysis, can be used in evaluating print materials, but in addition it is useful in reviewing audio, visual, games, and other forms of instructional media.

Readability Analysis. If the materials being evaluated utilize written narrative to any reasonable extent, it is critical to determine the readability level of the material. Readability is defined by most instructional materials developers as the relationship of the reading material to the abilities of the learner. Readable, commercially produced or teacher-prepared print materials (which could include texts, reference materials, workbooks, worksheets, or classroom tests) should have qualities that match the abilities of the learner in format, style, and level.

Numerous readability formulas have been developed to measure the reading difficulty level of printed materials. Figure 12-3 presents a worksheet for using the FOG Index (Weisman 1975), a measure that has become recognized as an efficient and reasonably accurate reading level measure of materials designed for use at the secondary level.

Utilization of the FOG Index. Three simple steps are required in using the FOG Index to determine the reading level of any instructional material. Calculations for each of these steps can be recorded on the worksheet.

1. Take several samples of 100 words each, spaced evenly throughout the material. Count the number of sentences in each sample. (Stop the sentence count with the sentence ending nearest the 100-word limit.) Divide the total number of words in the sample (100) by the number of sentences. This gives you the average sentence length. Record this figure.
2. Using the same samples, count the number of words that have three or more syllables. *Do not count* words that are:
   a) Capitalized
   b) Combinations of short, easy words (e.g., bookkeeper)
   c) Verb forms made into three syllables by adding -ed, -es (e.g., created)

   Record this number directly under the figure obtained in the first step.
3. The FOG Index is determined by totalling the two factors just recorded (average sentence length and number of three-syllable words in the sample) and multiplying the total by 0.4 (four-tenths). This gives you the approximate grade level of the written material. It should be noted, however, that this estimate tends to run somewhat high with more difficult materials.

In addition to assessing the reading level of materials, readability formulas such as the FOG Index can be used for the following:

1. To check the readability of worksheets and exercises given to students.
2. To point out lengthy sentence structure that may inhibit comprehension by some students.
3. To point out specific words that are likely to be problems for selected students.

FIGURE 12-3. FOG READABILITY INDEX WORKSHEET

Title ______________________ Type of material ______________________
(e.g., textbook, test, procedure manual)

SAMPLE 1 (100 words from page no. _____)

a. _____ No. of sentences in the sample

b. _____ Average sentence length (100 divided by a. above)

c. _____ No. of three-syllable words in the sample

d. _____ Sum of (b) and (c) above

X 0.4 Multiplication factor

[ ] Reading level for Sample 1

SAMPLE 2 (100 words from page no. _____)

a. _____ No. of sentences in the sample

b. _____ Average sentence length (100 divided by a. above)

c. _____ No. of three-syllable words in the sample

d. _____ Sum of (b) and (c) above

X 0.4 Multiplication factor

[ ] Reading level for Sample 2

SAMPLE 3 (100 words from page no. _____)

a. _____ No. of sentences in the sample

b. _____ Average sentence length (100 divided by a. above)

c. _____ No. of three-syllable words in the sample

d. _____ Sum of (b) and (c) above

X 0.4 Multiplication factor

[ ] AVERAGE READING LEVEL FOR ALL THREE SAMPLES

[ ] Reading level for Sample 3

4. As a tool for checking teacher-prepared materials after they have been developed or rewritten.

Other Readability Concerns. Specific reading level can only be considered one part of a readability analysis. Several other factors such as the following need to be considered in selecting printed materials to be used by special needs learners.

1. Double-column pages provide for easier eye movement and tend to be more legible.
2. Type face should be ten to twelve points in size in order to be easily read by most students. Enlarged print materials have been commonly used with visually impaired learners.
3. Black printing on dull-finish paper white paper tends to provide for optimum legibility.
4. Generous spacing between lines and wider margins are also conducive to increased reading comprehension.

Perhaps the most crucial consideration in selecting reading material is its compatibility with the learner's interest. Generally speaking, the reading ability an individual demonstrates can be expected to increase by as much as two full grades if reader interest is high.

Format and Content Analysis. In addition to readability analysis, all instructional materials should undergo at least an informal format and content analysis. This analysis would focus on such elements as content appropriateness, alternative uses of the materials, portability of the material, type and amount of illustrations used, and so on. These considerations are extremely important in considering all types of instructional materials for potential use with handicapped and disadvantaged learners.

Figure 12–4 presents a format and content checklist. Although many of the items included are appropriate criteria for reviewing and evaluating any instructional material, a number of the items pertain directly to special needs learners. When occupational educators utilize this or other similar lists to evaluate materials that will be used with special needs students, it is important that special educators, who are acquainted with the learner's needs, also

FIGURE 12-4. INSTRUCTIONAL MATERIALS CHECKLIST

Directions: Commercially-produced or teacher-prepared materials can be evaluated using the review criteria listed below. Both occupational and special educators should assess the material prior to purchase or final revision (if teacher prepared).

Title ______________________ Evaluators ______________________

Media type (film, book, etc.) ______________________

Source ______________________ Date ______________________

	RATING LOW HIGH	INAPPROPRIATE CRITERIA *(check)*
1. Is the instructional material potentially interesting for the learner(s) for whom it is intended?	1 2 3	________
2. Are the skills, knowledges, and attitudes it will develop appropriate for the learner?	1 2 3	________
3. Are the skills, knowledges, and attitudes it will develop consistent with the instructional objectives of the unit?	1 2 3	________
4. Does the material contain explicitly stated goals so that students and teachers alike will be able to evaluate their performance?	1 2 3	________
5. To what extent is the material controlled to provide the appropriate reinforcement for correct responses and near correct responses?	1 2 3	________
6. To what extent can students actively participate with the instructional material?	1 2 3	________
7. To what extent are the materials useful with both individuals and groups?	1 2 3	________
8. Are the directions for using the material too complex for teachers and/or learners to readily understand?	1 2 3	________
9. To what extent is the material flexible enough to permit additions, deletions, or modification of content?	1 2 3	________
10. To what extent is the material portable and readily available from the distributor or manufacturer?	1 2 3	________

FIGURE 12-4. *(Continued)*

	RATING LOW HIGH	INAPPROPRIATE CRITERIA *(check)*
11. To what extent has the material been pretested, pilot tested, and evaluated with different special needs populations?	1 2 3	________
12. To what extent does the material permit the teacher to evaluate diagnostically a student's level of performance to determine where the learner should begin?	1 2 3	________
13. Are there cost-benefit considerations to be made in using this material? Will the material produce results that outweigh the costs?	1 2 3	________
14. Will the material have to be adapted to another media form (e.g., braille, enlarged print) for visually handicapped learners?	1 2 3	________
15. Will the material have to be adapted to another media or format for orthopedically handicapped learners (e.g., self-instructional packages for homebound instruction)?	1 2 3	________
16. Will the material have to be adapted to another media (e.g., cassette or audio tapes to print) for hearing impaired learners?	1 2 3	________
17. Are the illustrations and pictures appropriate for special needs learners?	1 2 3	________
18. Is the material sufficiently durable for classroom or lab use?	1 2 3	________
19. Are sufficient and appropriate examples or applications used to present the information realistically?	1 2 3	________
20. Other considerations or criteria:		

FIGURE 12-4. *(Continued)*

21. DISPOSITION *(Check one):*

_________ Do not purchase or use

_________ Purchase and/or use "as is"

_________ Purchase and/or use after the following modification(s) are made:

22. Instructional Materials Modifications:

review the materials and offer their suggestions before materials are purchased or developed in final form.

Modifying Instructional Materials

Once the analysis or evaluation of materials is complete, it is then appropriate to consider specific modifications. Based on the evaluation of the material(s) and relevant information from the individual's learner profile or prescription, specific changes in the materials can be made. If you have not recently done so, it may be helpful to review the learning prescription(s) developed for the special needs learner in Chapter 6.

A number of guidelines can be provided for probable modifications of materials for use with students having specific disabilities. Guidelines for modifying materials for students with general learning problems, and physical, visual, or hearing impairment are provided in Figure 12-5.

FIGURE 12-5. GUIDELINES FOR MODIFYING INSTRUCTIONAL MATERIALS

FOR STUDENTS WITH LEARNING PROBLEMS

Be sure the language is at an appropriate reading level.

Keep words and sentences as simple and as short as possible.

Include as many visuals (drawings, pictures, illustrations) as possible.

Provide verbal reinforcement for the material in the form of individualized attention.

Be sure the examples used are concrete and meaningful for the learner.

Make extensive use of audio-visual aids.

Prepare audio cassette recordings of important printed materials.

Modify materials (such as workbooks) so that students can respond by drawing illustrations or recording on cassette tapes.

FOR STUDENTS WITH PHYSICAL IMPAIRMENT

For students who are frequently homebound, self-instructional materials must be available.

Students who have difficulty with writing should be permitted to tape record or type their responses.

For individual students with specific physical impairments (limited use of hands, for instance) be sure that the impairment does not limit access to or the use of tape recorders, large reference books, and so forth. Adjustments and modifications have to be made on an individual basis.

FOR STUDENTS WITH VISUAL IMPAIRMENTS

Printed instructional materials may have to be converted into braille, enlarged print, or thermoformed print.

Electronic scanning equipment can also be used; it transforms letters and words from printed material into raised images that can be felt.

Pertinent material can be transcribed onto records or cassette tapes.

Volunteer or paid reader services can be arranged for individual students.

Special or supplementary lighting may be needed for partially sighted students.

FIGURE 12-5. *(Continued)*

Utilize volunteer service agencies to tape record printed materials such as textbooks or reference books.

FOR STUDENTS WITH HEARING IMPAIRMENTS

Since hearing impaired students (especially the deaf) also frequently have learning problems, many of the suggestions offered under the learning problems section above will apply.

Captioned films, charts, overhead transparencies and other visual materials should be used extensively.

Written and simplified transcripts of cassette or audio taped materials can be prepared.

Arrange for an in-class tutor (deaf interpretor) to work with deaf students and others having problems.

MODIFYING FACILITIES AND EQUIPMENT

Many persons, including educators, parents, and others, are concerned about the adjustment of facilities, tools, and equipment used in occupational programs by special needs learners. Regrettably, in the past some special needs learners have not been admitted to or adequately served in occupational education programs because of existing, nonadaptive facilities or equipment. However, recent federal and state legislation has done a great deal to remove the architectural and other physical barriers that might prohibit or limit handicapped students from participating fully in occupational and all other educational programs.

Modifying facilities and equipment requires assessment of individual learner needs first of all. In order to provide appropriate programs and services for *all* special needs students, their specific, individual limitations must first be known. Once aware or informed of this, teachers, therapists, and others can begin the task of designing or adapting the necessary educational facilities and equipment so that the effect of the student's disability on the learning process is eliminated or minimized.

However, it is extremely important that the facilities or equipment not become too specialized or totally unique. Regular facilities, tools, equipment, and materials should be used whenever possible so as not to over coddle special students. Special provisions and adaptations should always be made in light of the facilities and equipment that exist in the real world. If the educational goal is to prepare the student for an independent adult working role, in most instances he will likely be required to use facilities and equipment that are of conventional, not special, design.

In considering educational modifications and adaptations for the special needs learner, teachers should address a series of general concerns as well as specific concerns for the physically handicapped. This section of the chapter will review a number of the general concerns, such as the use of color, and will offer a series of specific suggestions for modifying equipment for the physically handicapped.

General Learning Environment Considerations

Flexibility in designing environments, the use of color, class or group size, and types of special equipment are the major general considerations in planning or adapting the environment (including the tools, facilities, and equipment) in which the special needs student will learn most effectively and efficiently.

Flexibility. Probably the most important consideration in planning or adapting your classroom or lab to accommodate special needs learners is flexibility. Does the existing environment take into account that special needs learners will work at different rates? Will the environment enable the students to use different materials and different learning methods at the same time? Does the room have different subspaces for discussions, reading, lab work, listening, and viewing self-instructional media. Does the general environment offer several work surface heights to accommodate students who prefer to sit, stand, lounge, lean, or perch? In order for the environment to be attractive and stimulating for students who have had learning and behavioral difficulties, it must be flexible enough to tolerate the individual preferences and needs of such students.

Color. Color is an important factor in the learning environment. Room colors, as well as the instructional use of color, are important in shaping the behavior of students. Room colors have a significant influence on the moods and tone of the learning environment and need to be used to provide a positive effect. According to Wexner's (1954) research on colors and the moods or feelings they create, blues tend to suggest secure, comfortable, and serene moods that have a tender or soothing effect. Reds generally tend to stimulate excitement, but in some students red also suggests a contrary, defiant, or hostile mood. Orange is also a color that some find disturbing or upsetting. Yellow offers a cheerful and jovial mood, while purple represents a dignified or stately tone. Finally, black and dark shades of brown were found to conjure up masterful, powerful, and dejected moods.

Selection of basic colors and color combinations will be largely dependent upon the characteristics of the special students. Darker, depressing tones may be helpful in working with students who are hyperactive or have severe behavioral problems, while brighter colors (yellows and reds) may be helpful in stimulating students who are apathetic and despondent.

While it is important to recognize that while there appears to be a relationship between carefully planned color schemes and scholastic achievement, we still do not have research data to correlate specific color schemes with specific behaviors—attentiveness, for instance—or communication patterns.

Class and Group Size. The preceding chapter extensively emphasized the need for using individualized and small-group instructional techniques with special needs learners. One adaptation that should always be considered in working with special students is the size of the group. Although the determination of optimum group size is influenced by several other factors—the learning task, for example—there are some general principles that should be followed in establishing or adjusting group size. One study in particular involving special needs clients (Hutt and Vaizey 1966) is quite useful. Normal, autistic, and brain-damaged children were observed in play and learning situations where the size of the group varied from less than six to more than twelve participants. As the density (size of the group) increased, all groups showed deterioration of behavior, but the normal students were less affected. The autistic students tended to withdraw, while the brain-damaged students as well as the normal students reacted with increased aggressive or destructive behavior. These results in no way provide conclusive evidence on managing or adjusting the size of groups in the learning environment. They do, however, suggest the following:

1. The learner's behavior is influenced to some extent by the density or number of persons in the immediate area or group.
2. Larger groups (more than twelve) have a negative effect upon the learning of some handicapped students.

Types of Special Equipment. Physically and orthopedically handicapped students sometimes require specific modifications in educational equipment in both special classes and occupational classes. Yuker and his co-authors (1967) have identified four general types of school equipment that can be used to meet the individual needs of physically handicapped learners:

1. Standard unmodified school equipment
2. Standard equipment that has been modified
3. Specially designed, commercially available equipment
4. Specially adapted equipment for individual students

It is important to remember that special equipment and adaptations of regular equipment must be designed to meet each individual's need. Special or adapted equipment should only be modified to the extent necessary to facilitate learning for the special needs student of concern. As the student generates competence in the learning task (or tasks) at hand, special or adapted equipment should be replaced with regular equipment as soon as possible. Whenever possible, standard unmodified equipment should be utilized instead of special equipment to minimize any stigmatizing effects of special modifications in regular classrooms.

Standard unmodified equipment usually has greater utility and is less expensive than modified or special equipment and generally can be used by disabled as well as nondisabled students.

Some standard classroom or lab equipment can be modified by purchasing adaption kits or special components from the manufacturer. These modification kits, such as special guards for a grinder, are usually installed at the school or purchased on the original equipment. Manufactured modification kits are generally inexpensive when compared to specially designed equipment.

Most of the specially designed educational equipment for physically handicapped learners is intended for use in nonvocational classrooms at the elementary level.

Some manufacturers of school and vocational program equipment that is specially designed for use by physically handicapped learners include the following: special seating, desks, ramps, and small equipment such as special grip mixing bowls for students with dexterity problems in commercial foods classes and special typewriter keyboard plates for cerebral palsied students. Equipment supply catalogs, special education administrators, and local rehabilitation agencies are excellent sources of information on specially designed equipment.

For some physically handicapped students, the unique nature of their disability will require made-to-order special equipment. The types of equipment in categories will obviously vary widely. Because such equipment will usually be prepared at the school where it will be used, the cost is usually quite high.

Several states are now developing special equipment pools. Districts involved in these cooperative pools often share the costs for purchase or modification of special equipment and then make the equipment available to other cooperating districts for use with low incidence handicapped students.

Suggestions for Modifying Equipment for the Physically Handicapped

A number of general suggestions can be made for possible adaptions of equipment and facilities for students with different physical handicaps. It is important to remember, however, that specific modifications will be based on the needs of individual students and these physical adjustment needs vary greatly even among students having the same disability. Additional information on special devices and modifications can be obtained from the American Foundation for the Blind and other similar organizations that serve the physically handicapped.

Modifications for the Hearing Impaired. Few if any modifications are usually required for deaf or hearing impaired students in occupational education classes. Generally, the tools and equipment used by the regular students will be appropriate. Two specific modifications are suggested by Szoke and Vest (1975)[1], however:

> A red light installed next to the switch indicating when the machine is in operation.
>
> Bells connected to a light that turns on when the bell rings. This is applicable on typewriters, class bells, timers, fire alarms, and emergency stop procedures.

Modifications for the Visually Impaired. The degree of equipment modification required for visually handicapped students in occupational classes will depend upon the type and extent of vision loss. Surprisingly, however, the majority of equipment used in occupational instruction will not require modification.

An orderly and unaltered environment is important to the safety and mobility of blind students in a lab situation. Szoke and Vest offer a series of additional suggested modifications for students with visual impairments.

> Control dials and switches that are easily accessible; special control dials with tactile rather than visual markings—brailled tape or raised marks (dots of Elmer's glue) can be used.
>
> Auditory rather than visual warning signals.
>
> Guard plates (where feasible) on power equipment.
>
> Specially designed communication and measuring tools and other devices are available and should be considered for the visually impaired student on an individual basis. These include braille shorthand machines and stenotype devices, auditory calculators, equipment for preparing raised line drawings, light detectors that emit a sound stimulus, audible multimeter, audible electronic level, brailled micrometers, calipers and rulers, sound monitors for indicator lamps, automatic

1. C. O. Szoke and S. Vest, *To Serve Those Who Are Handicapped* (Springfield: Department of Adult, Vocational, and Technical Education, Illinois Office of Education, 1975). Used with permission.

fluid measuring devices for darkroom work, braille bevel protractors, vernier rules, transformer testers, and feed indicators for lathes.

Modifications for the Orthopedically Handicapped. Several important considerations are necessary when implementing occupational instruction for students in wheelchairs, on crutches, or with artificial limbs. Szoke and Vest (1975) have identified six potential modifications for facilities and four equipment modifications that should be carefully reviewed.

FACILITIES

Absence of obstructions, ample space between aisles and around power equipment, storage areas for students in wheelchairs.

Nonskid floor to facilitate handling of crutches and wheelchairs.

Alterations in height of work benches, storage cabinets, etc. Typically these have to be lowered and recessed to accommodate students in wheelchairs.

Simple handles rather than knobs on cabinets for amputees with artificial limbs or other devices.

Mobile demonstration table that can be moved from student to student.

Sinks and water controls should be accessible to students in wheelchairs. Batwing faucets that require minimal manual dexterity for manipulation and gooseneck spigots that allow for greater ease of operation by providing ample room between the sink and the spigot are especially helpful for those students with upper extremity orthopedic involvement.

EQUIPMENT

Guard plates (where feasible) on power equipment. Machine switches on power equipment may need to be moved for easier accessibility.

Semistationary equipment should be put on variable height bases.

Regular equipment may need to be adapted such as hand controls added to machines usually operated by foot controls.

Special light weight hand tools or tools with extra large handles for easy use by students with weak hands.

PROVIDING REINFORCEMENT AND FEEDBACK

In an instructional setting, the teacher or counselor is continuously providing some forms of feedback or reinforcement to the learner. Because of their typical learning and behavioral patterns, often the presence of special needs learners in regular classes tends to make the task of providing feedback to individual students more difficult. Many authors have suggested that managing feedback and reinforcement is the key to successfully remediating the academic and learning difficulties encountered by special needs learners in school.

Key Terminology

There are several terms that need to be defined prior to this discussion of techniques for providing appropriate feedback. Many of them have emerged from the field of behavioral psychology, which uses a somewhat different set of terms than educators do to describe behavior modification principles and other key concepts.

For our purposes, reinforcement and feedback can be considered as nearly synonymous. Reinforcement and feedback is that reaction that the teacher provides after the learner has acted or performed in some manner. Reinforcement may be verbal or nonverbal (gestures, facial expressions, and so on). It can be positive as well as negative in its effect on the desired performance. It is usually provided immediately after the performance but can also be provided on a continuing basis. In addition to teachers, others involved in the situation, for example, other students, provide feedback following a learner's performance (Gardner 1977).

Target behaviors are the positive goal performances the teacher hopes the learner will eventually demonstrate. Once identified, the target behavior is shaped or generated by the type and amount of reinforcement provided.

Behavioral management, the psychological discipline that has developed many of the feedback and reinforcement principles, is regarded as the systematic process of arranging the educational situation to produce a specific change in observable behavior (Wallace and Kauffman 1973).

Coordination of Feedback and Reinforcement

When reinforcements are to be provided for individual learners, it is important that occupational, special, and other teachers working with the student be aware of the reinforcement arrangements and scheduling. Coordination and communication is important both in planning and in implementing the use of such reinforcers as an opportunity to go to the shop during a study hall. If the special needs learner's occupational interest is to be maximized, independent projects and other meaningful opportunities in the occupational program can be used as reinforcers for successful completion of math or reading units in the resource room or other special education class. All of this, however, requires close coordination and daily communication among staff members. With some special needs learners it will also be necessary to coordinate reinforcement and feedback plans with parents and employers.

Guidelines for Providing Reinforcement and Feedback

Occupational and special educators informally practice a number of different feedback and reinforcement techniques in their teaching. In recent years, however, the development of behavioral management theory has enabled us to expand and validate a number of these essential principles. This section will present and discuss a series of guidelines and suggestions for teachers and other personnel as they implement their instructional plans.

1. The first consideration involves identifying the target behavior. A decision has to be made as to whether the target behavior is to be positively reinforced to strengthen it or negatively reinforced to eliminate it. Identification and specification of the target behavior is an essential first step.

2. Selection of the reinforcer to be provided for the learner is the next and perhaps most critical step. To be effective a reinforcer or reward must be a) Highly desirable in the learner's eyes and b) Not obtainable

elsewhere. In many instances, the best way to determine the appropriate reinforcer for a special needs learner is to simply ask what he or she would enjoy doing most from a range of possible activities. Special education teachers, counselors, and parents are also excellent sources of this kind of information.

3. Initially, reinforcement and feedback must be provided immediately following the behavior on a continuous schedule. At first, the reinforcement will probably be provided even though there might be only a small bit of demonstrated performance.

4. Managing the delivery of continuous, immediate reinforcement and feedback in a large class is virtually impossible. It is helpful to establish a secondary system of providing credit points that the learner can accumulate. A point system is a functional technique for reinforcing desired behavior. Accumulation of points influences the student to act in accordance with the desired outcome or goal. Point systems and charts can serve as functional secondary reinforcement systems and can be used for such purposes as increasing class attendance, decreasing tardiness, or increasing participation in shop cleanup activities.

5 When teachers are concerned with the development of *new skills or behaviors,* it is especially important that the learner be reinforced after every correct performance. Random or intermittent patterns of reinforcement and feedback should be used only after the new skill or behavior has stabilized.

6. Initially, it is important to use tangible reinforcers frequently such as an opportunity to tune up a car. Whenever possible, these tangible reinforcers should be paired with a social stimulus (positive recognition by teachers or peers). Gradually the tangible reinforcers can be removed and shifts made to reinforcers that are less artificial and more natural.

7. Modifying behavior for many learners involves the principle of *successive approximations.* A task analysis of the target behavior should be done to determine the different components or natural steps involved in acquiring the target behavior. Reinforcement is then provided as each of

these natural steps is attained. The initial performance requested of the student is a small, easy-to-perform part of the expected final performance. If the requested performance is too difficult or beyond the learner's ability or level of comprehension, no amount of reinforcement or reward will help.

For example, if you are concerned about getting a student to clean up the lab or classroom, have him or her begin by putting away the tools, then cleaning the machine, and finally sweeping the floor, as opposed to simply directing him or her to "clean up."

8. To eliminate certain behaviors, it is helpful to find and use behaviors that either oppose or are incompatible with the learner's undesired behavior. In a classroom or lab setting, when another learner nearby is performing the task correctly, a heavy dose of reinforcement for the correct performance will likely diminish the incorrect behavior. Quick elimination of reinforcing behavior is also effective. If teacher attention is reinforcing for the learner, such attention should not be provided when a performance is incompatible with the target behavior.

9. Whenever possible, stimuli that are competitive should be removed from the learning situation. If, for instance, the student encounters social difficulty when working in teams with certain classmates, it is best to arrange the team assignments so the problems are avoided; the student can work with team members who can provide positive reinforcement for desired behaviors. Removal of adversive stimuli diminishes the negative reinforcement that causes or perpetuates the undesired behavior.

10. Rewards and reinforcers should be keyed to performance and not obedience. Rewards given for accomplishment of desirable goals are much better than simply requiring students to comply with any standards of the system, which they do not see as desirable for themselves or the system. Rewarding students for accomplishment will lead to independence, while continuously rewarding them for obedience will tend to make them dependent.

11. A very simple and practical principle of behavioral management was developed by Premack (1959). The Premack principle states: "Any-

thing a learner likes to do more can be used to reinforce any behavior he likes to do less." Through observation and getting to know students, teachers are able to determine student preferences. Highly preferred activities can then be used to reinforce less preferred activities. The greater the difference in preference between the two activities, the greater the reinforcing power of the preferred activity. Listed below are two arrangements that could be used to operationalize the Premack principle in occupational programs.

LEARNER'S PREFERENCE	REINFORCEMENT ARRANGEMENT
Learner prefers working on his motorcycle to completing a welding exercise.	Provide an opportunity to work on the motorcycle contingent upon successful completion of the welding exercise.
Learner chooses to sit in the classroom and read instead of engaging in lab activities.	Make access to the reading materials contingent upon observation in the lab. Later make access to the materials contingent upon participation in lab activities.

12. Homme (1970) has developed an approach for providing reinforcers in the form of an agreement or contract. The learner benefits from an explicit statement of the relationship between present behaviors and the consequences of such behavior. A negotiated contract between the learner and teacher(s) states that the teacher will provide a desired reinforcer after the learner demonstrates the desired target behavior. A contingency contract can be either verbal or written but must be similar to any good business contract, that is, fair to both parties, clear and concise statement of terms, must be adhered to, and must provide a positive incentive. Figure 12–6 on the following page presents an illustration of a written contingency contract that could be developed and used with special and occupational educators jointly involved in monitoring the learner's performance.

13. There are several specific considerations in designing and implementing procedures for providing direct reinforcement or feedback. Gold

FIGURE 12-6. CONTINGENCY CONTRACTING FORM

Note: Contingency contracting can be done on either a verbal or written basis. This is an example of the less frequently used written contract form.

CONTINGENCY CONTRACT INVOLVING

Instructor(s) Candy Jenkins, Spec. Ed / Tom Powers, Auto   Learner Steve

Date Jan. 12

TARGET PERFORMANCE If Steve will 1) attend all of his classes for 6 weeks with no more than 2 excused absenses and 2 tardy reports, and 2) complete 4 exercises in occupational math in the resource room,

If the above stated target performance is successfully demonstrated by the learner, the incentives or rewards listed below will be provided by the appropriate instructional staff.

INCENTIVES/REWARDS Steve will be permitted to use the auto lab equipment and tools during his free period to 1) service his minibike and 2) build a motorcycle trailer.

SIGNATURES

Learner Steve   Instructor(s) Tom Powers / Candy Jenkins

Date 1/12

(1975) has identified one rule that is critical in providing feedback to learners as they perform manual tasks. The rule of diminishing feedback states that each time an instructor corrects an error that has been made previously, enough information to correct the error should be provided, but less information than the time before. If, for instance, a learner is having trouble setting the feed and speed on a machine lathe, the instructor might indicate what the appropriate combination of feed and speed is for the material being machined. Later, if the learner again encounters trouble with the feed and speed settings in a later operation, the instructor might indicate the appropriate speed, but suggest that the student consult a feed setting chart. Limiting the amount of feedback in this way provides an incentive for the learner to internalize the feedback when it is provided.

14. In certain situations teachers will find it useful to provide reinforcement on a group basis instead of an individual basis. In such instances, each member of the group must exhibit the desired behavior before the reinforcement is provided. This technique is commonly used by industrial education teachers who make dismissal of the class contingent upon the completion of each class member's cleanup responsibilities. In situations like this, peers will give encouragement or distract the learner as little as possible in order to obtain the reinforcement. Care must be taken, however, to insure that the failure of one student does not result in punishment for the entire class.

15. Once desired target behaviors are attained or obtained, there are several techniques that can be used to maintain them. These include:

a. Gradually reducing the frequency and/or amount of feedback and reinforcement provided
b. Gradually delaying the reinforcement after performance
c. Gradually fading from artificial to natural reinforcers
d. Reinforcing self-control behaviors

16. It is imperative that the reinforcement and feedback plan be coordinated with all of the student's teachers as well as the parents. If the target behavior is to increase school attendance and decrease tardiness when the student is in school, this will obviously require the cooperation and participation of school personnel, parents, and employers in providing the necessary reinforcement.

SUMMARY

Chapter 12 reviews four critical considerations for implementing individualized instruction for special needs learners. These are usually thought of as general teaching techniques.

Principles and techniques for arranging or rearranging the sequence of instruction are reviewed. Based on the individual's learning prescription, it may be appropriate to plan a sequence of instructional modules based on such primary factors as the student's interest, skill development patterns, frequency of occupational task performance, or increasing difficulty. Techniques for utilizing different sequences with different students are also presented.

Analyzing and modifying instructional materials is a second critical consideration. Readability, format, and content evaluation techniques for use with print materials are discussed. In order to appropriately select or modify instructional materials, personnel must frequently review and evaluate the student's learning style.

Modification of physical facilities and equipment is an extremely important consideration in providing a barrier-free environment for physically handicapped learners. Guidelines for modifying equipment, based on the assessed individual needs of visually, hearing, and orthopedically impaired learners, are presented. General concerns such as room colors, flexibility of the facility, and the use of special equipment are also discussed.

The final section of the chapter is devoted to strategies for providing continuous reinforcement and feedback to special needs learners. Techniques for developing a behavioral management system, such as the use of individual contingency contracts, are outlined.

REFERENCES

Gardner, W. I. *Children with learning and behavior problems: A behavior management approach.* Boston: Allyn and Bacon, 1972.

Gardner, W. I. *Learning and behavior characteristics of exceptional children and youth: A humanistic behavioral approach.* Boston: Allyn and Bacon, 1977.

Gold, M. W. *Task analysis.* Urbana: University of Illinois, College of Education, March 1975. (Graduate student seminar presentation.)

Homme, L., et al. *How to use contingency contracting in the classroom.* Champaign, Ill.: Research, 1970.

Hutt, C., and Vaizey, M. J. Differential effects of group density on social behavior. *Nature,* 1966, 209, 1371–72.

Johnson, S. R., and Johnson, R. B. *Developing individualized instructional material.* Palo Alto, Calif.: Westinghouse Learning Press, 1970.

Mager, R. F., and Beach, K. M. *Developing vocational instruction.* Palo Alto, Calif.: Fearon, 1967.

Popham, W. J., and Baker, E. L. *Planning an instructional sequence.* Englewood Cliffs, N.J.: Prentice-Hall, 1970.

Premack, D. "Toward empirical behavior Laws I. Positive reinforcement." *Psychological Review,* 1959, 66.

Smith, R. M. *Clinical teaching: methods of instruction for the mentally retarded.* New York: McGraw-Hill, 1974.

Szoke, C. O., and Vest, S. *To serve those who are handicapped.* Springfield: Division of Adult, Vocational, and Technical Education, Illinois Office of Education, 1975.

Wallace, G., and Kauffman, J. M. *Teaching children with learning problems.* Columbus, Ohio: Charles E. Merrill, 1973.

Weisman, L., et al. *A handbook for developing vocational programs and services for disadvantaged students.* Springfield: Illinois Office of Education, 1975.

Wexner, L. B. The degree to which color (hues) are associated with moodtones. *Journal of Applied Psychology,* 1954, 38, 432–35.

Yuker, H. E., et al. *Educational and school equipment for physically disabled students* (Human Resources Study Number 9). Albertson, N.Y.: Human Resources Center, 1967.

EVALUATING LEARNER PROGRESS

This, the final chapter, deals with procedures and techniques for assessing the educational attainment of special needs learners. Typically, assessment of learner progress has occurred after a period of instruction has been completed. As noted in Chapter 6, however, with special needs learners, monitoring and continuous evaluation of progress is essential throughout the instructional period and not just as its completion. ~ In this chapter we will discuss 1) special considerations that need to be made in developing and using evaluation instruments, 2) appropriate techniques for assessing progress, and 3) a format for monitoring and reporting learner progress data. This chapter will not deal with general measurement and test construction theory. While it does focus on measurement and evaluation, our specific intent here is to examine and provide suggestions for how measurement and

13

evaluation can be effectively conducted *for special needs learners.* The references at the end of the chapter should be consulted for detailed discussions of the general principles of educational measurement, assessment, and evaluation.

Evaluation of the special needs learner's progress involves several key issues and activities, two of which will be discussed in this chapter: 1) developing, selecting, and administering instruments, and 2) reporting and using progress information. Each of these activities will be discussed in light of evaluating the level of competency or achievement attained by the learner during and following instruction.

Several evaluation issues and concerns were discussed in Chapter 6. There, however, our emphasis was evaluation of specific learning prior to or during the early stages of instruction. Our primary purpose there was to determine the special needs of the learner in order to prescribe instruction that would be appropriate. In this chapter, evaluation is conducted with the purpose of determining how well the student does *following* instruction. For our purposes, "following" may be defined as any time after which a significant amount of instruction has been provided. For some teachers, this may be after one week, while for others it may be at the end of the marking period or the semester. Still others conceive of the ultimate evaluation of learner progress as occurring a year or so after schooling is completed, when a follow-up study is conducted (Wentling 1970). Evaluation of learner progress following any significant amount of instruction will be the focus of this chapter.

USING LEARNER PROGRESS INFORMATION

There are several uses for evaluation information that describes the progress of achievement a learner has attained. To illustrate some of them, let's take another look at Mark and the process used by his teachers in assessing his progress. Mark, you will recall from Chapter 1, is educable mentally handicapped, and his learning style and prescriptive educational program were discussed and described in detail.

Mark is currently enrolled in both agricultural mechanics and special education classes. Near the end of the first semester, Mark's special education teacher, Ms. Jenkins, and his agricultural mechanics teacher, Mr. Reese, met on two consecutive days to review and discuss Mark's achievements for the semester. They had been meeting informally every other week or so to evaluate his progress and plan instructional experiences. At this point, they felt it necessary to assess more closely what specific competencies Mark has attained and share this information with his parents, Mr. Ely who will be his co-op coordinator next semester, and other interested persons involved with Mark.

As they discussed their intended progress evaluation, they saw three major purposes for it:

1. *Assemble data that would let Mark know how he is doing and provide encouragement for additional learning.*
2. *They, as well as the other persons mentioned above, would have a more complete and accurate understanding of what occupational and basic skill competencies Mark has attained.*
3. *With this information, Mark's future teachers and other professionals involved with Mark could better address his learning problems and other special needs. They also felt that by carefully assessing Mark's achievement they would discover areas of their instructional programs and services that could be improved. This was especially important because they see the likelihood of greater numbers of special needs students enrolling in agricultural mechanics in the future.*

As they began to discuss how they might approach the evaluation of Mark's performance, a number of logical steps began to appear. First, they were concerned that whatever instruments or techniques they might use be appropriate for Mark. That is, they wanted to select or develop and use evaluation methods that assessed Mark's competencies accurately and reliably. They agreed that many of the paper and pencil tests Mr. Reese used with his nonhandicapped students would not accurately reflect Mark's understanding of certain concepts learned this semester. The possibility of using a series of performance tests, verbal identification quizzes, rating scales, or observation checklists in both the agricultural mechanics and special education class was discussed and felt to be more appropriate. (A number of basic considerations made by Mark's teachers in selecting, developing, and using evaluation techniques and instruments are presented later in this chapter.)

Another concern that Mr. Reese and Ms. Jenkins addressed was who might receive and use the assessment results in addition to themselves. More specifically, they were concerned with how *the outcomes could be most effectively conveyed to Mark himself and to his 1) future teachers, 2) parents, 3) work experience supervisors, 4) prospective employers, 5) counselors. In addition to these individuals, it was anticipated that the results could be shared with the directors of the special education and occupational education programs, as well as the building principal and counselors and case workers from local agencies such as vocational rehabilitation, mental health, social services, and the employment service.*

After considerable discussion it was concluded that the results should reflect as accurately and explicitly as possible the level of competency attained by Mark in specific areas. The traditional letter grade system was not totally appropriate for this purpose because it didn't describe Mark's accomplishments or abilities descriptively. After reviewing several possible formats for presenting progress assessment information, they decided that a one-page profile, which had appeared in a recent journal article, was appropriate. Although it was not exactly what they were looking for, they felt it could be adapted and used to include his achievement and specific talents and abilities. (The learner performance record and how it was adapted and used by Mark's teachers is discussed in the last section of this chapter.)

As Mark's teachers sat in the teacher's lounge and discussed evaluation, several other high school teachers became interested and involved in the discussion. One of the concerns expressed by the teachers was a need for follow-up information on the students after they graduated. One business education teacher commented, "One of the things I would like to know is where my students, including the special needs students from last year, are employed. If I knew more about the problems they encountered, I could improve my course tremendously. Certainly, I get feedback from a few students who come back to visit, but it's not enough nor is it an accurate sample of all the students."

As the conversation among the teachers continued, the principal entered and, after listening awhile, suggested that those teachers interested in doing a follow-up of their last year's students form a committee and conduct a follow-up survey. Two of the special education teachers indicated they would like to have a number of their students from last year included, and they offered to share their experiences from having previously done follow-up surveys.

While follow-up surveys of former students, their parents, and employers are a critical part of a total evaluation system, time and space considerations will not permit us to discuss adequately the organization and development of such surveys in this chapter. A number of references that include procedures and instruments for conducting these surveys may be found at the end of the chapter.

EVALUATION AND ASSESSMENT TECHNIQUES

Over the years a vast number of different evaluation and assessment procedures and techniques have been developed, many of which have been used with special needs learners. The decision as to which technique may be most appropriate for assessing the achievement of a special needs learner is not an easy one to make. It will depend upon two equally important key factors—the type of achievement being measured and the special needs of the learner.

Type of Achievement

There are three basic types of learner achievement that can be measured once well-defined objectives are written. They are identified by the three domains of human performance: cognitive (knowledge), affective (attitudes), and psychomotor (skills). Another variation of the last domain, known as the perceptual domain, is also sometimes considered a major classification of human performance.

The appropriateness of a specific measurement technique depends upon which domains of human performance are to be used. Wentling and Lawson (1975) suggest that items for eliciting and measuring cognitive achievement (commonly done via paper and pencil tests) fall into two categories: 1) *recognition items,* which include multiple choice, true-false, and matching items and 2) *constructed response items,* which include the completion, short answer, definition, and essay items. They also suggest a number of other techniques appropriate for assessing psychomotor/perceptual and affective achievement (achievement or changes in physical skills and attitudes).

Perceptual and psychomotor performance can be assessed by using such techniques as *rating scales* and *checklists.* Using these techniques, observers, supervisors, teachers, or, in some instances, students themselves have evaluated performance products or processes. Occupational educators have commonly used a number of different rating forms to evaluate a student's project or finished product. Observation checklists have also been used frequently to assess the procedure or process used by a student in accomplishing a specific task (Bloom, Hastings, and Madaus 1971).

Surveys or questionnaires are the most frequently used types of instruments for assessing attitudes. Informal questionnaires often use desirability/undesirability, agree/disagree, and pro/con or neutral scales to determine a person's feelings about a particular concept.

As most teachers recognize, a number of attitudes such as initial career expectations, world-of-work opinions, on-the-job attitudes, and basic attitudes concerning career advancement are extremely important for all individuals to internalize. They are especially important for special needs learners because experience has shown that these individuals have more frequently lost their job due to a lack of social skills rather than because they couldn't perform the skills required in the job.

Type of Disability

Because of the range of learning, behavioral, or physical problems encountered by special needs learners, it is impossible to identify specific evaluation techniques that may be appropriate for the group as a whole. For instance, paper and pencil tests may be highly appropriate for gifted or certain learning disabled students and yet highly inappropriate for mildly retarded individuals.

When considering the learner's disability, the key to selecting an appropriate evaluation technique (paper and pencil test, performance test, and others) is to select those that minimize the impact of the disability upon the outcome. If, for instance, you had a totally deaf student in a small engine mechanics class with other hearing students, you would not expect the student to be able to tune a two-cycle engine by ear on a performance test. While a performance test is definitely an appropriate technique, the deaf individual may need some special equipment such as a dwell meter or tachometer to provide him with the essential information the other students obtain by sound.

This is, of course, a simple and obvious example of selecting evaluation techniques that minimize the effect of the disability on the outcome of the evaluation. When one begins to examine disability areas that include reading, perceptual, and behavioral problems, the selection of appropriate techniques is seldom clear-cut. However, in order to determine accurately what competencies a learner has attained, it is critical that our evaluation procedures and instruments do not, in themselves, prevent the learner from demonstrating his or her level of competency attainment.

DEVELOPING, SELECTING, AND ADMINISTERING EVALUATION INSTRUMENTS

A number of special considerations may be necessary in the evaluation process. As with instructional planning and all of the other instructional development processes described, the key question is deciding how we must modify our procedures and techniques for evaluation to make them appropriate and usable with special needs learners. After reviewing the list of special considerations and modifications, you will see that, in most cases, the necessary modification or adjustments to be made are minor, not major.

Progress assessment of special needs learners must be focused on individuals. It is extremely difficult to generalize and conclude that, for example, tests printed in sixty-point or larger type will be needed for partially sighted students. Obviously, the size of enlarged type required will depend upon the type and degree of vision loss. Similar generalizations regarding appropriate evaluation strategies cannot readily be made for students with other special needs such as learning or behavioral disabilities.

Special Considerations in Selecting or Developing and Using Evaluation Instruments and Procedures

Listed below are a series of special considerations that teachers should carefully review prior to deciding on specific techniques, procedures, or instruments for evaluation. These are broad considerations, and are appropriate for any type of evaluation method or setting, and are equally as important in constructing performance or written tests as they are in designing follow-up interview guides or a questionnaire.

Some of the considerations involve procedures such as the writing of directions, questions, or items, while other considerations involve the format by which the special needs learner will respond. Still other considerations reflect different ways of administering evaluation instruments. While these are identified by disability area, this in no way implies that certain of the special considerations are not appropriate for other disability areas.

FOR THE MILDLY MENTALLY HANDICAPPED

Use vocabulary and language that is extremely simple and concise.

Make the sentences or test items as short as possible.

Verify that the test information to be read is at or below the learner's reading level in terms of difficulty.

Use nonverbal response scales whenever possible:

Permit oral presentation of questions to provide simplification and clarification. This can be done on either an individual or small group basis.

Permit testing to take place in short sessions over several days.

Provide simple directions and several examples for responding.

Use only concrete, meaningful items.

Repeat directions or other essential information until overlearning occurs.

Use some modes for responding other than writing whenever possible.

FOR THE BLIND OR PARTIALLY SIGHTED

Use test or other evaluative instruments prepared in braille.

Use test or other evaluative instruments with large print.

Use auditory modes instead of visual modes of communication, such as quiz questions on cassette tape.

Use special or supplementary lighting.

Design test situations using tactile discrimination.

Arrange for students to respond in braille or by using a cassette tape recorder.

FOR THE DEAF OR HARD OF HEARING

Use a total communication approach that includes lip reading, signing, and finger spelling.

Provide favorable seating for partially hearing students.

Employ necessary sound amplification devices.

Use special devices to improve acoustics.

Have the evaluation instrument reviewed for interpretation by manual communication.

FOR THE LEARNING DISABLED

Use modes for responding that do not involve extensive writing or speaking.

Have instruments and evaluation procedures reviewed by a learning disabilities consultant prior to use.

Watch the student carefully for cues that difficulty is being encountered.

FOR THE PHYSICALLY HANDICAPPED

Provide large response boxes for individuals who exhibit poor fine motor coordination.

Make sure that necessary modifications are made in tools, equipment, materials, work tables, or desks when performance testing is used.

When performance testing is to be used, arrange materials and tools so that the student's limited mobility doesn't limit his or her performance.

FOR THE EMOTIONALLY DISTURBED

Prior to testing or assessment take steps to insure that the test situation is nonthreatening to the extent possible.

Watch the learner closely during the testing to spot potentially disruptive situations.

FOR THE NON-ENGLISH-SPEAKING

Have tests or other instruments translated to the native language.

Use a bilinguist to administer the instrument.

Consider very carefully the cultural fairness of your tests or other instruments. To what extent do the evaluation procedures or instruments point out differences among cultural groups that are based on language, reading speed, or culturally loaded content?

MONITORING AND REPORTING LEARNER PROGRESS

As we have noted throughout this section the continuous evaluation and re-evaluation of special needs learners is critical. You will recall that in Chapter 6 we began by discussing assessment of the special student prior to or during the early stages of instruction. In Chapter 10 a checklist system for assessing learner progress using the instructional planning form was introduced. This section will focus on monitoring, compiling, and reporting information from the checklist system presented on the instructional planning form in Chapter 10.

Who Should Receive Learner Progress Information?

One of the initial considerations when reporting progress or achievement information is the audience who will receive and use the information. The information needs of the audience(s) should determine, to a large extent, the format and type of progress information to be reported. A number of different audiences exist who generally have use for the information describing the educational progress achieved by a special needs learner. These include:

The learner

Prospective employers

Counselors

Parents

Teachers and other personnel currently working with the student

Future teachers and educational personnel

Special service agencies (vocational rehabilitation services)

Other training agencies (sheltered workshops, manpower programs, or industrial training programs)

The Learner Performance Record

Traditionally, schools have reported educational progress information by assigning letter grades. Seldom has evaluation reporting been specific enough to describe the actual competencies or levels of competence attained by the learner.

In recent years, profiles and performance records have emerged as a more useful and functional method of reporting evaluative results for all students. This trend has occurred primarily because the traditional grade reports have often failed to meet our informational needs. Employers, in particular, have begun to ask for descriptive information on the student's attained level of competency. Reporting that the student is competent in operating a key punch machine tells an employer much more than simply reporting a grade of "C" for this student in a data processing course.

The learner performance record shown in Figure 13–1 is an example of a format for compiling and reporting progress information. While other formats could be used, this one is specifically designed to be used with the learner profile and progress monitoring system presented in Chapters 6 and 10.

FIGURE 13-1. LEARNER PERFORMANCE RECORD

Learner *Mark*
Program *Agric. Mechanics*
Instructional *Al Reese*
Team *Candy Jenkins*

Part A: Occupational Competency Assessment

LEARNER PERFORMANCE RECORD

Tasks	Learner Progress: Introduced	Involved	Productive	Employable		Descriptive Assessments	Date
Lubricate machinery and equipment			✓		1	*Can operate grease gun and cup greasers appropriately*	*9/17*
				✓	2	*Can change filters and locate all appropriate specifications*	*10/15*
					3		
					4		
Service tires	✓				1	*Unfamiliar with basic procedure*	*9/17*
		✓			2	*Can recognize all tools and equipment needed*	*10/15*
			✓		3	*Dismounts and mounts tires as per specifications*	*10/30*
				✓	4	*Can replace valve stems and make special repairs*	*11/11*
					1		
					2		
					3		
					4		
					1		
					2		
					3		
					4		
					1		
					2		
					3		
					4		
					1		
					2		
					3		
					4		
					1		
					2		
					3		
					4		
					1		
					2		
					3		
					4		
					1		
					2		
					3		
					4		

FIGURE 13-1. *(Continued)*

Learner *Mark*
Program *Agric. Mechanics*
Instructional *Al. Reese*
Team *Candy Jenkins*

Part B: Basic Skills/ Concepts Assessment

LEARNER PERFORMANCE RECORD

Basic Skills/Concepts	Learner Progress: Introduced	Learner Progress: Developing	Learner Progress: Competent	Descriptive Assessments	Date
Technical Vocabulary –		✓		1 *Can recognize 90% of terms in the unit*	*9/18*
Lubrication			✓	2 *Can recognize and accurately spell all of Unit I*	*9/25*
				3	
Measurement –	✓			1 *Is not aware of capacities of oil containers*	*9/18*
Volume and Weights		✓		2 *Can identify 1-quart and 5-quart oil cans*	*9/25*
			✓	3 *Can correctly label six different sizes of oil containers*	*10/2*
				1	
				2	
				3	
				1	
				2	
				3	
				1	
				2	
				3	
				1	
				2	
				3	
				1	
				2	
				3	
				1	
				2	
				3	
				1	
				2	
				3	
				1	
				2	
				3	
				1	
				2	
				3	
				1	
				2	
				3	

The learner performance record is designed to graphically portray the levels of progress achieved by the special needs learner. Part A of the form describes the learner's occupational competencies while Part B focuses on the basic skills. Ideally, the cooperating team can use this form to note the specific levels of achievement the individual has attained at different points during or following the instructional program. Figure 13–1 shows how the record was used by Mark's teachers.

Using the Learner Performance Record

Use of the performance profile format can be facilitated by a description of certain sections of the form. The form basically consists of a page of descriptive and interpretation information (the cover sheet) followed by two pages of assessment profile forms. The latter two pages can be printed on the front and back of a single piece of paper (thus placing the essential progress information on one page) and used with a cover sheet.

Cooperation. One of the most important factors in evaluating and reporting learner progress information is cooperation. All of the personnel involved with the student, including occupational and special educators, counselors, therapists, teacher consultants, or anyone else providing programming or special services, can and should be involved in preparing the learner performance record. Ideally, the individuals most directly involved in this will be those persons who were identified in the cooperative instructional arrangement (Chapter 9). Cooperative involvement of all appropriate professionals working with the learner can help to make the learner performance record data accurate, comprehensive, and useful to the team and others in improving their instructional efforts, programs, and services.

Cover Sheet. The cover sheet for the learner performance record, (see Figure 13–2) contains the basic descriptive information on the student, along with the information needed to interpret the levels of progress identified on the record. Obviously, this latter information is essential for the user in interpreting the ratings accurately and consistently.

FIGURE 13-2. LEARNER PERFORMANCE RECORD COVER SHEET

A LEARNER PERFORMANCE RECORD FOR

Mark

Occupational goal Mechanics helper Instructors ______

Cluster/program Agric. mechanics Al Keese, Agric. mechanics

School ______ Candy Jenkins, Spec. Ed.

The above-named student has demonstrated the occupational skills described by the attached form. The criteria described below can be used to interpret the level of skill development attained by the student.

OCCUPATIONAL PERFORMANCE

Introduced. The learner has become acquainted with the general task, as well as its function and/or purpose, through previous experiences or instruction. However, the learner has not yet begun to develop or demonstrate any significant, recognizable competency in performing the task.

Involved. The learner has begun to develop and/or demonstrate minimal competence in performing a few selected parts (subskills) of the task.

Productive. The learner has developed and/or demonstrates a minimal level of competence in performing several parts (subskills) of the task. The student learner would be employable in specialized, entry-level occupations requiring only minimal skills.

Employable. The learner has developed and/or demonstrates a level of competency that would make him or her employable in a normal, competitive work setting.

BASIC SKILLS/CONCEPTS CONTENT

Introduced. The learner has become acquainted with the basic skill or concept through previous experience and/or instruction.

Developing. The learner has demonstrated some capacity to perform the basic skill, and/or interpret and apply the basic concept.

Competent. The learner is capable of accurately and repeatedly performing the basic skill, or interpreting and applying the basic concept.

Part A: Occupational Competency Assessment. This section of the learner performance record focuses on the learner's progress relative to occupational tasks. "Task" refers to the specific titles of the instructional modules developed for the special needs student. Task or module titles such as "take and record pulse" or "applying for a social security card" would be appropriate here. Tasks, then, represent the major instructional units or modules the student has undertaken while in the occupational education program.

As noted before, these task titles should be worded to describe a behavior or performance. Preferably, single action words with concise, descriptive objects should be used to describe, as accurately as possible, what the learner is capable of doing at the conclusion of the unit or module of instruction.

Part B: Basic Skills/Concepts Assessment. You will recall that in each instructional module, a number of basic skills and concepts directly related to the occupational performance objectives were identified. Basic skills such as "counting" and "recording numerical information" were identified in the example module of "taking and recording pulse." These basic skills and concepts are often the performance areas in which special needs students are deficient. Thus, in evaluating a student's progress we frequently must be concerned with development of these essential, basic skills and the understanding gained of basic concepts, in addition to the occupational skills.

Part B of the learner performance record is designed to familiarize the reader with the degree to which certain basic skills and concepts have been attained. The basic skills and concepts typically included here are those that are interwoven in the occupational instruction. In occupational education programs in the health occupations, for instance, many of the basic skills and concepts involve human relations and interpersonal skills because of the regular and frequent contact with other persons in this field.

Since the special or basic education team member usually provides instruction relative to the basic skills and concepts, this person will likely have the primary responsibility for assessment of the learner's progress in this area.

Levels of Progress. For both Part A and Part B, different levels of progress are identified. Four levels are identified for the occupational competency assessment (Part A), and these are identical to the four levels used on the instructional module format (Figure 10–2). Three levels of progress in attaining the basic skills and concepts are presented from the instructional module format.

The most difficult aspect of developing any student evaluation system is deciding, as precisely as possible, what is meant by the various rating levels used. One teacher's definition of "competent" is often different from the next teacher's definition. It is critical, therefore, that the cooperating team determine several descriptive criteria for each criterion rating level they intend to use. In this way the members of the cooperating team can consistently and reliably rate the learner's performance level.

A series of descriptors for the various levels used in parts A and B of the learner performance record are shown on the cover sheet (Figure 13–2). These descriptors were developed by several groups of teachers who used the record in their classes for monitoring special needs learners.

Finally, it should be mentioned that the progress levels on the performance record are not standardized or validated in any way. If, for some reason, you find it more feasible or efficient to use three or five levels instead of four, the record form should be modified to fit your system or preference. The progress levels identified in the example have resulted from regular use and refinement of the learner performance record by practicing occupational and special education teachers. It is important, however, that concise and discrete levels of progress be identified and an operational definition for each level be developed by those who will be using the record for monitoring student progress.

Descriptive Assessment. To the right of the progress level columns on the learner performance record spaces are provided for further describing the learner's performance at different time intervals. In Part A, spaces are provided permitting assessments to be made at four intervals. The four intervals should be considered as stages covering preassessment, interim assessment, and postassessments.

As shown in the example performance record prepared by Mark's teachers, Mark was already at the "productive" level in two tasks when he entered the agricultural mechanics program. However, it is apparent that at the time of the preassessment (line 1) conducted by Mr. Reese, his agricultural mechanics teacher, he had only been "introduced" to the other task. One can readily see that this type of progress monitoring is based on the concept of performance evaluation that provides for frequent and regular assessments of the achievement made by students.

The open-ended descriptive assessment areas require teachers to define operationally the progress levels attained by the learner on specific tasks. This is the most difficult portion of the record to complete according to those who have used it. They have found it very worthwhile, however, for two reasons. First, it requires the evaluator to develop an objective, measurable description of what the learner has or has not demonstrated to deserve the rating. Second, open-ended, objective assessment statements convey a better understanding to the reader of what this learner is actually capable of doing. Instead of simply saying he or she is "employable," we are attempting to describe what "employable" means for this learner in this task.

SUMMARY

Evaluation of learner progress is a continuing activity that occurs prior to, during, and following instruction. Chapter 6 focused on assessment considerations to be made prior to instruction. This chapter focuses on techniques, instruments, and strategies to be used in evaluating the learner's progress once he or she has begun the instructional program.

Guidelines for selecting, developing, and using nondiscriminatory evaluation instruments for use with special needs learners are discussed. With the passage of recent federal legislation, all educational evaluation programs must now assess the actual performance of the learner and not be inherently discriminatory toward special needs learners because they are physically handicapped or speak a different language.

The learner performance record is presented as a format for monitoring and assessing learner progress. Techniques for maintaining rating consistency and objectivity in evaluation criteria are also discussed.

Throughout the chapter, strategies for using assessment information with appropriate audiences such as parents, prospective employers, the learner, and others are emphasized.

SUMMARY FOR PART II

Throughout Part II emphasis has been placed on several key concepts that need to be summarized here. First and most importantly, it is imperative that all special needs learners enrolling in career exploration and preparation programs be assessed and planned for on an individual basis. Through the development of individualized educational plans that contain objectives from a base curriculum, appropriate in-school and on-the-job instructional experiences can be provided. A system for providing continuous, objective evaluation data that describe the learner's performance prior to, during, and following instruction is essential for selection of instructional objectives and instructional media. In order to provide a full range of career exploration and preparation experiences, community resources and employment opportunities in local businesses and industries must be routinely and broadly examined. The need to evaluate annually both career exploration and preparation curricula for their relevancy to local and regional employment needs cannot be overemphasized.

You will recall that Chapter 5 presented a System for Developing and Managing Instruction for Special Needs Learners. This System contains operational activities designed to address the above concerns and others. After reading Part II, it is hoped that the reader will review this introductory chapter and have a positive and personalized feeling for how he or she should proceed with implementing one or several of the ideas presented in Parts I and II.

Finally, it is critical to recognize the importance of cooperative efforts. Only by engaging in open, frequent, and positive communication and cooperation can occupational and special educators (working in concert with parents, administrators, and others) provide broad-based, dynamic, and effective educational programs for special students. Such cooperative efforts result in programs and services that are far more effective than those that historically have been provided independently by special educators or occupational educators.

REFERENCES

Bloom, B. S., Hastings, J. T., and Madaus, G. F. *Handbook on formative and summative evaluation of student learning.* New York: McGraw-Hill, 1971.

Erickson, R. C., and Wentling, T. L. *Measuring student growth: Techniques and procedures for occupational education.* Boston: Allyn and Bacon, 1976.

Felstehausen, J. L. *A one-year follow-up survey: Occupational program alumni* (Final Report Project No. ROC-B4-079). Charleston: School of Education, Eastern Illinois University, 1974.

Gathany, N. A., and Coogan, J. P. Job profile your students. *School Shop,* 1975, 35, 40–41.

Gearheart, B. R., and Willenberg, E. P. *Application of pupil assessment information: For the special education teacher.* Denver, Col.: Love Publishing, 1974.

Pucel, D. J., and Knaak, W. C. *Individualizing vocational and technical education.* Columbus, Ohio: Charles Merrill, 1975.

Wentling, T. L. A report of the Illinois school for the deaf follow-up study. (Unpublished Report.) Jacksonville: Illinois School for the Deaf, 1974.

Wentling, T. L. Quality control for education: A closed-loop system. *Journal of Industrial Teacher Education,* 1970, 7.

Wentling, T. L., and Lawson, T. E. *Evaluating Occupational Education and Training Programs.* Boston: Allyn and Bacon, 1975.

APPENDIX

LEARNING RECORD FOLDER

The Appendix is intended to offer an example of a practical system for developing and monitoring curriculum by utilizing a separate file for each learner. The learning record folder, the tab of which is illustrated in Figure 1 (see end of Appendix), contains several nonconfidential assessment and curriculum materials that can be shared by the occupational instructors, special needs teacher, placement coordinators, administrators, parents, and the learner. Each member of the instructional team will probably need a duplicate set of the materials so mutual understanding and team effort is maintained. Several advantages of this system include:

Learning characteristics are identified.

Learner's occupational goal(s) are stated.

Concise descriptions of needed occupational performances are prepared.

Explicit contributions are identified for cooperating teachers.

Evaluation techniques are based on job readiness.

Assessment, instruction, and evaluation are individualized.

LEARNER PROFILE

Several basic components seem important for each person's learning record folder. One component would be the learner profile for finding out more about the learner's past school experience (see Figure 2). This assessment technique—described fully in Chapter 6—includes input from each member of the learner's educational planning and placement committee and focuses upon the difficulties and strengths of the learner. This activity attempts to surface learner characteristics through cooperative efforts of parents, teachers, and administrators so that reasonable goals can be identified and appropriate curriculum materials can be developed.

LEARNER PERFORMANCE RECORD

With the support and involvement of various school and community resources, described fully in Chapter 7, a second component, the learner performance record, is developed for each learner to identify his or her occupational goal and to outline the necessary tasks and performances needed for completion (see Figure 3). Chapter 8 provides a detailed explanation of how cluster/programs, tasks (or units), and occupational performances are stated and prepared. Several factors seem to make the process worth the effort. First, the organization and reorganization of course content tends to revitalize the curriculum writing style; second, it becomes possible to share ideas in an efficient manner; third—and probably the most critical—teachers are better able to fit the curriculum to the needs of the learner instead of the traditional approach of having the learner fit the already established curriculum.

Each of the instructors described in the episodes (Chapter 3) have developed an exhaustive listing of tasks within their cluster/programs that are supported by a series of performances. Due to the individual nature of the career preparation experiences, each learner has had a unique set of tasks prepared as a "learner performance record" by his educational planning and placement committee that relates to his or her specific occupational goal. Within each task or unit specific performances have been selected from the instructor's master list. The selection process accounts for the incomplete listing of all performance numbers within a given task. For example, since Ed's entry-level occupational goal is to be a draftsman for an engineering firm, the performances on his learner performance record will be consistent with what an employer expects (instead of listing the complete design and drafting curriculum). The learner performance record serves as a display of what the learner will be accomplishing and provides an area for monitoring progress. Chapter 13 describes a series of evaluation techniques that can be used to measure learner progress. Should the listing become unrealistic in terms of the learner's abilities and interests, the educational planning and placement committee modifies the plan.

INSTRUCTIONAL MODULE

A third component includes a series of instructional modules (see Figures 4 and 5). Each instructional module breaks down the content into a shared teaching relationship between the occupational and special needs instructors. On the first page (which can be the front side), the occupational performance objectives are stated for the occupational instructor and, after an analysis of the learner, each performance is broken down into basic skills/concepts and basic skill/concept content (explained fully in Chapter 10) by the occupational and special needs teachers. Thus, the special needs teacher can concentrate on improving the learner's inherent weaknesses so that he or she becomes competent. The words "cluster/program" are used to describe the content to be learned. *Cluster* fits most consistently with the career preparation areas, while *program* is most appropriate for career exploration. For example, general agriculture, general business, home economics, and industrial arts are general career exploration programs, whereas automotive service, child care, horticulture, and office occupations are career preparation clusters. Similarly, the terms "task" and "unit" relate to concepts to be learned. "Task" is more commonly used among occupational instructors, whereas "unit" is more familiar with the general agriculture, general business, general health, home economics, and industrial arts teachers at the career exploration phase.

While the cooperating teachers share ideas of instructional methods and knowledge of the learner's abilities, they list, on the back side of each instructional module, teacher activities, learner activities, and instructional resource materials that seem most appropriate. Both instructors are encouraged to monitor progress in the space provided and to meet on a regular basis to review and improve the module. The learner performance record and the instructional module have several obvious uses including a tool for communicating with an employer, and it is certainly more communicative for cooperating teachers than an A, B, C, D, or E grade in a course. This resume of the learning record folder is not intended to imply that there is included a complete listing on the learner performance record or a complete collection of instructional modules but, instead, it is an example of how to begin a learner performance record, and it gives a couple of examples of instructional modules that one learner is attempting to complete.

FIGURE 1. LEARNING RECORD FOLDER TAB

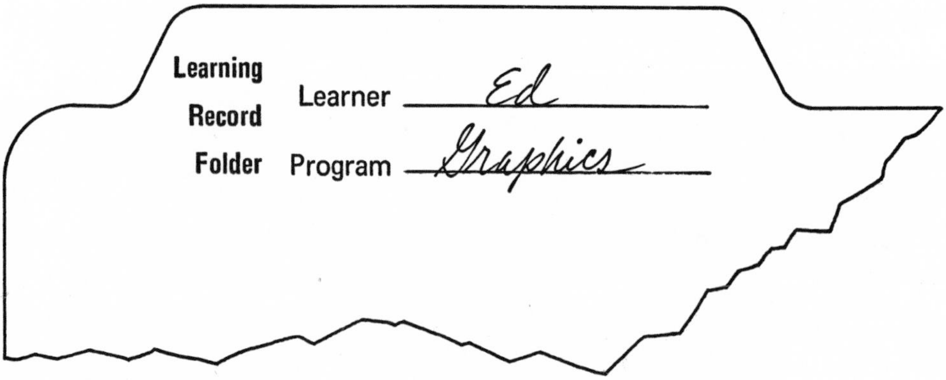

Learning Record Folder

Learner *Ed*

Program *Graphics*

FIGURE 2A.

LEARNER PROFILE

Learner *Ed*

School

Assessment/
Appraisal Team

Candy Jenkins — *Math teacher*
Principal
Greg Atwood — *Ed's father*
Ed's Coach

Special Needs Indicators	Learning (Strength – Difficulty)	Documentation/Observed Behavior
Quantitative/Numerical Skills Count and record Add/subtract Multiply/divide Measure General number use Money Other quantitative/numerical skills		• *Demonstrates excellent basic computational skills in mathematics* • *Scored at the 88th percentile in mathematical computation on the C.A.T.* • *Calculates gas mileage and route schedules while traveling with his uncle who is a truck driver.*
Verbal Skills Read Spell Record information Verbal communication Written communication Other verbal skills:		• *Expresses ideas fairly well on paper* • *Shows reluctance to engage in any form of teacher-planned discussions in class situations* • *Uses profanity, is insulting, and has caused havoc in several of his classes* • *Scored at the 64th percentile in language usage on the C.A.T.*
Cognitive Skills Retention Sequence Attentiveness Planning ability Mechanical aptitude Transfer Other cognitive skills:		• *Enjoys competing with his teachers for classroom attention, especially in the quiet lecture-type classes.* • *Basic ability to learn seems normal but is very disturbing to several of his teachers* • *Applies knowledge and skills learned in junior high school industrial arts to his drafting class.*

FIGURE 2B.

LEARNER PROFILE

Special Needs Indicators	Learning (Strength / Difficulty)	Documentation/Observed Behavior
Perceptual Skills Auditory discrimination Form perception Form discrimination Space perception Color perception Touch discrimination Other perceptual skills:		• Has excellent visual, hearing, and perceptual abilities • Excels in areas of physical and mechanical involvement • Received highest grades, B's, in industrial arts classes
Language Skills Listening Nonverbal expression Technical vocabulary Grammatical expression Other language skills:		• Has been characterized as being "bull headed" • Uses body language and gestures with unusual effectiveness • Has been punished severely for disrespectful gestures
Psychomotor/Physical Skills Physical strength Hand-eye coordination Manual dexterity Mobility Other physical skills:		• Possesses excellent physical strength and coordination • Has gone out for the junior varsity wrestling team • Expresses frustration with tedious and meticulous work in drafting

FIGURE 2C.

LEARNER PROFILE

Special Needs Indicators	Learning (Difficulty – Strength)	Documentation/Observed Behavior
Social Skills Sociability Cooperativeness Conformity Loyalty Safety Responsibility Sensitivity Other social skills:	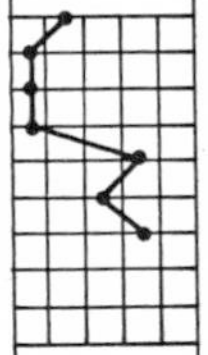	· Provides minimal appreciation to his teachers for extra help · Makes caustic remarks and insulting expressions to persons in authority · Reacts violently to accidents involving the loss of blood – fainted during a nosebleed · Expects teachers to stay away from him
Occupational Interests Agriculture/Natural Resources Automotive and Power Services Construction/Manufacturing Graphics/Communications Food/Clothing/Child Care Health Office/Business Other or specific occupational interests:	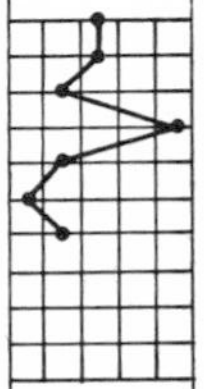	· Enjoys mechanical and physical activities · Performed well in junior high school art and industrial arts classes. · Expresses a strong interest in drafting and in graphic arts · Can't stand the sight of blood

FIGURE 3A.

Learner: Ed
Program: Graphic Arts
Instructional Team: Jenkins / Atwood
Principal / Ed's Dad
Math teacher /
Ed's Coach

Part A: Occupational Competency Assessment

LEARNER PERFORMANCE RECORD

Tasks	Learner Progress: Introduced	Involved	Productive	Employable		Descriptive Assessments	Date
Basic drawing			✓		1	Uses scale accurately (Entry skill)	9/6
			✓		2	Uses triangles efficiently (Entry skill)	9/6
			✓		3	Sketches quickly (Entry skill)	9/6
			✓		4	Knows uses of tools (Entry skill)	9/6
Basic dimensioning			✓		1	Observes basic dem. rules (Entry skill)	9/6
			✓		2	Makes lines and symbols (Entry skill)	9/6
					3		
					4		
Engineering lettering			✓		1	Makes letters accurately (Entry skill)	9/6
			✓		2	Makes numbers accurately (Entry skill)	9/6
			✓		3	Uses mechanical devices (Entry skill)	9/6
					4		
Geometric construction	✓		✓		1	Draws lines tangent to arcs and circles	9/8
	✓	✓			2	Draws a line tangent to two arcs	9/9
	✓		✓		3	Divides a line into equal parts	9/10
					4		
1. Multiview drawing	✓			✓	1	Sketches simple blocks	9/14
	✓		✓		2	Sketches blocks with inclined surfaces	9/16
	✓	✓			3	Sketches blocks with hidden surfaces	9/21
	✓	✓			4	Sketches blocks with arcs and circles	9/23
2. Multiview drawing	✓		✓		1	Draws views of simple objects	9/28
	✓	✓			2	Draws views of objects with inclined surfaces	9/30
					3	Draws views of objects with hidden surfaces	
					4		
3. Multiview drawing					1		
					2		
					3		
					4		
					1		
					2		
					3		
					4		
					1		
					2		
					3		
					4		

FIGURE 3B.

Part B: Basic Skills/ Concepts Assessment

LEARNER PERFORMANCE RECORD

Basic Skills/Concepts	Learner Progress: Introduced	Learner Progress: Developing	Learner Progress: Competent		Descriptive Assessments	Date
BASIC DRAWING			✓	1	ED REVIEWED ARCHITECTUAL SCALE EXERCISES FOR PRETEST.	9/2
NUMERICAL SKILLS			✓	2	ED PRACTICED TRIANGLE AND INSTRUMENT EXERCISES FOR PRETEST.	9/2
PERCEPTUAL SKILLS			✓	3	ED SKETCHED OBJECTS FROM JR. HI. IND. ARTS FOR PRETEST.	9/2
BASIC DIMENSIONING		✓		1	HE DISCUSSED HANDOUTS FROM JR. HI. IND. ARTS FOR PRETEST.	9/3
NUMERICAL SKILLS		✓		2	WE REVIEWED HIS WORK FROM IND ARTS FOR PRETEST.	9/3
LANGUAGE SKILLS				3		
ENGINEERING LETTERING		✓		1	HE PRACTICED MAKING LETTERS FOR PRETEST.	9/3
TOUCH CONTROL				2		
FORM PERCEPTION				3		
GEOMETRIC CONSTRUCTION		✓		1	WE REVIEWED STUDY SHEET FROM GREG.	9/8
NUMERICAL SKILLS		✓		2	ED STUDIES WORDS LISTED ON THE TASK MODULE.	9/9
TECHNICAL VOCABULARY				3		
MULTIVIEW DRAWING		✓		1	ED PRACTICES SKETCHING ASSIGNED PROBLEMS.	9/15
SPACE PERCEPTION		✓		2	WE REVIEW THE VERBAL CONCEPTS FROM TASK MOD.	9/16
TECHNICAL VOCABULARY				3		
				1		
				2		
				3		
				1		
				2		
				3		
				1		
				2		
				3		
				1		
				2		
				3		
				1		
				2		
				3		
				1		
				2		
				3		
				1		
				2		
				3		

FIGURE 4A.

CLUSTER PROGRAM: GRAPHICS
task: GEOMETRIC CONSTRUCTION

Learner: ED

I.D. No.: GC - 1

Learner Progress

			Competent
✓		✓	Developing
			Introduced

Basic Skill/ Concept Content

DETERMINE LENGTH OF A LINE
LOCATE THE CENTER OF A LINE, CIRCLE, ETC.
INTERPRET CIRCULAR DIMENSIONS IN:
DEGREES
MINUTES
SECONDS

BISECT, DIVIDE, CONSTRUCT, ANGLE, LINE, TRIANGLE, SQUARE, TANGENT, HEXAGON, OCTAGON, PENTAGON, ELLIPSE, SEGMENT, CENTER, FLAT-POINT ARC

EXAMPLES OF INDUSTRIAL APPLICATIONS OF THESE BASIC PRINCIPLES MAY BE NECESSARY TO MAINTAIN ED'S INVOLVEMENT.

Basic Skills/ Concepts

QUANTITATIVE / NUMERICAL SKILLS:
MEASUREMENTS

LANGUAGE SKILLS:
TECHNICAL VOCABULARY

OCCUPATIONAL INTERESTS AND APTITUDES:
OCCUPATIONAL INTERESTS

Occupational Performance Objectives
Given the necessary materials, tools, equipment, and requisite knowledge, the learner will:

1. DRAW A LINE TANGENT TO A CIRCLE, AN ARC TANGENT TO A STRAIGHT LINE, A STRAIGHT LINE TO TWO ARCS, AND DIVIDE A LINE INTO EQUAL PARTS.

Learner Progress

	Employable
	Productive
✓	Involved
✓	Introduced

FIGURE 4B.

CLUSTER PROGRAM:
task:

I.D. No. ____________

Occupational Instruction	Basic Skill/Concept Instruction
Teacher Activities: · DISCUSS CONSTRUCTION PROCEDURES WITH EACH STUDENT · DEMONSTRATE PROCEDURES AT THE CHALK BOARD · UTILIZE TRANSPARENCIES	Teacher Activities: · work with drafting teacher to become familiar with basic drafting tools · Prepare overhead transparencies with pictures of basic drafting tools · Refer to drafting text for illustrations
Learner Activites: · COMPLETE GEOMETRIC DESIGNS USING APPROPRIATE TOOLS · WORK ON DIFFICULT PROBLEMS WITH A BUDDY · DISCUSS UNCLEAR PROCEDURES WITH THE INSTRUCTOR	Learner Activites: · Explain and demonstrate to teacher the correct and incorrect way to use basic drafting tools · Identify orally to teacher the basic drafting tools on overhead transparencies

Instructional Resource Materials

Name / Title	Media	Source	Name / Title	Media	Source
"GEOMETRIC CONSTRUCTION"			Drafting instruction basic text		
			Board, T-Square, Triangles, compass, dividers, scales		

FIGURE 5A.

CLUSTER PROGRAM: GRAPHICS
task: MULTIVIEW DRAWING

Learner: ED

I.D. No.: MD 1, 3, 4

Basic Skills/Concepts	Basic Skill/Concept Content	Learner Progress: Competent	Learner Progress: Developing	Learner Progress: Introduced
PERCEPTUAL SKILLS: SPACE PERCEPTION	DETERMINE SCALE OF AN OBJECT ON A DRAWING ONE (1) FOOT (') OR ONE (1) INCH (") EQUALS WHAT FRACTIONAL PART OF AN INCH INCH FRACTIONS LENGTH HEIGHT DEPTH		✓	
LANGUAGE SKILLS: TECHNICAL VOCABULARY	LANGUAGE OF INDUSTRY VIEWS FRONT TOP SIDE PROJECTION ORTHOGRAPHIC CENTER SPACING LINES OBJECT CENTER DIMENSION CONSTRUCTION		✓	

Occupational Performance Objectives

Given the necessary materials, tools, equipment, and requisite knowledge, the learner will:

Occupational Performance Objectives	Learner Progress: Employable	Learner Progress: Productive	Learner Progress: Involved	Learner Progress: Introduced
1. PRODUCE A DRAWING WITH THE USE OF ORTHOGRAPHIC AND THIRD ANGLE PROJECTION		✓	✓	✓
3. USE THE CORRECT NUMBER OF VIEWS TO COMPLETE AN OBJECT AND USE A HIDDEN LINE TO COMPLETE A FEATURE OF THE OBJECT		✓	✓	✓
4. LAY OUT A THREE VIEW DRAWING AND/OR OBLIQUE SURFACES IF NEEDED			✓	✓

FIGURE 5B.

CLUSTER PROGRAM:
task:

I.D. No. ______

Occupational Instruction

Teacher Activities:

- ACQUIRE AND PREPARE STYROFOAM MODEL BLOCKS FOR STUDENT USE
- GIVE CHALKBOARD DEMONSTRATION OF CONSTRUCTION PROCEDURE
- DEMONSTRATE EXERCISE ON MISSING LINE DRAWINGS
- UTILIZE A GLASS BOX TO ILLUSTRATE MULTIVIEW PROJECTION

Learner Activities:

- CUT AND FORM STYROFOAM MODELS TO VISUALIZE SOLUTIONS OF MULTIVIEW PROJECTIONS
- SKETCH TOP, FRONT, AND SIDE VIEWS OF OBJECTS
- COMPLETE ASSIGNMENTS INCLUDING MISSING LINE PROBLEMS

Basic Skill/Concept Instruction

Teacher Activities:

- Drill students technical vocabulary
- Consult with drafting instructor to become more familiar with hidden line drawings
- Get styrofoam from drafting instructor and have that instructor explain technique for cutting, etc.

Learner Activities:

- Complete sketching and drawing assignments
- Orally give definition or example of each word listed under language skills: technical vocabulary
- Show other students how to cut out styrofoam blocks. Show how the different views will look on paper.

Instructional Resource Materials

Name / Title	Media	Source	Name / Title	Media	Source
STYROFOAM BLOCKS			Textbook and workbook used by drafting teacher		
"TWO VIEW ORTHOGRAPHIC - NEEDLE VALVE"			Styrofoam, board, T-Square, triangle, Square		
MISSING LINE PROBLEMS FROM WORKBOOKS OR TEACHER PREPARED					

INDEX